blue smoke curled up from somewhere. He swung his survival pack over one shoulder. He'd better move now -- just to one side of this planet's magenta sun something flickered: an ~~query~~ Omerge huntership coming to finish him off.

Smith forced his way into the surrounding grey-green spore-forest. From space it seemed to be the best cover available. From somewhere at once far above and deep inside him, Smith heard a voice: "What about an ambush? That would be dramatic!" An author, Smith thought to himself. And using one of the banned metaphysical typewriters! Smith trudged on, saying nothing.

"What of the 'thirst for adventure'?" asked his author.

"Lost it -- oh, ages ago," said Smith.

"Adventure may find you yet."

Smith heard the unmistakable sound of the suspense key of a metaphysical typewriter. Seconds ~~Moments~~ later, he heard another sound, echoing through the spore-trees

ON WRITING
SCIENCE FICTION

ON WRITING SCIENCE FICTION

(THE EDITORS STRIKE BACK!)

by

GEORGE H. SCITHERS, 1929–

DARRELL SCHWEITZER

and

JOHN M. FORD

Öwlswick Press
Philadelphia

Published by the Owlswick Press, Box 8243, Philadelphia PA 19101;
Typeset by the Twin Company of Holyoke, Massachusetts; printed
and bound by Bookcrafters, Inc., of Chelsea, Michigan; all in the
United States of America.

The stories "A Simple Outside Job," "Perchance to Dream," "African Blues," and
They'll Do It Every Time" are © 1977 by Davis Publications, Inc. The stories "Bat
Durston, Space Marshal," "Born Again," "The Adventure of the Global Traveler,"
"The Tryouts," "Scrap from the Notebooks of Johann Wolfgang von Goethe," and
"Heal the Sick, Raise the Dead" are © 1978 by Davis Publications, Inc. The Foreword,
under the title "Hints," and the stories "Someone Else's House" and "Tank" are ©
1979 by Davis Publications, Inc. All appeared for the first time in *Isaac Asimov's
Science Fiction Magazine*®, the title of which is a registered trademark of Davis
Publications, Inc. All appear here with the permission of their respective authors and
of Davis Publications, Inc.

International Standard Book Number 0-913896-19-5

iv

To
Robert A. Heinlein,
Frederik Pohl,
and George Lucas

for showing us all
how to write,
how to edit,
and how much fun science fiction can be.

The authors wish to thank Alan Lankin, John Ashmead, James Gunn, Larry Shaw, Sharon Webb, Algis Budrys, Shawna McCarthy, Susan Groarke, Elana Lore, and Lee Weinstein for all their assistance with this work. We are especially grateful to Joel Davis, publisher of *Isaac Asimov's Science Fiction Magazine,* who suggested that we put our experience editing the magazine into a book.

TABLE OF

CONTENTS

FOREWORD

Every once in a while I get a letter from some eager young would-be writer asking me for some "hints" on the art of writing science fiction.

The feeling I have is that my correspondents think there is some magic formula jealously guarded by the professionals, but that since I'm such a nice guy I will spill the beans if properly approached.

Alas, there's no such thing, no magic formula, no secret tricks, no hidden shortcuts. It's a matter of hard work over a long period of time. If you know of any exceptions to this, that's exactly what they are—exceptions.

There are, however, some general principles that can be useful, to my way of thinking, and here they are.

1. You have to prepare for a career as a successful science fiction writer—as you would for any other highly specialized calling.

First, you have to learn to use your tools, just as a surgeon has to learn to use his.

The basic tool for any writer is the English language, which means you must develop a good vocabulary and brush up on such prosaic things as spelling and grammar.

There can be little argument about vocabulary, but it may seem to you that spelling and grammar are just frills. After all, if you write great and gorgeous stories, surely the editor will be delighted to correct your spelling and grammar.

Not so! He (or she) won't be.

Besides, take it from an old war-horse, if your spelling and grammar are rotten, you won't be writing a great and gorgeous story. Someone who can't use a saw and hammer doesn't turn out stately furniture.

Even if you've been diligent at school, have developed a vocabulary, can spell "sacrilege" and "supersede" and never say "between you and I" or "I ain't never done nothing," that's still not enough. There's the subtle structure of the English sentence and the artful construction of the English paragraph. There is the clever interweaving of plot, the handling of dialog, and a thousand other intricacies.

How do you learn that? Do you read books on how to write, or attend classes on writing, or go to writing conferences? These are all of inspirational value, I'm sure, but they won't teach you what you really want to know.

What *will* teach you is the careful reading of the masters of English prose. This does not mean condemning yourself to years of falling asleep over dull classics. Good writers are invariably fascinating writers—the two go together. In my opinion, the English writers who most clearly use the correct word every time and who most artfully and deftly put together their sentences and paragraphs are Charles Dickens, Mark Twain, and P.G. Wodehouse.

Read them, and others, with attention. They represent your schoolroom. Observe what they do and try to figure out why they do it. It's no use other people explaining it to you; until you see it for yourself and it becomes part of you, nothing will help.

But suppose that no matter how you try, you can't seem to absorb the lesson. —Well, it may be that you're not a writer. It's no disgrace. You can always go on to take up some slightly inferior profession like surgery or the presidency of the United States. It won't be as good, of course, but we can't all scale the heights.

Second, for a science-fiction writing career, it is not enough to know the English language; you also have to know science. You may not want to use much science in your stories; but you'll have to know it anyway, so that what you do use, you don't misuse.

This does not mean you have to be a professional scientist, or a science major at college. You don't even have to go to college. It does mean, though, that you have to be willing to study science on your own, if your formal education has been weak in that direction.

It's not impossible. One of the best writers of hard science fiction is Fred Pohl, and he never even finished high school. Of course, there are few people who are as bright as Fred, but you can write considerably less well than he does and still be pretty good.

Fortunately, there is more good popular-science writing these days than there was in previous generations; and you can learn a great deal, rather painlessly, if you read such science fiction writers as L. Sprague de Camp, Ben Bova, and Poul Anderson in their nonfictional moods—or even Isaac Asimov.

What's more, professional scientists are also writing effectively for

ISAAC ASIMOV

the public, as witness Carl Sagan's magnificent books. And there's always *Scientific American.*

Third, even if you know your science and your writing, it is still not likely that you will be able to put them together from scratch. You will have to be a diligent reader of science fiction itself to learn the conventions and the tricks of the trade—how to interweave background and plot, for instance.

2. You have to work at the job

The final bit of schooling is writing itself. Nor must you wait till your preparation is complete. The act of writing is itself part of the preparation.

You can't understand completely what good writers do until you try it yourself. You learn a great deal when you find your story breaking apart in your hands—or beginning to hang together. Write from the very beginning, then; and keep on writing.

3. You have to be patient.

Since writing is itself a schooling, you can't very well expect to sell the first story you write. (Yes, I know Bob Heinlein did it, but he was Bob Heinlein. You are only you.)

But then, why should that discourage you? After you finished the first grade at school, you weren't through, were you? You went on to the second grade, then the third, then the fourth, and so on.

If each story you write is one more step in your literary education, a rejection shouldn't matter. Editors don't reject writers; they reject pieces of paper that have been typed on. The next story will be better, and the next one after that still better, and eventually . . .

Then why bother to submit the stories? If you don't, how can you possibly know when you graduate? After all, you don't know which story you'll sell.

You might even sell the first. You almost certainly won't, but you just might.

Of course, even after you sell a story, you may fail to place the next dozen, but having done it once, it is quite likely that you will eventually do it again, if you persevere.

But what if you write and write and write and you don't seem to be getting any better and all you collect are printed rejection slips? Once again, it may be that you are not a writer and will have to settle for a lesser post such as that of Chief Justice of the Supreme Court.

4. You have to be reasonable.

Writing is the most wonderful and satisfying task in the world, but it does have one or two insignificant flaws. Among those flaws is the fact that a writer can almost never make a living at it.

Oh, a few writers make a lot of money—they're the ones we all hear about. But for every writer who rakes it in, there are a thousand who dread the monthly rent bill. It shouldn't be like that, but it is.

Take my case. Three years after I sold my first story, I reached the stage of selling everything I wrote, so that I had become a successful writer. Nevertheless, it took me seventeen more years as a *successful* writer before I could actually support myself in comfort on my earnings as a writer.

So while you're trying to be a writer, make sure you find another way of making a decent living—and don't quit your job after you make you first sale. And don't think, either, that what I have said is enough for you to move ahead on. You need more detail and, in particular, you need examples of what is right and wrong. So don't stop here; keep on going. What I have written is prolog; the rest of the book you are now holding is the thing itself. Turn the page—

—Isaac Asimov

ON BEING A WRITER

"Are you really A.E. van Heinlein? Well, look; I have this great idea for a story; and if you'd write it, we could split the money fifty-fifty . . ."
"I've been working on a novel since college, and . . ."
"I'd like to be a writer someday, if only I had the time! I have lots of great ideas, but I never get them down on paper."
"Just how does one become a writer?"
"Do I need an agent to get published?"

Oh, no; *not **that** again,* writers often find themselves groaning when they encounter one of these remarks for the fiftieth time. Many writers have short, standard answers to cope with them. When asked how to become a writer, Raymond Chandler used to say, "Type on one side of the page, double-spaced, and leave an inch margin." Harlan Ellison explains he gets his ideas from Poughkeepsie: "There's a post office box there. You send them three bucks and they send you an idea."

The magical, mysterious, hidden Truth Of The Matter is very simple: a writer is one who writes. You become one by writing. There is no transitional stage. The purpose of this book is to help you teach yourself to write at a publishable level of competence and to dispel some of the superstitions that are all too common among not-yet-published writers.

It is not, for example, necessary to have an agent in order to sell a short story—or even a novel—in the science-fiction field. Every editor in the business receives huge piles of manuscripts every day, virtually all from complete unknowns. Maybe one in two hundred is agented. All are read. All are evaluated. Those which are worth buying are bought, no matter who wrote them or who submitted them. Every story in this book is a first SF sale, by a writer who was totally unknown at the time and consequently not represented by an agent.

Agents are primarily for full-time writers who write books, and are an absolute necessity only for writers whose work is being used for movies or TV. An agent can frequently get a better contract and more money for such works; but since the rates and terms for short stories are usually firmly fixed, the writer doesn't really need an agent there. If you are unpublished, virtually no reputable agent will want you as a client because your money-making ability is unproven. (We think you should *stay away* from agents who charge "reading fees" and remember the old observation that no good agent has to advertise.) When you are selling stories regularly and are starting to tackle novels, then it is time to think about agents.

Anyone still convinced that a writer needs an agent to sell a short story should consider the simple fact that nowadays most of the big names in the field are writing novels (and keeping their agents busy selling them), so that, if a magazine or anthology editor wants to fill pages, she or he will have to buy lots of stories from people who have never sold before. The continued existence of these publications shows that such purchasing goes on all the time, often with as many as three or four stories per issue from beginners. Stories *are* being bought from people like you.

Another common superstition is that the beginning writer's story will be stolen. The novice fears that if he lets an editor see it, it will vanish . . . until the story appears in print with somebody else's name on it. But there is no case of this ever happening in the history of science-fiction publishing. If it ever did, the whole field would quake with cries of, "By the stars, how can that editor have been so *stupid?*" That editor's reputation would be ruined utterly, and no one would send another story to him.

Furthermore, *a writer is worth more to an editor the second time around,* and still more the third, and so on. The last thing any sensible editor wants to do is to drive off his contributors, and surely someone from whom a publishable story has been stolen will never submit another one to that editor. Instead, every editor wants to turn his beginning writers into well-known names. No matter how you look at it, it isn't worth anyone's while to steal your story, as far as the domestic magazine and anthology markets are concerned.

(Movie and TV sales are another matter entirely; there, you *must* have an agent, and a good one at that, not only to protect you from possible sharp dealing but also to protect the studio from being unfairly sued for sharp dealing when in fact there has been none.)

The one kind of stealing that does go on in the science-fiction field works in the other direction: some nitwit copies a published story by a successful writer, puts the nitwit's name on it, and sends it in. Usually, the editor spots the story as an old one at once. Should he not recognize the story and publish it, the readers will always catch the deception and point it out. The nitwit's career, of course, is forever ruined, since nobody will ever take the risk of buying *anything* from the nitwit again.

Another important point: science fiction is a literature of ideas—and new ones at that. Therefore, the superstition that you have to write "safe," formula stories in order to get published is utterly, totally *wrong*. This may be so in TV, but science fiction is not TV. Instead, the new writer often makes the biggest splash—and the most assured continuing success—by being breathtakingly original. Consider such debuts as Stanley Weinbaum's "A Martian Odyssey" or Philip José Farmer's "The Lovers," or almost anything that John Varley has written. If the field did not constantly renew itself this way, it would have stagnated and died out long ago—as, in fact, almost all other American short fiction already has.

What are your chances of actually being published? The answer varies with publishers, but the percentage of stories actually bought to those submitted is—alas—very low, from perhaps one in thirty on down to one in a thousand, depending on the markets. *However,* these are overall statistics, and editors do not buy statistics; they buy stories. In fact, the only time that chance comes into the matter is when your story happens to arrive when an editor is overstocked with exactly the same kind of story. Even then, some other editor won't be overstocked when you get to him.

If you write prose that is at all competent, if your ideas show any novelty, your characters any believability, your backgrounds any color, then your chances are very good indeed, because you will be better than 90 to 99 percent of the people who think they are writers. Any writer of good science fiction will have no difficulty selling virtually all the material he can create.

What about "solicited" manuscripts? How does one get "solicited?"

A solicited manuscript is one the editor specifically asks for, as when an editor of an anthology might call up Ursula R.R. Silverberg and ask for a 5,000 word story on intelligent space-barnacles to fit a hole in a project he's working on. The overwhelming majority of manuscripts, even those from the biggest names you can think of, come in unsolicited. This means each is a surprise. When a story by anyone, including *you,* is good enough to publish, the event is a pleasant surprise. It is one of the joys of editing.

That little phrase you see on most magazines' contents page, "not responsible for unsolicited manuscripts," merely means that the editor is not to be held liable if a manuscript is lost in the mails or otherwise. It means you *must* keep a good copy of every single story you send out; it most certainly does not mean you have to ask permission before you can send in a good story!

What about "inspiration" and ideas? We're not going to give you the address of that post office box in Poughkeepsie; you'll have to come up with ideas yourself. Far more people have ideas than will ever write stories, because ideas are so easy to come by. You can research them in scientific periodicals, or they can simply come from life or from your imagination. The important points are that you collect the ideas, in memory or—better—on paper, that you assemble them into stories, and finally that you *write* those stories.

On a wintry afternoon, let's say, you look through your window and see a shed almost entirely buried by the drifting snow. You imagine an exaggerated, eternal winter, a new Ice Age smothering civilization. That is an *idea*. It is the basic idea from which John Christopher's novel, *The Long Winter,* and Arthur C. Clarke's short story, "The Forgotten Enemy," grew.

Or you put together a mental picture (say, a black-hooded stranger sitting on the sand looking at a fire), a "what-if" (a society where all news is transmitted by professional "newstellers"), and a chance remark from a TV show ("Everybody wants to be a critic")—and you have something like "The Tryouts," which appears later on in this book.

Now you can see why an author at best will brush off politely anyone who comes to him with one of those "split the money fifty-fifty and all you have to do is write my idea" offers. Idea and story are not the same. *Story* consists of character, plot, dialog, setting, and the less tangible elements like tone, imagery, and so on. An author doesn't sit around doing nothing until "inspiration" hits like a bolt of lightning, whereupon the entire story pours out as fast as he can type. There is a large amount of deliberate craftsmanship involved.

While it is true that you can't write a good story if you have nothing to say, you also can't write one if you don't know how to say it. This is what you can learn from books like this one: technique, or at least how to avoid certain obvious blunders.

In 1947, there first appeared a small volume entitled *Of Worlds Beyond: The Science of Science Fiction Writing,* edited by Lloyd Arthur Eshbach; the book is still in print from Advent:Publishers. Robert A. Heinlein's contribution to this collection was a brilliant essay, "On the Writing of Speculative Fiction," which probably contains more common sense and essential information about the art of science fiction than anything else ever penned in comparable length. In it Heinlein listed five Rules for Writing, which we cannot emphasize too strongly. They follow:

1. You must *write*. If you don't, for all the talk and sound and fury, you're not a writer. You may be reading this book for amusement; but if you don't actually practice your craft, all the advice in the world isn't going to do you any good. People who "would like to find time to write someday" probably never will, and thus are removed from further consideration here. You have to *make* time to write.

2. You must *finish* what you write.   Equally essential. Nobody will publish a promising fragment. You have to stick to a story until you are done.

3. You must refrain from rewriting except to editorial order.   See above. This taken on face value may horrify your English Literature teacher. What does Heinlein mean by *finish?* What does he mean by *rewriting?*

You can't expect to set the typewriter's line-feed to double-space, put in two sheets and a carbon, and just tap out final copy. A story may take several drafts before it is finished, especially while you're still a beginner. It may have to be set aside for a while, then completely overhauled. You may have to junk most of it and try a new approach to the same material.

Finishing means getting the story as good as you can reasonably make it, through whatever drafts and revisions are necessary to get it there. But once it is finished, you have to call it quits until someone who is willing to pay you money tells you to make a specific change. Some obsessive perfectionists go on rewriting and rewriting the same story for years, until it has been beaten to death. Others seek the advice of friends or relatives, and rewrite to their suggestions; this is just as bad.

What about revision to *editorial* order? This means the editor, having read your story, writes back to you something like: "Dear Joe, I like your story; but when the heroine steps out into the street and is run over by a spaceship at the end, everything she has done before seems rather pointless. Can you fix this?"

The implication is that if you "fix this" (and do it right), the editor will buy the story. But, you might protest, it is your story; and as it is, it says what you want it to say. Well, the editor *could* be wrong. But it's far more likely that the person you're dealing with has years of experience you don't have, and has read enormously more science fiction than you have, while you're just beginning. No one can run a successful magazine, anthology, or book publishing operation without knowing what makes a story work. Nine times out of ten, at least, the editor's request for changes should be followed. After all, the object is to *sell* this story and get on to the next one.

4. You must put it on the market.   This means you must put a copy of your manuscript in an envelope; enclose a stamped envelope, addressed to yourself, which is big enough to bring your manuscript back to you; and mail it to someone who might publish it. Our observation is that literary talent is not rare, but the will to do something with that talent *is*. For every writer who gets to the stage of submitting his material, there are dozens who are afraid of rejection, convinced there's a plot to keep new writers out, ignorant of what's being published and by whom, or otherwise inclined to procrastinate. Many simply have never thought in terms of publication before. This is the reason for the Marine drill-sergeant approach to this chapter; if we can shake a few of you into becoming published authors, it will have been worth it.

In another essay in *Of Worlds Beyond,* John W. Campbell, who was the greatest SF editor, remarked:

The reason 99% of all stories written are not bought by editors is very simple. Editors *never* buy manuscripts that are left on the closet shelf at home.

If you take the trouble to write a yarn—*send it in!* Returning to Heinlein's Rules,

5. You must keep it on the market until it is sold. Heinlein goes on to say, ". . . you will find some editor, somewhere, sometime, so unwary or so desperate for copy as to buy the worst old dog you, or I, or anybody else, can throw at him." For the new writer this is not always true. Many beginning efforts are *not* publishable. They are learning experiences. You learn that they are no good, and (one hopes) why, by the rejections you get on those stories and the comments editors make.

When Ray Bradbury began to sell regularly, he got out about a million words of his unsold and unpublished fiction and made a bonfire of it. Frederik Pohl tells how he sat up one night with his first novel, reading it page by page and understanding why it was bad, and tossing each page into the fireplace as he did. These writers could have sold some of their pre-professional work later, after they had become famous; but they knew it wouldn't do their reputations any good to do so. Heinlein was not talking about early efforts, juvenilia, and the like, but about professional-level stories which somehow didn't make it to the top markets. Of course, his worst is often better than other people's best.

Please, at this point, remember Scithers's Saving Statement: **Editors do not reject people; they reject pieces of paper that have typing on them.** And for all that it *feels* that you, your heart and soul, or your children have been turned down—it isn't so. You can pick up whatever part of yourself is on one set of pages that have been typed on and put it—in more interesting form—into another draft or another story.

For the new writer, the sensible strategy is to make up a list of all possible markets for each story. You can get this information from publications such as *Locus, The SFWA Bulletin,* and *Writer's Market.* Arrange the possible markets in a descending scale, according to what each pays. Exclude those with unreasonable contracts—that is, those that buy "all rights," that specify that yours is a "work for hire," or which take an unreasonable time to respond. Then work your way down the list.

Painful though you may find rejections to be, in spite of Scithers's Saving Statement, your object here is to maximize income, not to minimize rejections. Aim high; you may be a better writer than you think, and *this* story might make it.

To each market, submit stories one at a time, lest you find yourself competing with yourself. (If an editor is moderately interested in your work, he may buy several stories if they appear in his mailbox one at a time, whereas if you send them in a batch, he will be more likely to take the best one and send the rest back.)

If you've reached the bottom of the list and the manuscript has been turned down by every science-fiction magazine and anthology in the United States, Canada, Great Britain, and Australia, *and* by every magazine that publishes an occasional science-fiction story from a beginner, the story may still be publishable, though the odds are against it. Thereafter, you can try it on whatever new markets may appear from time to time. Meanwhile, while this story has been wandering from doorstep to doorstep, *of course* you have been busy writing another, and another, and another . . . Eventually, you may decide to retire some of your earlier efforts because, with growing experience, you see how to recycle the best of the ideas in those stories into new ones.

Again: once you've written a story and started it on the rounds of markets, get going on the next. Your time's better spent working on a new one than agonizing over what's happening to the last one. Not only does this make a rejection easier to take if that happens, but also you're that much better prepared when an editor's acceptance includes the question, "When can I see more of your work?"

STORIES: THROUGH THE
VALLEY OF THE SHADOW

*"Editors also know that the people who are really readers want to read.
They hunger to read. They will forgive a vast number of clumsinesses and
scamped work of every sort if the author will delight them just enough to
keep them able to continue."*

—*William Sloane*

And here you were thinking that the goal of writing was artistic
perfection, or creating a monument for posterity, or illuminating the
halls of Time with the strong light of Truth.

No. These are not the goals. They are desirable, but they are mere
side effects (and excuse us for calling perfection and truth "mere"
things) that are sometimes—rarely—achieved in the pursuit of the
real goal, which is to hold the willing interest of a reader. To succeed,
a story must first *entertain,* in the broad and complete sense of the
word.

To be sure, there are some people out there who are writing not
for real living people but for something called "posterity." That is
rather sad, because this purely hypothetical posterity can give them
nothing that a reading public does not give in full measure—and while
the writer is around to enjoy it, to boot. If you wish to be renowned
and praised long after you are gone, that is all right—but remember
that real literary immortality is to have future generations take your
book down from the shelf and read it, and be delighted in it. Homer
and Aristophanes and Chaucer and Shakespeare live, not because
scholars discuss them, but because they are *read.*

All right, how do you "get read"? If you write a work that is thrilling
and exciting, people will want to read it—and will forgive a great

number of mistakes if the author has this talent. An editor will recognize this and publication will follow as a natural consequence—after all, he's a reader too. If the work is not readable, it does not matter how perfectly polished its prose may be; it is a failure—and unpublishable.

But how do you write to get read? Well, helping to explain that is the purpose of this book: teaching you to write a story.

The process of storytelling is more than simply relating a set of invented facts. The amazing thing about storytelling is that it has a universal pattern; the elements of *story* are the same for an American, a Frenchman, and a Pathan from faraway Hind. Of course there are differences in language and the cultural decoration of the story, but these things are superficial. American children have no trouble at all with the tales of Nasr-ed-din Hodja (Persian), or Anansi the Spider (African), or Baba Yaga (Russian), or Bre'r Rabbit, or John Henry.

It is this universality that makes the writer's task possible. You must fit your imagined facts into this great pattern, which isn't that simple a process. The elements of a story don't all come from the conscious mind; many come from deep in the subconscious where one must navigate by instinct and touch.

But you can train your instinct, and learn to interpret what your touch is telling you. You learn this through practice and by gaining an understanding of story structure. What follows is an outline of what is needed in a story; that is, a series of steps, after James Gunn, for casting your raw ideas into **A Story.** We explore these rules in greater depth throughout the rest of this book. You should visualize these steps when reading the more detailed chapters that follow.

1. Since science fiction is a literature of ideas, a literature that has something to say, begin with an idea. An entirely new one is best, but you can work an interesting new twist or insight on an idea which hasn't already been worked to death. (This is covered in more detail in Chapter 3.)

2. An idea by itself won't carry more than a thousand words or so, and sometimes not even that many. Bring the idea to life with a conflict, which means: intelligent wills pitted against obstacles, not just chase scenes and blaster fights. Challenge your characters with enough of a problem to make them suffer, and thus drive them to action and to a resolution of problem and of story. (Conflict is covered in more detail in Chapter 4.)

3. Pick characters who will best dramatize the conflict you've set up. To do this, John M. Ford suggests: **Observe, don't imitate.** Watch, listen to, *understand* real people rather than depending on someone else's literary character. People don't change often; nor, when they do, by very much. But if they *do* change through the events of the

story, as by learning better, or growing up, or falling in love, the story becomes important, and interesting, and memorable. (Character is covered in more detail in Chapter 5.)

4. Lay out a sequence of events—a plot—which will show all the necessary steps of your character working out his main problems to a resolution. (Plot is covered in more detail in Chapter 6.)

5. Work out a self-consistent background for all this, colorful enough to hold interest, but not so obtrusive as to overwhelm the story's basic idea. You need not, and almost certainly should not, display every point that you have worked out; but you must have absolutely clear in your own mind just how your story-world works. (Background is covered in more detail in Chapter 7.)

6. Start the story in the middle of things; Homer began the *Iliad* thus, and it's good advice to this day. As H.G. Wells taught: **[You] must trick [the reader] into an unwary concession to some plausible assumption and get on with [your] story while the illusion holds.** Shoot the sheriff in the first paragraph. Backtrack to explanation or flashback only if you must, and then only when the material is immediately relevant *in* the story, as when your heroine naturally (and briefly) recalls just how she got in her present fix.

7. Select the best point of view from which to tell *this* story. Shift from one viewpoint to another only when you absolutely must do so.

8. Write in scenes that are conceived completely, like the scenes of a play. At every scene, put your characters, and thus your readers, firmly into the time and place of that scene. Appeal to the senses; go beyond what one can see, to the smell and sound and feel of your setting. But don't overdo it. Omit anything that doesn't advance the story; chip away everything that isn't *story*.

9. Dramatize everything possible—again like a play. Since your space is limited, get the maximum effect from everything. And remember that exposition is dead matter: avoid it as much as you can.

10. Avoid clichés like the plague! Learning to avoid triteness, not only in word and phrase but also in ideas, plots, characters, and settings, is easily half the task of becoming a good writer. *Use* the freedom that SF gives you to invent—to invent slang and profanity, the parables and idioms, the very clichés of your world. (They won't be clichés to your readers, of course, but will add to the unobtrusive touches of verisimilitude that make your narrative convincing.)

11. Revise the story, rejecting all unneeded diversions and irrelevant details, thus strengthening the real story. Remember that the criteria are *need* and *use*, not prettiness or how much you liked writing the passage. Fix any awkwardness, replace approximate words with precise ones, and smooth the flow of the story. But only revise as necessary—you *must* know when to stop revising.

12. Type the story, using the correct physical format, and mail

it to a paying market. (Format and submission are covered in detail in Appendix A.). When you have achieved the synthesis, fulfilled the patterns, created a story—*then* you must show it to an editor who will share it with an audience. That's what writing is all about.

You may have noticed that none of these points was concerned with the "style" of the story. Many beginners are obsessed with something they call style; some even send cover letters that say, "I know the story isn't very good—but what about my style?" The unkind but correct answer to this question is, "It's not styles we're buying, it's good stories."

There are in fact two kinds of style. One, personal style, is what most people think of when they use the word: the choices of words and rhythm, of image and symbol that make a paragraph of, say, Faulkner different from one of Hemingway. Unfortunately, personal style does not come automatically when one begins to write. You can't be taught it. Worse yet, you can't even *learn* it. It must *develop*, over many stories and many years. Some writers never do develop a single style—and there is nothing wrong with that. Who cares whether one can identify an author's work from a single random paragraph? That's what by-lines are for. Who in fact *wants* to be so stereotyped?

If it sounds as if we're telling you to forget about personal style—we *are*. If you have a long, productive writing career (and please remember how few people ever do), your style will come. Or it won't. You really won't have anything to say about it.

There is another kind of style, and this one can be taught; in fact, you *must* learn it if you hope to succeed. It is the art and skill of using the right word rather than the approximate one—its second cousin, as Mark Twain said—and of perfect rhythm in punctuation, sentence length, and paragraphing. It is an art, because the right word cannot simply be picked out of a dictionary or thesaurus. And it is a skill, because you must know your tools—language and punctuation—precisely in order to use them precisely. Think of a symphony conductor, who can pick a single false note from a hundred-piece orchestra; you are looking for false words among the thousands, and tens of thousands, of words in your story. It sounds terribly difficult. It *is*—all the more so because you are hunting for flaws in your creation. But you have to do it; and you cannot dodge the issue by talking about "protecting your art," because without the exhausting application of craft your art will not work.

Style is that use of language that creates a vivid, full-color image, with sound and smell and other sensory effects, in the reader's mind; and that is *all* it is. It has no existence for its own sake, nor is it to show off your brilliance to the reader. If you truly write brilliantly, the readers will notice without having it pointed out to them. Remember: what lasts in the reader's mind is not the phrase but the effect created by the phrase: laughter, tears, pain, joy. If the phrase is not affecting the reader, then what in the name of the Scatterer's Hangman is it *doing* there? Cut it! Without mercy or remorse or anguish—because deadweight words are traitors to the art you are trying to create.

Welcome to the Valley of the Shadow. No one said this was going to be easy.

CHAPTER 2

IDEAS: THE GAME OF IF

"A writer will seal his own coffin,
And the interests of readers will soften,
* If the author insists*
* On the usual twists,*
And he goes to the Wells once too often."

—*Mark Grenier*

"The best way to have a good idea is to have lots of ideas."

—*Linus Pauling*

About one-quarter of the stories we reject as not suitable for *Isaac Asimov's Science Fiction Magazine* suffer from idea problems: the idea content is old, or too thin to carry the story, or lacking altogether. Another one-fifth of the total of those rejected are sent back for a related problem: being essentially pointless. To keep your stories out of these depressing statistics, keep in mind James Blish's Rule: **Science fiction must have content; it must be about something.** Ours is a literature of ideas, and new ideas at that.

On the other hand, about one-eighth of rejections are of stories that are nothing but ideas, to the exclusion of plots, characters, and other important elements of story; they are tours of wonders, or sermons, or both. Obviously whatever process ran dry in the former two categories is in full flood in the latter.

What, then, is this process? Well, it isn't magic. As a rule, SF writers don't believe in magic; it's too erratic and unpredictable. The properly tuned idea mechanism runs very reliably—almost too much so. It will drive you from a warm bed to a cold typewriter, make you mumble while you're riding streetcars and ferryboats, and convince the neighbors that writers are even crazier than they're reputed to be—but nobody told you that writing was going to be easy!

Nor is the process an inborn gift. Some factors of writing apparently *are*—but ideation can be learned, even as spelling, grammar, and punctuation can.

Call it a game. There are obstacles to cross, pitfalls to avoid, tasks to accomplish. And there are rules to follow, the most important being John M. Ford's **Observe, don't imitate.** You must start with things that you can see and hear and smell and feel—precisely that, not things that you read about someone else seeing, smelling, and so on.

To illustrate the distinction, consider an episode of the TV series "Star Trek." What you are observing, when you see James Doohan as Chief Engineer Scott, is a capable actor playing the role of a Scots engineer; you are *not* by any means observing a Scots engineer. And since the creation of a television character is a joint effort by writer, director, and actor, what you are observing is only a small part of the process of creation.

To put a believable Chief Engineer aboard *your* starship, you must start earlier than this. Find a real chief engineer—of a ferry or tugboat, for instance. Observe him, get to know him, and then combine what you know of him with the spaceship you have as carefully laid out. Which need not be patterned after a U.S. Navy vessel. . . . Are you getting the point?

Story ideas follow exactly the same process. Observe, combine that observation with something else—usually a concept such as "change with time." And then fill in the details. The first step is *what if:* thereafter, *what then.* And the basic difference between SF writers and ordinary folk is that the SF writers actively remember or write down the best of their *what ifs* and **then** go on to the *what thens.*

The classical application of this process in science-fiction writing is to combine some present trend with the concept *if this goes on* . . . and thus produce an idea of the future that is different from the present. This is also (alas!) the most abused idea-generator in the business—first, because too many people copy someone else's "prediction" instead of really looking for a trend on their own; and second, because a straight-line extrapolation from what's happening now doesn't really predict the future.

Thus, editors are plagued with untidy heaps and piles of oh-how-awful-pollution-will-be-in-the-future stories. These stories seldom say anything on the subject that G.K. Chesterton didn't say better in *Tales of the Long Bow* in 1925, and are seldom based on real observation, for in point of fact, pollution is generally decreasing or at worst remaining constant, and was far worse a few years or decades ago.

As for straight-line predictions, editors get smaller heaps of stories that depend on the assumption that society will continue its trend toward greater permissiveness, especially in matters sexual. Most people throughout history have assumed that the world around them would *not* change, so any story based on the idea of change is an enormous advancement over the concept of a static world. However, the good writers have moved on from simple, linear prediction to an understanding that *rates of change* will themselves change with time. Thus, the careful observer can find signs that the permissive trend is slowing, here and there; is even, in some places and with some subjects, already reversing.

Other trends—such as population shifts from farm to city and city to suburb, or the proliferation of bureaucrats and lawyers, or even the exhaustion of natural resources—also show signs of cresting and reversing direction here and there.

Consequently, *if this goes on* must be applied with intelligence. Don't settle for imagining what it will be like when society is even more permissive (or short of resources, or oversupplied with bureaucracy, or . . .) than it is now, but look even further, to when this trend has crested and is in full ebb, to when, for example, children are ashamed of the loose-living, profligate ways of their parents. Even more invention and hard thinking is required of the writer who has picked out an *if-this-goes-on* trend that no one else has spotted (and which everybody will call "obvious" once the writer has written of it). That writer must then think through *why* the trend is trending and figure out all the *then whats* that are needed to bring his future to believable life.

John W. Campbell's Observation applies here: **The future doesn't happen one at a time.** *If this goes on* is but the first step in your ideation; next comes *if this, then what.* For, having assumed the one major change that distinguishes your story-future from the present, you must work out all the other changes that are the result of (or which must have preceded) your key change.

Another idea generator—a particular favorite of John W. Campbell's—is to select some fact or assumption that "everybody knows," that is widely taken for granted, and then combine just the reverse of that fact or assumption with as much of the rest of the known universe as will fit that one reversed item. *What if,* for an example, all of science is an enormous hoax perpetrated by wizards bent on concealing their witchcraft from the public; *what if* a future war between the United States and Mexico ended in a swift Mexican victory? (Sorry; both of these *what ifs* have been used—and in both cases, the real story turned on the *if this, what thens* that the basic ideas spawned.)

The ideas generated by this reverse-reality system tend to be wild, even outrageous. They work only if they can be made—for the duration of the story, at least—convincing. H.G. Wells had a Rule to fit these ideas: **The thing that makes such imaginations interesting is their translation into commonplace terms and a rigid exclusion**

of other marvels from the story. In the terms we've been using, this means you may use only one *what if,* one independent wonder per story—but then put in all the *what thens* that are needed to make the original wonder convincing and the story work.

A particularly elegant variant of the reversal system is to take something that almost everybody vaguely assumes—but which *actually* is not so—and to make the story turn on that. The technique is particularly well fitted to the hard-science, scientific-puzzle science-fiction tale. Whether so built, or simply built on the best scientific knowledge of the physical universe, the hard SF story is still a difficult form; it is correspondingly rare and sought after by editors.

But even the solidly scientific tale involves ideation, and thinking up new ideas can always be seen as a kind of synthesis: take one idea, fact, personality, or *anything,* then combine it with another or with several others. Generally, the more contrast there is in this synthesis, the more interesting the combination. Thus an imaginary chief engineer and an imaginary spaceship is—well—imitative. Far better, a real chief engineer played against an imaginary spaceship, the real conditions on, say, Titan and an imaginary project on that satellite, or a real literary mystery and—oh, let's try a wholly fictional arch-villain. Here, then, a pair of examples of the idea-centered story.

A SIMPLE OUTSIDE JOB
by Robert Lee Hawkins

*The author tells us that he was born
23 years ago and raised on a small farm
in Ohio. He is, he says, of that unique
breed, American-hillbilly/Japanese (the
latter on his mother's side of the family).
He has a B.S. in physics from Ohio State
and is now studying upper-atmosphere
physics at Denver University. Hobbies
include basketball and football, com-
puters, and the philosophy of science.
Mr. Hawkins reports that our purchase
of this story—his first sale—was
especially cheering since it reached him
in the middle of final exams week.*

Jeffrey Castilho used the mirrors in one corner of the airlock to
check the back of his lifepack, his eyes going from the checklist
painted on the wall to the fasteners and connectors of his suit, speaking each item out loud just as he'd been trained. Static muttered in
his earphones, from the fusion generator equipment working outside
on Titan's surface and inside Titan Pilot Project's lifedome. Then
the earphones popped and Jeff heard, "Castilho, this is Rogers. You
sure you don't want someone to come with you?"

Jeff tried to scowl and tongue the transmit button at the same
time. He caught sight of his face in the mirror, with the stringy
beard he'd started to grow when he'd found that no one outside of
translunar space shaved, and realized he had just looked funny. He
took a breath to be sure he kept the irritation out of his voice and
said, "No. It's just a matter of plugging in a new black box, and I
know you have other things to do."

"Okay. You need help, just holler."

"Sure. Thanks." Jeff tongued the button off and said to the dead
microphone, "You don't have to baby me."

Then he looked over the front of his suit: the replacement box for
the broken icecube maker, test socket and adaptor, flashlight, screw-
drivers, emergency oxygen tank. He'd be damned if he'd take a
chance on leaving something behind and asking Rogers to bring it
out. He planned on being an asset to Titan Pilot Project, not a
liability.

Jeff punched the cycle button and felt his pressure suit become
full as the airlock was evacuated. *Anyway,* he thought, *I might be
fresh out of engineering school, first time past the orbit of Luna, and
Earthgrown, but anyone short of a Self-Fulfillment Class dropout*

could handle this job. No matter what the shift supervisor thinks.

The outer door opened and Jeff stepped onto the orange-yellow surface of Titan. He felt the cold—not with his skin, but with his eyes: the dim light of the sun casting unnaturally sharp shadows, the fanciful shapes of melted and refrozen ice, orange-yellow snow drifted by the thin methane wind. Jeff looked closer. It wasn't snow, but chips of eroded ice.

Irritation fell away. This was his dream. Space-living man was self-sufficient in metals, oxygen, and silicon, but short of carbon, nitrogen, and hydrogen—especially hydrogen to be thrown away in his inefficient fusion drives. Titan had all three, carbon in the atmosphere as methane, nitrogen frozen in the ground as ammonia, hydrogen in everything. If Titan Pilot Project proved the feasibility of using these resources, dependence on Earth for organic chemicals would end. Jeffrey Castilho was proud to be part of the Project, even if it only meant fixing broken icecube makers.

He found the broken machine a few hundred meters from the lifedome. It was an irregular, dull-silver box, the size of the front half of a railroad boxcar. It had cut a geometrically perfect trench, just wide enough for its caterpillar treads and one-and-a-half meters deep. A double row of transparent water-ice cubes, as tall as Jeff, lay in the trench behind it.

Jeff carefully pushed in the safeties at the snout end of the machine, making sure the lasers wouldn't cut back in when he replaced the bad circuit. The lasers, radiating at a wavelength in the infrared strongly absorbed by water but not by methane, were supposed to melt the orange-yellow ice just ahead of the snout. The machine would then suck in the water, separate the dissolved ammonia and organic contaminants, let a cube start to freeze and drop it out the back. The cubes were shells of ice twenty or thirty centimeters thick filled with liquid water, but quickly froze solid. Plastic balloons of frozen ammonia were dropped off to one side.

But a monitor circuit in the laser control box had gone bad ten minutes before. The icecube maker's brain had turned the lasers off, signaled the main computer, and waited. The job had gone on the job board and Jeff had grabbed it.

Jeff moved to the snout end, shuffling in the low gravity. The lasers were mounted in blisters, connected by a thick wedge that formed an overhang over a pit where the melted water lay. He used his flashlight to find the access hatch, on the lower surface of the wedge.

There was a thin layer of ice covering about fifteen centimeters of liquid in the pit. The ice broke when Jeff dropped into the pit and crawled between the blisters, but he ignored it. His boots were well insulated.

CHAPTER 3

Replacing the module should have been simple enough; but crouched down under the snout, in a pressure suit, trying to work in the crowded circuit compartment by the light of a flash velcroed to one leg, it took a frustratingly long time. Finally Jeff got the black box out and wired into the test socket. Then he plugged the socket into his suit radio and let it talk to the main computer in high-pitched whistles that changed almost too fast to hear. It sounded like a cage full of birds speeded up by a factor of ten. The computer replied vocally:

"Test: module micro 1777496 dash LOC5028: module defective: failure parameters follow. . . ."

Well, he had the right one. Jeff noticed that his helmet was fogging up. The icecube maker's internal heaters were still going, and he was getting vapor—probably ammonia—condensing and freezing on the faceplate. He turned up the faceplace defogger and went back to work, plugging in the new module and checking its operation. Then he hung the old module on his belt, fastened the access hatch shut again, and started to shuffle out from under the snout.

Except his feet wouldn't come.

He swore peevishly and jerked his left foot. The foot shifted inside the boot but the boot didn't move. Jeff twisted to see past his space-suited legs and swore again.

He had little experience in swearing, but he gave it his best shot. The water in the pit that had been fifteen centimeters deep was now only half that, and there was a thick cylinder of ice around his boots all the way to the ankles.

For a second Jeff felt as cold as if he'd been naked in the methane wind. In the next second his tongue went automatically to the transmit button, but he took it back.

"Wait a minute. I must look like an *idiot*." If he called for help, would Rogers volunteer to come get him? What would the rescue party say when they saw him, crouched between the laser blisters, face in the corner, ankle-deep in dirty ice? "He expected me to screw up. Son-of-a—"

Jeff took three deep breaths. Then he tried chipping with a screwdriver, but the orange-yellow stuff was incredibly tough. He suspected new ice was freezing as fast as he chipped it off. "Couldn't wait for all the water to freeze? Had to jump right in and go wading, eh? Gahhh." Jeff stuck the screwdriver back on his belt. It might be even stupider not to call for help. Still . . .

He took his flashlight apart and shorted a wire from the test socket across the battery terminals. The wire glowed a cherry red in the dimness and was almost white-hot when Jeff applied it to the collar of ice around his right ankle. As far as he could tell, it sank right in, losing its glow, but the water seemed to freeze behind it as fast as it melted. Then the wire came loose from one terminal, sparking briefly, and was stuck fast in the ice.

"Great. I should have brought a blowtorch with me." Jeff crouched in the darkness for a while, still not willing to use his radio. And then he started to straighten up with a jerk, thumping his helmet on the overhang, and looked down at his emergency oxygen tank in a wild surmise.

The inner airlock door cycled open. With the green emergency tank dangling from his left hand, Jeffrey Castilho stepped into the cloakroom. While he was racking the pressure suit, Rogers stopped in.

"Took you a long time to finish that job, Castilho. No trouble, was there?"

Rogers's face was hard to read behind his thick black beard. Jeff made a vague motion with one hand. "Well, uh—"

Rogers saw the empty emergency tank. "What's that empty for?"

"Well—" Jeff bit the bullet. "I emptied it. I, uh, used it to build a fire."

"A fire."

Jeff's thumb indicated the outside. "People on Earth used to burn methane all the time. So I burned some because my feet were stuck in the ice."

"Ah ha. So. You were stupid enough to get stuck." Jeff winced. "But smart enough to get loose." Rogers looked at Jeff for a moment. "I guess we'll settle for that.

"Now, we've been having some trouble with the methane compressors. . . ."

CHAPTER 3

THE ADVENTURE OF THE GLOBAL TRAVELER

or:

THE GLOBAL CONSEQUENCES OF HOW THE REICHENBACH FALLS INTO THE WELLS OF INIQUITIE

by Anne Lear

Most of the author's professional sales heretofore have been in popular history. With this sale, she has won a contest with her husband to see who can sell a mystery first; this is also her first SF sale. Shakespeare and Sherlock are their household gods.

All I wanted was to find out who the Third Murderer in *Macbeth* really was. Well, I know now. I also know the secret identity and the fate of one famous personage, that the death of another occurred many years before it was reported to have done, and a hitherto unknown detail of Wm. Shakespeare's acting career.

Which just goes to show what a marvelous place to do research is the Folger Shakespeare Library in Washington, D.C. In the crowded shelves and vaults of that great storehouse are treasures in such number and variety that even their passionately devoted caretakers do not know the whole.

In my quest for the Third Murderer I started at the logical place. I looked in the card catalog under M for Murderer. I didn't find the one I had in mind; but I found plenty of others and, being of the happy vampire breed, switched gleefully onto the sidetrack offered.

Here was gore to slake a noble thirst: murders of apprentices by their masters; murders of masters by apprentices; murders of husbands by wives, wives by husbands, children by both. Oh, it was a bustling time, the Age of Elizabeth! Broadsides there were and pamphlets, each juicier than the last.

The titles were the best of it, perhaps. Yellow journalism is a mere lily in these declining days. Consider:

A true discourse. Declaring the damnable life and death of one Stubbe Peeter, a most wicked Sorcerer, who in the likeness of a Woolf, committed many murders . . . Who for the same fact was taken and executed . . .

or

Newes from Perin in Cornwall:
Of a most Bloody and unexampled Murther very lately committed by a Father on his own Sonne . . . at the Instigation of a merciless Step-mother . . .

or the truly spectacular

Newes out of Germanie. A most wonderful and true discourse of a cruell murderer, who had kylled in his life tyme, nine hundred, threescore and odde persons, among which six of them were his owne children begotten on a young woman which he forceablie kept in a caue seven yeeres . . .

(This particular murtherer is on record as having planned, with true Teutonic neatness of mind, to do in precisely one thousand people and then retire.)

Eventually I found myself calling for *The moft horrible and tragicall murther, of the right Honorable, the vertuous and valerous gentleman, John Lord Bourgh, Baron of Caftell Connell, committed by Arnold Cosby, the foureteenth of Ianuarie. Togeather with the forrofull fighes of a fadde foule, uppon his funeral: written by W.R., a feruant of the faid Lord Bourgh.*

The pamphlet was sent up promptly to the muffled, gorgeously Tudor reading room, where I signed for it and carried it off to one of the vast mahogany tables that stand about the room and intimidate researchers.

As I worked my way through the blackletter, I found the promising title to be a snare and a delusion. The story turned out to be a mediocre one about a social-climbing coward who provoked a duel and then, unable to get out of it, stabbed his opponent on the sly. Pooh. I was about to send it back, when I noticed an inappropriate thickness. A few pages beyond where I had stopped (at the beginning of the forrofull fighes) the center of the pamphlet seemed thicker than the edges. 'Tis some other reader's notes, I muttered, only this and nothing more.

So, it appeared when I turned to them, they were. There were four thin sheets, small enough to fit into the octavo pamphlet with more than an inch of margin on every side. The paper was of a good quality, much stronger than the crumbling pulp which had concealed it.

I hadn't a clue as to how long ago the sheets had been put there. They might have gone unnoticed for years, as the librarians and users of the ultra-scholarly Folger are not much given to murder as recreation, even horrible and tragicall murthers of the vertuous and valerous, and therefore they don't often ask for the bloody pulps.

Further, the descriptive endorsement on the envelope made no mention of the extra sheets, as it surely would have done had they been any part of the collection.

I hesitated briefly. People tend to be touchy about their notes, academicians more than most, as plagiarism ramps about universities more vigorously than anyone likes to admit. The writing was difficult in any case, a tiny, crabbed scribble. It had been done with a steel pen, and the spellings and style were for the most part those of *fin de siècle* England, with a salting of unexpected Jacobean usages. The paper was clearly well aged, darkened from a probable white to a pale brown, uniformly because of its protected position, and the ink cannot have been new, having faded to a medium brown.

My scruples were, after all, academic, as I had inevitably read part of the first page while I examined it. And anyway, who was I kidding?

"On this bleak last night of the year I take up my pen, my anachronistic steel pen which I value highly among the few relics I have of my former—or is it my future?—life, to set down a record which stands but little chance of ever being seen by any who can comprehend it.

"The political situation is becoming dangerous even for me, for all that I am arranging to profit by my foreknowledge of events as well as from the opportunities civil confusion offers to those who know how to use it. However, my prescience does not in this or any other way extend to my own fate, and I would fain leave some trace of myself for those who were my friends, perhaps even more for one who was my enemy. Or will be.

"To settle this point at once: those events which are my past are the distant future for all around me. I do not know what they may be for you who read this, as I cannot guess at what date my message will come to light. For my immediate purpose, therefore, I shall ignore greater realities and refer only to my own lifeline, calling my present *the* present and my past *the* past, regardless of 'actual' dates.

"To begin at approximately the beginning, then, I found it necessary in the spring of 1891 to abandon a thriving business in London. As head of most of Britain's criminal activities—my archenemy, Mr. Sherlock Holmes, once complimented me with the title 'The Napoleon of Crime'."

At this point my eyes seemed to fix themselves immovably. They began to glaze over. I shook myself back to full consciousness, and my hand continued to shake slightly as I slipped the pamphlet back into its envelope and the strange papers, oh so casually, into my own notes. After an experimental husk or two I decided my voice was functional and proceeded to return the pamphlet and thank the librarian. Then I headed for the nearest bar, in search of a quiet booth and beer to wash the dryness of astonishment and the dust of centuries from my throat.

The afternoon was warm, a golden harbinger in a gray March, and the interior of the Hawk and Dove, that sturdy Capitol Hill saloon, was invitingly dark. It was also nearly empty, which was soothing to electrified nerves. I spoke vaguely to a waitress, and by the time I had settled onto a wooden bench polished by buttocks innumerable, beer had materialized before me, cold and gold in a mug.

The waitress had scarcely completed her turn away from my table before I had the little pages out of my portfolio and angled to catch the light filtering dustily in through the mock-Victorian colored window on my left.

"... I had wealth and power in abundance. However, Holmes moved against me more effectively than I had anticipated, and I was forced to leave for the Continent on very short notice. I had, of course, made provision abroad against such exigency, and, with the help of Colonel Moran, my ablest lieutenant, led Holmes into a trap at the Reichenbach Falls.

"Regrettably, the trap proved unsuccessful. By means of a Japanese wrestling trick I was forced to admire even as it precipitated me over the edge, Holmes escaped me at the last possible moment. He believed he had seen me fall to my death, but this time it was he who had underestimated his opponent.

"A net previously stretched over the gulf, concealed by an aberration of the falls' spray and controlled by Moran, lay ready to catch me if I fell. Had it been Holmes who went over the edge, Moran would have retracted the net to permit his passage down into the maelstrom at the cliff's foot. A spring-fastened dummy was released from the underside of the net by the impact of my weight, completing the illusion.

"I returned to England in the character of an experimental mathematician, a *persona* I had been some years in developing, as at my Richmond residence I carried out the mathematical researches which had been my first vocation. I had always entertained there men who were at the head of various academic, scientific, and literary professions, and my reputation as an erudite, generous host was well established. It was an ideal concealment for me throughout the next year, while my agents, led by the redoubtable Colonel, tracked Mr. Holmes on his travels, and I began to rebuild my shadowy empire.

"During this time I beguiled my untoward leisure with concentrated research into the nature of Time and various paradoxes attendant thereon. My work led me eventually to construct a machine which would permit me to travel into the past and future.

"I could not resist showing the Time Machine to a few of my friends, most of whom inclined to believe it a hoax. One of the more imaginative of them, a writer named Wells, seemed to think there might be something in it, but even he was not fully convinced. No matter. They were right to doubt the rigmarole I spun out for them about what I saw on my travels. Mightily noble it sounded, not to say luridly romantic—Weena indeed!—although, as a matter of fact, some few parts were even true.

"Obviously, the real use to which I put the Machine during the 'week' between its completion and my final trip on it was the furtherance of my professional interests. It was especially convenient for such matters as observing, and introducing judicious flaws into, the construction of bank vaults and for gathering materials for blackmail. Indeed, I used 'my' time well and compiled quite an extensive file for eventual conversion into gold.

"As I could always return to the same time I had left, if not an earlier one, the only limit to the amount of such travelling I could do lay in my own constitution, and that has always been strong.

"My great mistake was my failure to notice the wearing effect all this use was having on the Time Machine. To this day I do not know what part of the delicate mechanism was damaged, but the ultimate results were anything but subtle.

"I come at last to the nature of my arrival at this place and time. Having learned early of the dangers attendant upon being unable to move the Time Machine, I had added to its structure a set of wheels and a driving chain attached to the pedals originally meant simply as foot rests. In short, I converted it into a Time Velocipede.

"It was necessary to exercise caution in order to avoid being seen trundling this odd vehicle through the streets of London during my business forays, but there was nothing to prevent my riding about to my heart's content in the very remote past, providing always that I left careful markings at my site of arrival.

"Thus did I rest from my labors by touring on occasion through the quiet early days of this sceptered isle—a thief's privilege to steal, especially from a friend—ere ever sceptre came to it. Most interesting it was, albeit somewhat empty for one of my contriving temperament.

"It was, then, as I was riding one very long ago day beside a river I found it difficult to realize from its unfamiliar contours would one day be the Thames, that the Velocipede struck a hidden root and was thrown suddenly off balance. I flung out a hand to stabilize myself and, in doing so, threw over the controls, sending myself rapidly forward in time.

"Days and nights passed in accelerating succession, with the concomitant dizziness and nausea I had come to expect but never to enjoy, and this time I had no control of my speed. I regretted even more bitterly than usual the absence of gauges to indicate temporal progress. I had never been able to solve the problem of their design; and now, travelling in this haphazard fashion, I had not the least idea when I might be.

"I could only hope with my usual fervency and more that I should somehow escape the ultimate hazard of merging with a solid object—or a living creature—standing in the same place as I at the time of my halt. Landing in a time-fostered meander of the Thames would be infinitely preferable.

"The swift march of the seasons slowed, as I eased the control lever back, and soon I could perceive the phases of the moon, then once again the alternating light and dark of the sun's diurnal progression.

"Then all of a sudden the unperceived worn part gave way. The Machine disintegrated under me, blasted into virtual nothingness, and I landed without a sound, a bit off balance, on a wooden floor.

"A swift glance around me told me my doom. Whenever I was, it was in no age of machines nor of the delicate tools I required to enable my escape.

"Reeling for a moment with the horror of my position, I felt a firm nudge in the ribs. A clear, powerful voice was asking loudly, 'But who did bid thee join with us?'

"The speaker was a handsome man of middle age, with large, dark eyes, a widow's peak above an extraordinary brow with a frontal development nearly as great as my own, a neat moustache, and a small, equally neat beard. He was muffled in a dark cloak and hood, but his one visible ear was adorned with a gold ring. As I stood dumbly wondering, he nudged me again, and I looked in haste beyond him for enlightenment.

"The wooden floor was a platform, in fact a stage. Below on one side and above on three sides beyond were crowds of people dressed in a style I recognized as that of the early seventeenth century.

"Another nudge, fierce and impatient: 'But who did bid thee join with us?'

"The line was familiar, from a play I knew well. The place, this wooden stage all but surrounded by its audience—could it possibly be the Globe? In that case, the play . . . the play must be . . . 'MACBETH!' I all but shouted, so startled was I at the sudden apprehension.

"The man next to me expelled a small sigh of relief. A second man, heretofore unnoticed by me, spoke up quickly from my other side. 'He needs not our mistrust, since he delivers our offices and what we have to do, to the direction just.'

" 'Then stand with us,' said the first man, who I now realized must be First Murderer. A suspicion was beginning to grow in my mind as to his offstage identity as well, but it seemed unlikely. We are told that the Bard only played two roles in his own plays: old Adam in *As You Like It,* and King Hamlet's ghost. Surely . . . but my reflections were cut off short, as I felt myself being covertly turned by Second Murderer to face upstage.

"First Murderer's sunset speech was ended, and I had a line to speak. I knew it already, having been an eager Thespian in my university days. Of course, to my companions and others I could see watching from the wings most of the lines we were speaking were spontaneous. 'Hark!' said I. 'I hear horses.'

"Banquo called for a light 'within,' within being the little curtained alcove at the rear of the stage. Second Murderer consulted a list he carried and averred that it must be Banquo we heard, as all the other expected guests were already gone into the court. First Murderer proffered me a line in which he worried about the horses' moving away; and I reassured him to the effect that they were being led off by servants to the stables, so that Banquo and Fleance could walk the short way in. 'So all men do,' I said, 'From hence to th' Palace Gate make it their walk.'

"Banquo and Fleance entered. Second Murderer saw them coming by the light that Fleance carried, and I identified Banquo for them, assisted in the murder—carefully, for fear habit might make me strike inconveniently hard—and complained about the light's having been knocked out and about our having failed to kill Fleance.

"And then we were in the wings, and I had to face my new acquaintances. Second Murderer was no serious concern, as he was a minor person in the company. First Murderer was a different matter altogether, however, for my conjecture had proved to be the truth, and I was in very fact face to face with William Shakespeare.

"I am a facile, in fact a professional, liar and had no trouble in persuading them that I was a man in flight and had hidden from my pursuers in the 'within' alcove, to appear among them thus unexpectedly. That Shakespeare had been so quick of wit to save his own play from my disruption was no marvel; that the young player had followed suit as matter for congratulation from his fellows; that I had found appropriate lines amazed them all. I explained that I had trod the boards at one time in my life and, in answer to puzzled queries about my strange garb, murmured some words about having spent time of late amongst the sledded Polack, which I supposed would be mysterious enough and did elicit a flattered smile from the playwright.

"As to my reasons for being pursued, I had only to assure my new friends that my troubles were of an amatory nature in order to gain their full sympathy. They could not afford openly to harbor a fugitive from justice, although players of that time, as of most times, tended to the shady side of the law, and these would gladly have helped me to any concealment that did not bring them into immediate jeopardy. As I was but newly arrived in the country from my travels abroad, lacked employment, and could perform, they offered me a place in the company, which I accepted gladly.

"I did not need the pay, as I had observed my customary precaution of wearing a waistcoast whose lining was sewn full of jewels, the universal currency. However, the playhouse afforded me an ideal *locus* from which to begin making the contacts that have since established me in my old position as 'the Napoleon of crime,' ludicrous title in a time more than a century before Napoleon will be born.

"As to how my lines came to be part of the play's text, Will himself inserted them just as the three of us spoke them on the day. He had been filling the First Murderer part that afternoon by sheer good luck, the regular player being ill, and he found vastly amusing the idea of adding an unexplained character to create a mystery for the audience. He had no thought for future audiences and readers, certainly not for recondite scholarship, but only sought to entertain those for whom he wrote: the patrons of the Globe and Blackfriars and the great folk at Court.

"I am an old man now, and, in view of the civil strife soon to burst its festering sores throughout the country, I may not live to be a much older one. I have good hopes, however. Knowing the outcome is helpful, and I have taken care to cultivate the right men. Roundheads, I may say, purchase as many vices as Cavaliers, for all they do it secretly and with a tighter clasp on their purses.

"Still, I shall leave this partial record now, not waiting until I have liberty to set down a more complete one. If you who read it do so at any time during the last eight years of the nineteenth century, or perhaps even for some years thereafter, I beg that you will do me the great favor to take or send it to Mr. Sherlock Holmes at 221B Baker Street, London.

"Thus, in the hope that he may read this, I send my compliments and the following poser:

"The first time the Third Murderer's lines were ever spoken, *they were delivered from memory.*

"Pray, Mr. Holmes, who wrote them?

"Moriarty

"London

"31st December 1640"

We wrote to each of the authors of the stories in this book, asking how they came to write the stories, what changes they made as they were writing them, and how they would do things differently now.

CHAPTER 3

Robert Lee Hawkins replied, of "A Simple Outside Job," as follows:

"When I took another look at the first draft of 'A Simple Outside Job,' I noticed that the only dialog was at the very end. Well, the final draft didn't really have any more dialog, but I disguised the fact by having Jeff Castilho talk to himself. Besides breaking up what had been solid exposition, this let Jeff provide some of the information and kept him on stage much more than he had been in the first draft. The second thing I noticed was that I had originally spelled out the solution to the problem in much more detail. I remember worrying quite a bit about whether I had removed too much detail in the final draft, although it seems obvious now that if there is any joy in reading a story like 'A Simple Outside Job,' it is in figuring out the solution, not in being told the solution.

"The problem and the solution were the same in both first and final draft, as were most of the details (e.g., pushing in the safeties to prevent the lasers from coming on when the new part was put in place). Most of the changes were in the presentation. . . .

"If I were rewriting this story today, it seems to me that the ending suggests that Rogers expected Jeff to get stuck and let him go out as some kind of test, but it doesn't make a definite statement. I think I'd rewrite the ending one way or the other, probably to leave out the suggestion of a test.

"To me, the most important thing about this story is that I finished it and mailed it out. For five years I had been thinking up stories, starting them and not finishing them. I might rewrite the first quarter of a story four times and then drop the project. When I started 'A Simple Outside Job,' I told myself that I would write a first draft all the way through, no matter how much I wanted to go back and straighten out a twisted phrase or an unclear description. Then I would write a second draft through, if necessary a third; and the third draft would go in the mail. Of course, I was helped by the shortness of the story."

Anne Lear wrote us about "The Adventure of the Global Traveler":

"The story actually did come out of the Folger and the Third Murderer problem. During the time when I was working on *Macbeth* I tended to pester friends and acquaintances with the question, 'Who do *you* think is the Third Murderer?' Most of them could not have cared less if they had tried with both hands for a week, and one night at the National Press Club bar a guy named Lee Egerstrom finally shut me up by saying firmly, 'Professor Moriarty, of course.' Of course! I still have not finished the scholarly piece I set out to write. Thus the Genesis.

"I did a lot of checking of dates in Wells and the Sherlock Holmes Canon to be sure they meshed as I hoped they would, did more checking on details of the historical people involved (which is to say that I stole from Holinshed just as Shakespeare did), wrote the story, and sent it off to the magazine, to which I had been trying for some time to peddle a tale.

"The editor returned it with a list of suggestions, most of which improved it. I have what Hemingway called a 'well functioning crap detector,' right enough; but it has a delayed action so that I am virtually blind to the most glaring lapses of plot and style until some time has gone by after I have finished a story. Good editing always helps me tighten, as it did in this case.

"However, there were some points at which I could not make the requested changes. For example, the editor wanted me to stay in the library, instead of shifting to the Hawk and Dove; and this I simply could not do. I think it was mainly the thought of the awesome fuss the discovery would have kicked up in the majestic Folger. Professor Moriarty and—more especially—the filching of items however accidentally in the collection simply did not belong in the Tudor reading room, although both were at home in the saloon.

"That one worked out, but the editor and I never did agree on his demand for the excision of an entire third of the story. I had Moriarty actually going back to 11th century Scotland and *being* the original Third Murderer, in response to Banquo's having treated him with unconscious arrogance which the Professor resented. This was to have been the first stop on the uncontrolled forward progression of the Time Velocipede. Ah well.

"Perhaps one day I shall persuade someone to print the entire story and let the reader be the judge. Aside from this one cavil, I would not make any changes, as I have always liked this story better than any other I have written.

"And this brings me to the reason why I am delighted to have this opportunity. For some time I have squirmed under a sense of plagiarism and wished to give credit where it is due. The ending I wrote for 'The Global Traveler' was terrible, a dreary dribble that wound up nothing and left the reader, not to mention the writer, irritated and unzapped. It was an editor who came up with the paradoxical gloat that tied up everything into a neat, maddening package; and I am very grateful indeed."

The basic idea for "A Simple Outside Job" is that methane (essentially the natural gas of your gas range) will burn when oxygen is available, whether the methane is blown into an oxygen atmosphere or vice versa. From there, the *then whats* build rapidly toward a story: Titan, a moon of the planet Saturn, has an atmosphere mostly of methane, and is covered with water ice. There could be a research station built by men on Titan, and the workers at that station would

CHAPTER 3

be working outside the station in pressure suits with their breathing oxygen in tanks. Since water—as ice—is plentiful on Titan's surface, they'd probably use that instead of shipping supplies of water from Earth. . . .

And so the story builds. It could, of course, as easily have built from a different direction; if the writer decided first what the emergency would be—getting frozen into Titan's surface ice—a way could be invented toward the solution that methane burns in oxygen.

And from the central scientific puzzle, the story involves human elements—as it must, to *be* a story. Castilho, the new guy in the station, is trying to prove himself and is acutely aware that old hand Rogers thinks he'll get into trouble outside. Now, a stock trick in writing is to up the stakes, to make the problem ever more serious and menacing to the participants. The author resisted the temptation to do so here. He could have made getting free a life-or-death proposition for Castilho; he could have made it even more important, could have had Castilho carrying a message essential to the defense of the Galactic Empire against . . . and the story might have collapsed under the weight of the buildup necessary to make the situation and the suspense convincing.

This story-idea could be used as one of many adventures in a sweeping, *Star Wars* kind of space epic; here, however, we're concerned with a simple, short story built on a bit of science. Instead of elaborating on an invented Empire, the author has built believability into the story by using familiar—and hence wholly convincing—human elements around the puzzle. The reader knows what it's like to be the new guy, knows the need to prove oneself in the face of the old hand's skepticism—and the story takes both its believability and its novelty from the *contrast* between familiar, wholly human motives and the exotic landscape of Titan.

In her story, "The Adventure of the Global Traveler, or: The Global Consequences of How the Reichenbach Falls into the Wells of Iniquitie," Anne Lear tackles a kind of story that is much harder to write than she makes it appear. The very basic idea here, explaining some or other quirk of history by science-fictional means, has been used so often that it's very difficult to do anything fresh with it. And finding another long-lost manuscript on Sherlock Holmes has become a cliché even outside our field.

In general, this kind of *literary* idea is a tricky business. You can't use the characters of most twentieth-century authors lest you infringe their copyrights. If you take something from a public-domain source such as Shakespeare or Wells, you have another problem. Stories derived from literature rather than life tend to have a second-hand quality about them. Frequently they are no more than commentaries on a type of writing or else they are elaborate in-group references. This one, too, succeeds as an elegant joke on the sheer audacity of its ideas. The amazing thing, the thing that made the story good enough to publish, is that it comes to life *in addition* to being a clever gag. It works as a *story*.

Again: an idea is not enough. This particular collection of ideas is marvelous as a cocktail party (or press club bar) joke: "Hey, imagine a story with Sherlock Holmes and Macbeth and H.G. Wells's Time Machine!" But pulling the story off is an entirely different matter. Strictly taken as ideas, these elements are hardly a guarantee of success; all are over-familiar, to say the least. It would be all too easy to write a bad, tedious story about them.

Only, that's not quite what Anne Lear is writing about. Note the distinctions: she's writing not about Holmes, but Moriarty; not about Macbeth, but about the Third Murderer and Wm. Shakespeare himself; and—for the duration of the story at least—it's Moriarty's Time Machine, not Wells's (thus, Moriarty becomes Wells's unnamed Time Traveler). Note also the careful juxtaposition of elements: the Folger Library with the divers murthers of Elizabethan broadsides and pamphlets; the Hawk and Dove, another Capitol Hill landmark, with Moriarty's narrative. And this accuracy of detail does much to make the story effective. Both the Folger Library and the Hawk and Dove *are* accurately captured here; so too are the eccentricities of Elizabethan spelling and the late-Victorian phrasing of Moriarty's letter.

Our objection to the materialization of Moriarty in Scotland, as the story was originally written, was the staggering coincidence of hitting, quite by chance, both the original, real murder *and* a performance of it in Shakespeare's *Macbeth*. We also believed that the story worked perfectly well without the Scottish episode. Our objection to the shift from the library to the saloon, for the reading of Moriarty's letter, was that it appeared to be an unnecessary complication. There are times when the editor is right; there are times when he isn't.

As for the editorial addition—the little twist at the very end that the author so liked—that should be credited to John M. Ford, who was visiting the editorial offices when the manuscript came in, and consequently had been put to work copy-editing. (We do, be assured, check such changes with the author before a story is actually printed.)

CONFLICT: WINDING THE MAINSPRING

*"Fortunately, [psycho]analysis is not the only way to resolve inner conflicts.
Life itself remains a very effective therapist."*

—*Dr. Karen Horney*

Simply put, conflict or tension of some kind is an absolute essential of every story. Without conflict, one may have a descriptive travelog or a prose vignette; but not a *story*. Conflict—pressure from within and without—is what causes characters to take their actions, heroic and cowardly, great and terrible; it causes the events of the story to matter to the characters; and when the conflict is resolved, the tension released, the story is over (and the story is *not* over until that resolution occurs).

The elements of a work of fiction can no more operate in isolation than the organs of a body can live independently. But we can provide the following interdependent definitions:

Plot—the story line—is what happens.

Conflict—the driving force—is why it happens.

Background—the setting—is where it happens.

Character—the cast of players—is the nature of those to whom or because of whom it happens. Note that different people—and in stories, different characters—produce wholly different resolutions to an identical conflict. Hamlet tends to hesitate and to deliberate, while Othello impetuously acts first and thinks later. If the two swapped places, neither play would be a tragedy: Hamlet would watch and wait long enough to discover Desdemona's innocence, and Othello would run King Claudius through with a rapier at the first opportunity in Act 1. And Shakespeare's King Richard II, who never seemed to understand much or to get anything done, would have bumbled around feeling sorry for himself in either situation, resolving nothing.

A *protagonist* is someone who faces a problem or an obstacle and must deal with it. An *antagonist* is the person who set up that problem, the one who caused all the trouble. The protagonist is often the hero, narrator, or viewpoint character of a story, which makes his opponent the villain; but this isn't always the case. The protagonist, however, is always the person most directly involved in the conflict.

In the discussion of Shakespeare above, note that we transposed protagonists between conflicts, leaving undisturbed the antagonists, Claudius and Iago, who started all the trouble because of their own natures.

Consider an exchange of protagonists between "A Simple Outside Job" and "The Adventure of the Global Traveler." Swap Jeff Castilho for Moriarty. Moriarty, finding himself unexpectedly in the rôle of the inexperienced newcomer, would play out that part exactly as the people around him—Rogers and the rest—expected he would. Finding himself stuck in the ice, Moriarty would have called for help at once. On the other hand, if Castilho were traveling by time machine, he'd never let the machine deteriorate unnoticed; his training and experience were that machines are *important*.

But even in a story as short as "A Simple Outside Job," there is a protagonist, a conflict, and an antagonist. To find the protagonist, ask "Who hurts?" (Who is under pressure; who is at the center of things?) To find the conflict, ask why that character is under stress. These conflicts may be with other people (or intelligent beings, of whatever sort) or with things (environment, machines, or animals) or even within the protagonist himself. In one obvious way, Jeff Castilho is in conflict with the environment: his feet are frozen in the ice and he wants to get loose. At the same time, he's in conflict with Rogers: Rogers expects Castilho to get into trouble and Castilho wants to prove him wrong. And that leads to the third conflict: Castilho wants to call for help and at the same time wants to free himself unaided.

"The Adventure of the Global Traveler," for all its greater length, has far less conflict throughout; consequently it comes close to being a simple tour of wonders. But there *are* conflicts, and they make the story go. First the narrator battles the Folger card catalog in search of the Third Murderer, then struggles with her own conscience over the sheets hidden in the pamphlet. Then Moriarty's conflicts take over: first with Sherlock Holmes, then with his sudden Elizabethan predicament, and finally with Holmes again, as he poses the question one doubts even the Great Detective can answer.

Thus, conflicts come in all shapes and sizes. There is one thing that conflict is *not*, however, and that is slam-bang action for its own sake. A struggle has to mean something; it must be relevant to the development of character, advancement of plot, and resolution of the overall situation. If your hero is chased by a dinosaur for ten pages or stops to shoot it out with the Galactic Space Marines for a while and then goes on with the story, unchanged by his experiences, that isn't conflict; it's padding. Conflict *can* be physical, and it *can* be resolved by a violent act, but it doesn't have to be. The story may end with a simple decision to do or not do something *and* an understanding of why. It may be something as quiet (and *apparently* glossed over) as Rogers deciding that Castilho isn't so stupid after all. But the conflict *must* be resolved, and the tension relieved, or the story hasn't *done* anything—inviting that most painful of all criticisms, "So what?"

In the example that follows, note particularly how the point-of-view character, "Marian Warren," gains allies by resolving internal conflicts in two of the people around her.

SOMEONE ELSE'S HOUSE
by Lee Chisholm

*Ms. Chisholm is Canadian-born, married,
and now living in the beautiful
Monterey area of California. She broke
into print in the late '60s in* Alfred
Hitchcock's Mystery Magazine. *She's
since sold to* Cavalier *and* Cat Fancy.
*(She's a cat person, obviously.) This
is her first sale to an SF magazine, but
some of her recent sales to* AHMM
have included strange touches.

"How are you, Marian?"

The face hanging above her own assumed shape, dark mists clearing to reveal cold, gray eyes and a neat moustache centered exactly above a thin upper lip; with nose, cheekbones, and forehead cast in neat, middle-aged symmetry topped by iron-gray hair, stiff and short as iron filings. There was a coldness and remoteness about the face that had nothing to do with her emerging consciousness.

"Well, Marian?"

Impatience was there too, barely disguised by the show of concern. Obviously she was being a drain and a burden again, just as she had always been. First to her parents who had wanted a boy as their firstborn, not a sickly girl-child, and then later to her sister Viola, with whom she roomed. Viola and her husband Henry needed the room rent, while barely tolerating her physical presence.

She could get out; she knew that. But it was the headaches that frightened her. At least Viola understood; got her to bed and called the doctor. Got her the shot that killed the pain. Obviously she was just coming out of one of those shots now. She didn't know the doctor. He must be new.

"Can you hear me, Marian?" he repeated impatiently.

"Who," she asked, her mouth dry and cottony, "is Marian?"

"You," he replied, "are Marian."

"Oh, no I'm not. I'm . . ." She heard her voice stop and hang there. She was— Who was she? My God, her own name! Gone! It was funny, of course. Later on she would tell . . . Surely there was someone she could tell, some friend at the library where she worked. She struggled for the image of a friend, some familiar face among the stacks of books, wall-to-wall and floor-to-ceiling, that had been her life. But no image came. Just the books themselves—dry, lifeless; all the wisdom, passion and dreams of the world reduced to symbols on the printed pages. She knew then that she had no friend, just the books. And the books were cold. . . .

"My name is not Marian," she insisted again.

"I was afraid of this," the doctor said, turning to two people who came slowly into focus behind him. A young man and a woman. "It's the new drug. Being used with great success now for migraines, but it affects the memory center of the brain."

"For how long, doctor?" the woman asked. She was in her forties, blond, chic, and carefully made-up. The young man at her side, in a navy blazer with a longish haircut, seemed barely out of his teens. But they were obviously related. The shape of the faces was the same, sharp with high cheekbones and slanted, almost Slavic eyes.

She gazed up at them with interest. It went without saying that they were Rich with a capital **R,** something she herself had never been. But she recognized it when she saw it. The good clothes, the haughty air, the boredom that sufficiency can bring.

"Maybe a day, maybe a week. Depends upon the metabolism of the subj— er, patient. She could throw it off with another few hours' sleep. It's hard to say."

"But the drug *was* worth trying, doctor. I've never seen my sister in so much pain."

"It was one of her worst, yes," the doctor agreed dryly.

She listened, intrigued. It was a dream, of course. These people, the "doctor," even the room. Her eyes roamed around the darkened interior: rich mahogany furnishings from another era, all stiffly feminine. A woman's room. Floral wallpaper, heavy drapes and the four-poster bed in which she lay. She wouldn't be surprised to see a canopy appear overhead. Anything could happen in dreams.

But no canopy materialized. Instead, the three faces remained hanging above her own. She closed her eyes. Visions and dreams, distortions of time and space were no strangers to her. She'd had migraines since childhood, and in her sufferings, altered by the half-light world of drugs, she had seen many things. Devils and demons, distended furniture, upside-down rooms. She would sleep and the dream would pass. It always did.

But it didn't. When she awoke again the bed was the same with the four posts spiraling upward. The floral wallpaper remained, immutably imprinted with fat cabbage roses, and the room was still battened down by the heavy furnishings. Only now a grim-faced nurse, middle-aged and white-capped, with the visage of a minor bulldog, stood above the bed.

"Are you awake, Miss Warren?" asked the bulldog.

She'd experienced this before, too. The continuance of dreams. One awoke, floundered to the bathroom surrounded by a miasma of pain, then came back, fell into bed and resumed the dream. However strange or grotesque, the dream simply waited for the dreamer to pick up the threads. She closed her eyes. She would sleep the bulldog away.

But the bulldog stayed. "Miss Warren," she repeated in a voice flat with professionalism, "the doctor thinks you should get up now. Just for a little while. Start to get your bearings again."

"I don't want to get up, and I'm not Miss Warren!"

The nurse's opaque brown eyes showed a flicker of interest, as though she'd been told to expect this denial of identity. Her expression said, "Here it comes!"

"I want to see my sister, Viola," she said pettishly. At least that was one name she could remember.

"There's no person by that name here," the nurse said. "Your sister Mrs. Palmer's first name is Grace. *Grace*," she repeated, as though to write the word indelibly on this slow patient's brain.

Grace! It was laughable. Viola had always looked like a Viola. Dark-eyed and dark-skinned with curly black hair. The exact opposite of herself really, with her drab blond hair and fair skin that refused to tan.

"My sister's name is Viola," she said with dignity, then added, "Where am I? In some kind of nursing home? Was I that bad?"

"You are in your own home, Miss Warren."

"My own home?" She glanced around distractedly at the heavy, ornate room. "This is not my home; not my room. This is somebody else's house."

But the nurse was equal to the situation. Undoubtedly she'd been chosen for just that reason.

"It may seem strange now. You've been under very heavy medication. Disorientation's not unusual, but you'll find that little by little, the room and your surroundings will look familiar again. Now ups-a-daisy." The nurse got one strong arm between pillow and shoulders and hoisted. Then, reaching under the sheets, she dragged the reluctant legs forward. "There now, isn't that better?"

She sat on the edge of the bed; the room swam. When it cleared she found herself staring down at her own lank limbs. "Too tall and skinny," her mother used to say. Viola was the cute one. But afterwards, in later years barely out of her teens, Viola went to fat, whereas she had stayed gaunt. But gaunt was "in" by then. A model's figure, some friends said enviously, but she had never made the most of it. Heavy, dark stockings and plain skirts and sweaters had been her standard fare. It had been fixed in her mind that she wasn't "cute." The world's opinion, kinder and grander, mattered little. . . .

Could it be that she wasn't in a nursing home at all, but an asylum? Could the pain of the last headache have driven her crazy? She wouldn't put it past Viola and Henry to stick her in an asylum. Anything to get rid of her.

CHAPTER 4

"We'll go to the bathroom now, Miss Warren." The nurse helped her up. The floor swayed. She felt wobbly, but she was prodded forward to a door at the far side of the room which opened to reveal a baroque bathroom in imitation marble. The towels hung in thirsty richness, deep blue and thick as rugs, and in one corner a luxurious, white shower robe waited to accommodate its owner. This, most surely, was not hers! She wondered again when the dream would end.

The toilet flushed (the bodily functions were certainly real), and the nurse reappeared.

"How about a tub, Miss Warren?"

Miss Warren this, Miss Warren that. Was it possible that she *was* Miss Warren? Some new person in a new house, undertaking a new life? She leaned over the sink and looked into the mirror; same thin face, skin gray from weakness, eyes cloudy with drugs. But undoubtedly herself.

"Yes," she said. "Perhaps a warm tub. . . ." She had heard people talk like that in movies. Joan Crawford looking lofty in padded shoulders, or Myrna Loy, rich and pampered. A tub always seemed to improve things for people who had houses like this and bathrooms to themselves. There was no Henry here to knock on the door and tell her to hurry it up, or Viola to wail about the hot water running out. "Yes, perhaps a tub. . . ." she murmured, and was helped back to her bed to await the filling of same.

She was sitting on the side of the bed trying to sort out her thoughts when the door burst open and the young man who had hung over her earlier bounded in, a combination of high spirits and youthful fashion in a melon shirt and gray slacks.

"Hello, Auntie dear!" he said blithely, bending to kiss her on the cheek—the air-light landing of a butterfly. She drew back, startled.

He laughed, showing fine white teeth in the thin, narrow face. His brilliant blue eyes creased to oriental slits above the high cheekbones. A strange face. Interesting. Different. And one aware of its power to charm.

"You know," she said sternly, "that I am not your aunt."

"Since when?" he teased.

"Since never at all."

"Wishing me away won't work," he said, plopping himself down beside her. "I'm your nephew. You're stuck with me. Look, Auntie, . . ." The young man prepared to look serious. "I know your headaches are bad, but this last one was a complete wipe-out. Dr. Martin, your fancy medic, had to resort to some kind of miracle drug. Do you know you were out for three days?"

Three days! Seventy-two hours! Somewhere in there she had lost her identity and obviously gained a nephew.

"What's your name?" she asked.

"Auntie, are you asking *my name?*" He looked stricken. "Little Huey, whom you adored from the moment I was born, and spoiled silly for the next nineteen and three-quarter years?"

"Did I really?" *Wouldn't it be nice if I had?* she thought. If someone could hand her a dream come true, this would be it. Herself a wealthy matron of obviously unlimited means with a favorite nephew to indulge and love.

"What's your last name, Huey?" she asked.

Huey made a small exploding sound with his mouth. "Auntie, you can't mean it! My last name? Crompton, of course. Huey David Crompton, the Third."

"Your mother, I take it, is supposedly my sister, Grace?"

"You're getting good, Auntie. Only Mother's last name isn't Crompton any more. After Father died, Mother married Mr. Jarrett, very cold, very correct. Then she married Mr. Van Ness, not cold, not correct at all. Then she married Mr. Palmer. None of her choices were wise, but he was the worst. His skin was walnut-colored and he sang calypso in nightclubs. He managed to drain off what was left of her personal fortune. So, money gone, she came home to you. As for me, I've been here all along, except for school. I was 'inconvenient,' you see, for Mother and the parade of new husbands. Besides, you wanted me to yourself, didn't you, Auntie?"

He gave her a hug, encircling her thin shoulders with his strong, young arm. She drew away slightly, some habit from her cold, prim past, but it really was a pleasant sensation to be somebody's warmly loved aunt. Even if she wasn't. . . .

"Miss Warren's bath is ready." The nurse made a granite-faced reappearance.

"Go get cleaned up, Auntie," said Huey boyishly. "Then why don't you come downstairs for cocktails? It's only . . ." he studied his expensive wristwatch, "ten past four. The sun's over the yardarm and all that. You do feel okay, don't you?"

"Yes," she said. "I feel fine. Weak but fine."

"Good-o. Nursie here can bring you downstairs and keep an eye on you."

The nurse nodded her unsmiling assent.

She allowed herself to be helped down the broad staircase, knowing it was a game of "let's pretend" they were all playing. Not the nurse, perhaps, who seemed sincere in her rôle, but the rest of them, herself included. The only problem was, the game was so much fun! For the first time in her life she felt her real self emerging from some bleak, half-remembered shell.

Her dress was a tomato-colored print with an electric blue bodice

CHAPTER 4

and matching blue cuffs. On the hanger in the bedroom closet, yawning with department-store munificence, it had looked too young, too blatant. But the nurse had reached for it unerringly, insisting that she "slip it on." The effect of it slithering over her slim figure had been almost sensual, and once zipped up, the effect of its mellow color next to her pale skin was simply magical. It lent life, even radiance to her face.

The nurse had sprayed her straggly hair with dry shampoo and pulled the clean strands back from her face. A touch of tomato-colored lipstick completed the picture. She was sure she had never looked so good in her whole forgotten life.

At the bottom of the stairs Huey enfolded her in strong arms.

"Auntie, you look sensational! Wait till Franklin sees you."

"Franklin?"

"Oh come now, don't tell me you've forgotten Franklin, your faithful old butler? We had to keep him away from your bedside; you know how he likes to hover! So we sent him to the city for a small holiday. He thought you were dying, Auntie."

She wondered if the real Marian Warren were indeed dead and she had been brought in to take her place. She'd read of such things in mystery novels. Of course, it would be hard to fool the butler.

Grace was there; the sleek, slant-eyed blonde who was Huey's mother. She wore a floor-length dress of cream-colored silk that swirled softly about her lovely figure like the shimmer of a waterfall.

"Marian darling," she purred, drifting forward, the handsome library behind her a mere stage setting for her elegance. "You're up!"

"I'm up," she acknowledged, "but I'm not 'Marian darling,' as you know, of course."

"Well, if you say so, dear." Grace took her elbow and helped her to a damask-covered wing chair beside the fireplace.

"There, dear, your favorite chair. And Huey has made a dry Rob Roy for you."

"Right here, Auntie. On the rocks."

Huey brandished an amber-colored drink. Out of curiosity she sampled it and found it delicious, but potent. She recognized the taste of good Scotch. They always served Scotch at Christmas parties in the library. The other ingredient mystified her. But she liked it.

"Very good, Huey," she murmured.

"I imagine you would like a small sherry, Nurse," Grace said to the nurse, who had tried to make herself inconspicuous in a deep chair in a corner of the room.

The nurse nodded her acceptance. "Dry, if you please," she said sedately.

How awful to be in service like the nurse. To be accepting "suggestions" in somebody else's house. She knew. She had been doing it all her life. First in her parents' home until they both died. She was fuzzy on the details, but she knew they were dead. Then her sister Viola's house. And always, she had been the lonely hanger-on. The unwanted. Until now, when by some marvelous and obviously illegal set of circumstances, people bowed and deferred to her. And, however long it lasted, she was going to enjoy it to the full. Even if the dénouement was death. After all, she reasoned, she had been brought onto the scene for a purpose. That purpose accomplished, she would be removed. Or, at least, they would try.

"We have a surprise for you, Marian darling," Grace said, all catlike charm. "Bill Darrick said he might stop by this evening for cocktails."

"How interesting," she heard herself say. "Especially when I don't know who Bill Darrick is."

"That's what comes of being rich, Auntie love," said Huey with a chuckle. "You can conveniently forget your high-priced lawyer."

"My lawyer; hmm...." She studied Grace through narrowed eyes. Unless Bill Darrick turned out to be ninety and doddering, she could pretty well guess whose lawyer he was—by inclination if not by retainer. Well, another piece of the fresco was daubed in. She would wait and see.

The doorbell chimed in the distance. No lowbrow scurry to answer the door here. Grace, Huey, and herself, and even the nurse, continued sipping like gods on Olympus.

In a few moments the library door was silently opened and an old butler stood in the doorway, his chest sunken, his waistline rounded. But his face was beautiful. An aquiline nose, pinched with old age, preserved its authority beneath gray eyes sunken into seas of flesh. His head was bald, but the angle noble. She could see he was but a memory of his former grand self, doubtless resisting retirement, obscurity, and the grave.

"Madam," he said, "Mr. William Darrick, solicitor, has come to call."

"Very good, Franklin." Grace's voice was a blend of honey and cream. "Show him in."

Franklin looked toward her chair, his blurred eyes focusing on the warm, tomato-colored presence. He obviously assumed her to be Marian Warren.

"Madam...." He stepped forward, his voice cracking.

"How are you, Franklin?" she said graciously. "It's only fair to tell you that I'm not Marian Warren. Maybe a stand-in who looks like her; my memory is very clouded. However, I've heard of your devotion, and I wish to commend you for it. It's a very lucky mistress who has such a butler."

"Thank you, madam," said Franklin. Eyebrows were raised all

around, but not in horror. She was obviously being very much Marian Warren. Befuddled, befogged, forgetful, but every inch a great lady. And it was a source of considerable pride to have filled the rôle so nicely. After all, she was just a librarian. From what library, city, place or time in the world, she could not remember. However, a librarian she was. But she was not Marian Warren.

"Well, Marian. Finally dragged yourself out of bed, I see." The voice speaking from the doorway was deep and joyful—a voice designed to sway juries, woo ladies, and have its own way.

Bill Darrick came toward her, hands outstretched, a handsome, fortyish man with a deep tan, a white-toothed smile, and dark eyes limpid as a Venetian lover's.

"Are you by any chance Italian?" Marian Warren, rich eccentric, could say any mad thing that popped into her head.

He stopped, amazed, then recovered himself. "Why, I thought you knew that, Marian. I was born in Italy, but raised in this country by my aunt. The war years, you know. Later she legally adopted me, so I took the name 'Darrick'—which, of course, is an English name."

Well, you aren't fooling anyone, she wanted to say, but for the sake of good manners she let it go. He was in on the plot; she knew that. He came right up to her and got a good look at her pale face—similar to Marian Warren's, she was sure, or else she would not be here, but not Marian Warren. And he was not half blind like old Franklin, or a newcomer like the nurse.

"I suppose you have my power-of-attorney?" She enjoyed seeing his dark Italian skin go pale.

"I believe that is also a matter of record," he said stiffly, some of his buoyancy falling away.

"For how long?"

"For eighteen months now, ever since your headaches got so bad. You checked into the clinic for six weeks, if you remember, then a month at the Faith Healing Center, then two months in Spain on the theory that it might be your sinuses—"

"Never mind all that," she said.

"I'm merely pointing out, my dear Marian, that bills had to be paid in your absence and this entire estate had to be kept up plus—"

"An allowance for Huey, and doubtless ample funds for Grace."

"Well, yes." He looked at her askance, then shot a questioning glance at Grace, who seemed to have turned into a human statue, a drink halfway to her mouth. Even Huey had temporarily forgotten his role of charming boy-nephew.

"I understand perfectly," she went on, "but none of that will be necessary now. I'm feeling quite my old self again. In fact, much better!" She chuckled inwardly. Her old self, she was sure, had never had so much fun.

CONFLICT 47

"I will be at home from now on, my dear Mr. Darrick. And quite able to carry on my affairs. So first thing tomorrow morning please appear here with the papers drawn up to relinquish your power-of-attorney. My nurse here, Miss . . . er?"

"Finney," the nurse supplied.

"Miss Finney," she continued, "and Franklin, my beloved butler, will be the witnesses."

Franklin, who had been making a slow circle of the room, near-sightedly checking glasses and bottles, bowed formally.

"Very good, madam," he said.

"Let's make it ten o'clock then," she said with an authority that brooked no resistance. "Unless I happen to be dead tomorrow morning of so-called natural causes. In that case, call in the police, because I have no intention of dying during the night. Do you understand, Franklin?"

"Yes, madam," said Franklin, backing out of the room. The deadness of routine and old age were gone from his features. He'd been told something and he knew it. The Mistress must live, and if she died, he would know what to do.

"And you, Nurse?"

"Very good, Miss Warren." The nurse looked at her with new respect.

"How about another drink?" Huey said brightly into the silence.

"I think I will," she replied. "These Rob Roys are terribly good."

The nurse helped her back upstairs, and she went gratefully to bed, weak but happy. Someone, she realized, had chosen her to stand in for the missing, probably dead, Marian Warren. Someone with a supreme knowledge of practical psychology had matched her up. But little did they know how well. All her life she'd waited for something like this—an opportunity to be Someone. She'd always wanted it. The knowledge stirred like a live thing in the gray ashes of her half-forgotten self. And now she had it! The new Marian Warren would not be so easily displaced as the old.

She accepted her dinner on a tray with the élan of someone to the manor born and with the trust of a small babe. They wouldn't dare make a move against her tonight. Propped up in bed, she nibbled toast and chewed steak cut up into baby squares and drenched in milk gravy (the cook would have to go). She smiled reflectively. The morning meeting with Bill Darrick should prove interesting.

The nurse helped her downstairs at five till ten. Although she felt much stronger, she needed the moral support. The nurse was now definitely on Her Side; only one person could sway her, and rounding the bend in the stairs, she saw he had arrived. Dr. Martin was just handing his hat to Franklin.

"How much do you make a year?" she murmured in the nurse's ear.

The nurse looked startled. "That depends. I'm a private duty nurse. Fourteen thousand in a good year."

"How much in a bad?" She fixed the woman with an autocratic stare.

"Well. . . ." The nurse floundered. "Nine thousand, maybe ten."

"I'll give you fifteen thousand a year straight salary to stay on with me as secretary-companion. All the time off you need. Travel allowance for foreign lands."

"Wha–at?" the nurse looked stunned.

"All you have to say is 'yes' and you pass into my direct employ as of this moment. You can consider your responsibility to Dr. Martin and the others ended. I'm perfectly well anyway, as you can see. There's nothing left but to dismiss you. However, as my secretary-companion, you can consider yourself employed indefinitely."

"I . . ." The nurse reached for an answer.

"Just say 'yes' or 'no.' "

"Yes, Miss Warren." The nurse was a trifle breathless.

"Good. Then we know where we stand." She smiled, satisfied.

They were all assembled in the library, the same grouping as the night before with the addition of the doctor. He sprang up as she entered.

"Marian, you shouldn't be up and around so soon, especially when the drugs had such a powerful effect on you."

"Yes," she agreed with heavy humor while being helped to "her" chair. "They made me into a *new* woman."

"That isn't what I meant. Nurse, you should have let me know. . . ."

"I saw no reason to contact you, Doctor." The nurse was obviously offended. "Miss Warren reacted exactly as you said she would: a little forgetful at first, perhaps a bit disoriented. But when she rallied so quickly last evening, remembering who she was and joining the family for drinks, I thought you would be pleased."

"It's quite unfair to jump on Nurse Finney," she said, raising an imperious hand (as she was sure the real Marian Warren would do). "She followed orders exactly, and since I'm now quite well, I've dismissed her as my nurse and hired her as my secretary. So you see, Doctor, her allegiance to you is now at an end."

"But this is outrageous! A sick woman dismissing nurses, trying to call her own tune?"

"I am not sick. I am Marian Warren, surrounded by my beloved family in my beautiful ancestral home. All is as it should be. Besides, this meeting was to be between my lawyer and myself; I can't imagine what the *rest* of you are doing here. . . ."

Bill Darrick rose with white-toothed aplomb.

"Of course, of course. This is a business meeting like any other. A little unusual, perhaps, due to Marian's rapid recovery, but nothing to, uh, fear. Why don't you all, er. . . ."

"Clear out," she supplied.

"Right. Clear out. We'll call you if we need you. You too, Franklin. And Miss Finney."

"Franklin and Miss Finney are to be my witnesses."

"Yes, yes . . . when we need them." She could almost see him rolling up his mental sleeves.

As the door closed behind the others, Bill sat down opposite her, briefcase on his knee.

"Well now, Marian. . . ."

"No need for a long discussion," she cut in. "I merely want to sever your power-of-attorney. So if you would be good enough to give me the papers. . . ."

"You propose to sign your own checks?"

"Certainly."

He considered this, obviously framing a reply.

"You realize," he said finally, "that your signature and the old Marian Warren's signature would not compare."

"Why not?"

"Because you're not Marian Warren."

"Really? Since when?"

"Since always, which I'm sure you realized as soon as you got your wits about you. Unfortunately, we had to take you on a Quick Eradication basis. Nothing of your old life was to remain. After thirty-six hours of constant Computer Erasure and Supplant Input, you were supposed to be a different person with different memories, notions and opinions. In about one percent of the cases it doesn't work, due to the mental tenacity of the . . . er, subject. It wasn't expected of you, a somewhat pallid, fortyish librarian living in a fantasy world of books and dreams. However, in coloring, manner, size, and general appearance, you were almost a double for Marian Warren."

"The *late* Marian Warren, I presume."

"Yes, sad to say. She died of a brain tumor. One of her 'headaches.' The one real doctor she consulted didn't spot it. The other medical quacks and faith healers simply wished it away. 'Pray yourself well' was their theme."

"So you say. She could be dead of a bullet in the brain."

"That is also true." Darrick shifted his briefcase. "However, be that as it may, the dear woman is gone without a trace, and you are here, quite ostensibly she. You've been accepted by the help. . . ."

"Such as they are," she intoned, "half-blind and brand new."

"But accepted, nevertheless."

"So Marian Warren alive is worth more to you than Marian Warren dead?"

"Yes."

"Either you're covering up a murder, or the Will cuts Grace off without a cent and leaves young Huey dangling at the end of a trust allowance."

"You're shrewd," he said. "It could be a little of each, or a bit of all. However, you need only coöperate to get your share. Go on being Marian Warren and you'll have all the luxury to which you've been, ah—unaccustomed. Clothes, a generous allowance. . . ."

"Through your largesse, of course."

"Of course."

"And in the meantime, I take it, the estate will be given a more equitable division, so that when I do 'pass on' the Will will be practically a toothless document. With your power-of-attorney, certain large sums will be safely invested for Grace and generous gifts made to Huey—not to mention special rewards to yourself and the good Doctor Martin."

"Something of the sort, yes." He grinned, and she saw the malice behind the charm.

"So you need me," she said.

"Yes, we need you. For the moment. A long moment. These things cannot be done in a day. It takes time. Nor do we have any wish to involve ourselves in your untimely demise. Staying within certain reasonable guidelines, you can expect to live out your life as Marian Warren."

"I see." And she did. "Then I think cooperation is the order of the day. You keep the power-of-attorney and I stay very much alive with Nurse Finney as my secretary-companion."

"If those are your terms," he said agreeably.

"There's one more thing," she said. "How did I get here?"

He considered her intently, his dark eyes thoughtful. "Since we're going into business together, I see no reason for not telling you. Or at least, giving you an outline. Do you remember your name?"

"No," she answered truthfully.

"Or where you were born?"

"No."

"Or where you were living?"

"No."

"But you do remember some things?"

"Yes. I was a librarian. I had a sister named Viola. Viola was married to a lowbrow named Henry."

Bill Darrick smiled indulgently. "You are, then, a woman without a past, except for such past as we choose to give you. You came to us through an organization known as the PRS, or People Replacement Service. There's one in every major city, both here and abroad. They go by various names and guises, of course, but they are all linked to the World Bank Computer System.

"Say a girl wants to meet a personable young man. She goes to a dating service. On her computer reference card she puts down the most intimate information; but to her it's nothing—merely facts. Her age, weight, coloring, size. Her education, her preferences in food, clothes, men. Place of birth, languages, little defects like 'wear glasses to read' or 'leg once broken in skiing accident'. Hopefully, she'll be put in touch with some willing male who also likes to ski. So much for the girl. Maybe she will find true love at the end of a computer printout, maybe not. Regardless, she has paid a handsome fee and stripped herself bare. All the information goes into the World Computer Bank."

"But I haven't been to a dating service. Nor would I ever lower myself to such a degree."

"No, you haven't, but your sister and brother-in-law have. Only they answered the practical come-on of a 'Renters Exchange': *Can't stand Uncle Irwin, but rent him the spare room? Small fee to exchange him for more compatible roomer. Our listings guarantee top exchange. Bring photo and Unc's pref's. We do the rest.*"

"So they exchanged me?" She wasn't really surprised. No matter how low Viola and Henry sank, their depths had yet to be plumbed. "But how?"

"They merely waited until one of your 'headaches' struck, then had you removed to a kind of nursing-home boarding-house within commuting distance of your job. Meanwhile, they rented your room." He smiled sardonically.

"And my job?"

"When one is dead, one no longer needs a job."

"You mean?"

He nodded.

"But whom did they bury?"

"Guess," he said with a pleased grin.

"My God!"

"Yes, it worked out remarkably well. But that's not always the case. Sometimes the replaced people just wander away; amnesia, they call that. Or sometimes they meet with unfortunate accidents and have to be buried in potter's field. But you, my dear Marian, are alive and well, and getting the best of the bargain. What d'you think?" He ran the words together in a most unlawyer-like fashion.

"I suppose you're right," she agreed, "except that I have a lawyer who has my power-of-attorney and may dispose of me any time."

CHAPTER 4

"But won't."

"But won't," she repeated. "But what if you were to get amnesia, or be hit by a truck? What then?"

"Then a very sick Marian Warren will have to practice a very sick, shaky forgery of the real signature and try to carry on."

"I see."

"But," he assured her, "I have no intention of wandering off *sans* memory into the fog, or doing battle with a truck."

"I quite understand," she said sedately.

"Then I believe we understand each other." He collected his briefcase and rose. "I will tell the others that things will continue as planned and advise your two faithful retainers, Franklin and Nurse Finney, that no witnesses will be necessary today."

"Yes." She tried to give the appearance of dutifully accepting the inevitable.

Only Nurse Finney came to check on her.

"I've changed my mind about revoking Mr. Darrick's power-of-attorney, at least for the present. Right now, I'd like a good strong cup of tea and a copy of today's paper."

She looked at the paper's masthead with interest; she'd never seen it before. She was not only in a different city, she decided, but a different country.

When tea arrived she was deep in the want ads.

"Thank you, Franklin. I appreciate your standing by today. I'm holding off for a while, but I may need your witnessing signature in other matters, very soon."

"Very good, madam."

Ah-hah! There it was, under the Business Personals. Disguised, but there could be no doubt about the organization behind it.

A-1 Theatrical Service: Ashamed to introduce Cousin Charlie to society? His manners atrocious and accent all wrong? Contact us for a stand-in. Bring photo. We do the rest.

She picked up the desk phone and dialed. After a number of preliminaries she was put through to a voice-in-charge.

"I have a relative," she said, "a cousin, Italian born, but using an English name, who doesn't quite fit in. I would like to have him replaced. Just for a very important social event, of course. And I thought if I could also arrange a little vacation for him at the same time . . ."

The voice murmured assuringly. It so happened they were associated with a travel bureau.

"Of course, if he wanted to stay on vacation indefinitely, I would have no objections."

The voice murmured further assent.

"As for the fee, . . ." She paused meaningfully. "I could make a large deposit, but I wouldn't be able to pay in full until, well, until *after* my . . . er, cousin had been replaced."

The voice asked a question.

"Yes, indeed," she replied. "You were recommended by someone who has used your services. Very, very highly recommended. . . ."

The author sent us the following comments on her story:

" 'Someone Else's House' was written in 1974 and sold in 1978. Four years of making the rounds. And yet the story sold in essentially the same form as it was written. There was no character change or variation in the sequence of events. What was the trouble? Eight hundred words of flab. The original manuscript weighed in at 6800 words. The version that sold was a slimmed-down 6000 words.

"Many editors wrote favorable comments, but none bought the story. I rewrote it, cutting out 300 words. Again rejections. Finally, because I believed in the story, I sought professional help. I paid a reading fee and sent it to a reputable agent recommended by a friend. The result was 500 more adjectives, adverbs, and clichés blue-penciled out of my already 'trim' manuscript. First time out, it sold. Lesson learned."

An important point: in all the stories of this volume—except this one—the reader has been firmly put into the time and place of the story, the when and where, and usually introduced to the principal characters as well, within the first 100 to 200 words of text. Thus, in "A Simple Outside Job," the reader encounters Jeffrey Castilho, airlock, earphones, Titan's surface, the Titan Pilot Project's lifedome, and Rogers, all in the first paragraph.

"Someone Else's House" only *appears* to be an exception, however. In this story, the reader is—just as firmly—placed in the mind of a woman who doesn't know where she is. And, since the story adheres strictly to that woman's point of view throughout, the reader comes to know where that character is only as the character herself does. The author doesn't tell the reader, "she doesn't know where she is." Instead, the author *shows* us, from the *inside*, the character not knowing, and then slowly finding out.

This is the initial conflict: the middle-aged librarian finding herself in a strange and possibly hostile environment. She doesn't know what it can do to her if she doesn't play along, and she doesn't know what is expected of her. A strange environment, against which the protagonist must struggle, isn't always an alien world populated by monsters; here, that strange environment is a luxurious mansion. Our protagonist has clearly been whisked away against her will for some purpose which, if it weren't sinister, she would have been told about.

She also wonders if she has gone mad. She cannot remember much of her former life, or even her name. Is it possible that she *really is* the millionairess, and that these memories of a sister named Viola and a career as a librarian are delusions? This is a conflict going on entirely inside her head, which she must resolve before taking action to deal with the larger one. Having done so, she finds her real opponent is Darrick, the lawyer. In a direct contest of wills, he wants her to do one thing and she wants another. And even if she acquiesces to what he wants, he remains an enemy, who can (and probably will) dispose of her whenever she becomes inconvenient. Thus the overall conflict, on which her survival depends, is not resolved at the "business meeting" at all; it is only tabled temporarily. But during that truce, the librarian filling the place of Marian Warren uses the time she has gained to find out more about the situation, enough to resolve the problem truly by setting in motion the disposal of Darrick.

A *resolution* is more than just "an ending." It is the release of the original pressure that forced the protagonist into action. Note too that, as in this case, once the primary resolving action is taken, the subsequent action does not have to be described on stage.

There is a lesser but crucial conflict within the nurse. She is not part of the original plot. Her training and her nature direct her to look after the welfare of her patient: the woman she thinks is Mrs. Warren. It is obvious to her that something strange is going on, and she is uneasy about the situation. It is not difficult for "Marian" to win her over, then, for this makes her patient and her employer the same person, and her conflict of responsibility is resolved.

Similarly, the butler's doubts vanish when "Marian" begins to assert herself, putting him firmly into what he feels is his proper role:

> . . . The deadness of routine and old age were gone from his features. He'd been told something and he knew it. The Mistress must live; and if she died, he would know what to do.

A resolution, like any other part of the story, must fit the character(s) involved or it will ring false. Had the nurse preferred scheming to nursing, she would have relieved her inner tension by going along with the plotters. This would have at once placed "Marian" in a hopeless position, and shoved the story down the long bleak road toward futility. (For more on this, and why not to do it, see Chapter 9.) Conflict is not mere violence; it is also not cruelty—the piling on of unpredictable horrors until the protagonist collapses. If the pressure just *keeps coming* despite every effort to stop it, the reader will eventually decide that the protagonist's actions are meaningless . . . and the story is meaningless . . . and quit reading.

CHARACTER: HUMAN PROBLEMS, HUMAN SOLUTIONS

"A science fiction story is a story with a human problem, and a human solution, that would not have happened at all without its scientific content."
        —Theodore Sturgeon

"For above all else, a story—science fiction or otherwise—is a story of human beings."
        —John W. Campbell

"You see, *Watson, but you do not* observe.*" —*
        —Sherlock Holmes

John Beynon Harris (better known by his pen name of John Wyndham) was once telephoned by an editor—obviously not Campbell—and asked, "Hey, can you write stories about airplanes?"

"No," Harris replied. "Stories are about people."

Exactly.

In order to be meaningful to a human audience, a story must deal with human experience. This applies even—especially, in fact—in the most exotic settings of SF and fantasy.

This is especially apparent to those people who find themselves living for a time *in* an SF story. Mark Hamill, who was doing just that during the filming of *Star Wars*, feared that his role of Luke Skywalker would be overwhelmed by the movie's special effects. Sir Alec Guinness reassured Hamill thus: **In every kind of fantasy . . . there must be an anchor in reality, to contrast with all the bizarre elements.**

This is why *Star Wars* works: among all the swoops and dives and exploding planets are a group of human, identifiable characters, to whom the audience can respond.

One does not, of course, have to identify with Luke Skywalker; some people prefer Ben Kenobi, or Han Solo, or the Princess. . . .

. . . Or Chewbacca, or the robots, or Darth Vader. Because a protagonist in SF does not have to be commonplace, or even human. The dogs in Clifford Simak's *City;* the sentient rocks in Roger Zelazny's "Collector's Fever"; the floating naval mine in Murray Leinster's "The Wabbler"—all these have emotions and feelings recognizable to human beings. Simak's dogs respect the memory of mankind, and they know wonder. Zelazny's rock resents being carried off by a collector, especially since it's almost time to reproduce. And Leinster's mine seems to know and sense and feel as it goes about its mission to sink an enemy warship. These are all human elements, human thoughts, without which a story cannot reach a human audience. And you have no other.

Simple description is not characterization; putting a funny hat on someone doesn't make that person real. We *hope* you don't believe in such ancient clichés as "beady criminal eyes" and "cruel mouths."

Characterize by reaction, not description. A paragraph detailing how stunningly lovely a character is will slow the story's action down intolerably, not to mention being less than completely effective—your reader may not *like* black hair and violet eyes, for instance. Worse yet, in SF one frequently has to deal with totally nonhuman societies and beings. Imagine describing a beautiful intelligent dinosaur—"Her scales were like polished malachite under the glorious desert sun. Flicking her tongue coyly, she. . . ." You get the idea.

Instead, describe the *reactions* of other characters to this staggering display of beauty. If another intelligent dinosaur responds to those malachite scales in a fashion we can recognize as romantic, both the fact and the background to make it understandable will be communicated without silliness or lecturing.

Characterization can begin with a label—"Nitley was brilliant"—just as a story line starts with a single *what if*. But just as the *what if* must be followed by a chain of *then what*s, the label must be amplified and expanded until all the consequences of the original, essential character element are known. Nobody is *just* brilliant. Some are brilliant and arrogant. Some are brilliant and shy because they were treated unkindly when small, so that underneath the shyness is a monumental anger. This is a little trite, but a good enough example.

Now comes the hard part: once you have worked out Nitley's brilliant history, *don't tell it.* **Show** him acting: in the laboratory, hiding from the overbearing Institute Director, dodging his coworkers, brooding constantly over what he might do when the prototype death ray is working. The character profile you have created is your roadmap, your prompt-sheet; when Nitley must react to a new plot development, refer back to it, to determine just how he should react.

As we said, this example is pretty trite. The mousy-genius-with-a-grudge is a cardboard figure, and the cardboard is worn very thin. Names like "Nitley" don't help much, either, unless it's important that the character has had to live with an unpleasant name. Never rely on prejudices for characterization, no matter how popular those prejudices are. Not all big muscular people are stupid or bullying; not all retired generals are endlessly reliving the Battle of Omdurman; and relatively few Texans, or Arabs for that matter, own oil wells.

Another sort of stereotype starts out as an attempt to *avoid* typing: in a reaction to Pollyanna-ish saccharine romanticism the author makes everyone in the story vicious, cynical, cowardly, depraved, and so forth. This is no more than the substitution of one stereotype for another. Schweitzer's Law: **Ugliness for its own sake is not realism.** Real human beings have both faults and virtues—which means more than a "good side" and a "bad side" fighting for control; we all have many natures, some of them contradictory, and all our actions are compromises with ourselves.

Ursula K. Le Guin comments that the platitude, "There's a little bit of good in the worst of us and a little bit of bad in the best of us," is a dangerous oversimplification; the truth is that everyone contains an almost limitless capacity for good and evil.

For heaven's sake, *look* at the world: the awful people may seem to be in charge, even in the majority, but they're not *everyone*. (If they are, then you're one too.) A writer must be able to look at a situation—*any* situation—and see both beauty and ugliness. If you can learn to see both at once, you will never want for story conflicts.

The mechanics of characterization are subtle and elusive. Why is this? After all, you've been observing people all your life. . . .

Haven't you? Or have you (in Holmes's phrase) just been seeing them?

Think about a person you know very well, someone you would recognize from a crowd instantly. *Why* would you recognize that person? What would you notice? Think past outward appearance and dress. Think of mannerism, speech pattern, responses. Recognition is a gestalt idea, a whole greater than the sum of its parts; you are trying to learn how to assemble fictional parts to form a true-seeming whole. This is part of the "writer's eye," a not entirely natural sort of vision that is *essential* to the creation of anything new.

Robert Heinlein has pointed out that there are only three basic kinds of plot (he originally knew of only two, until L. Ron Hubbard pointed out the third to him). John Brunner has further explained that these derive directly from the three ways that people can change or be changed. In terms of an overall story, especially a long one, each character of consequence may have one such plot attached to him; some may have more than one.

One plot is the Man Who Learns Better: a person learns the hard way that one of his strongly held ideas or principles is wrong. When we say "the hard way," we *mean* it. This is not a casual lesson, but object learning in the school of life, in which the passing grade is survival.

The second basic plot is Boy Meets Girl: more precisely, someone becomes emotionally involved with someone else. The "someone else" need not be a person, or even a living being; it can be an inanimate object—think of the attachments people develop to their cars, houses, teddybears, and so forth—or it may be an idea, a philosophy.

The third plot is the Little Tailor: a character goes through a change in status and must adapt to it. (For those who have forgotten the original fairy tale, it concerned a fly-swatting tailor who acquired an undeserved reputation for giant-killing—then found himself with a real giant to kill.) This adaptation is often a kind of growing up—learning to use one's capacities and live with one's limitations, learning to take responsibility for one's actions.

Several things are common to all these plots. One is that the changes induced in the protagonist must be meaningful; they must cause a significant change in the character's life. Otherwise—who cares?

The change must be believable. Sudden changes of heart are unrealistic and unconvincing. People who seem to change their minds ceaselessly are usually uncommitted to any choice; thus the change has no emotional cost to them. This is not the desired fictional effect. It is perfectly all right, and in fact desirable, to put most of the accumulated pressure to change in the story's background, so the tale begins with the protagonist fuzed to explode; but make certain that the reader is aware of the prior buildup.

Part of making the change believable is presenting an adequate, credible penalty for not changing. The **or else** can be anything from a loss of face to the destruction of the Universe; often it is death, which *is* the end of one's personal Universe. If the threat is small, you must make the reader understand why it matters so much; if it is grotesquely large—blowing up the Galaxy—you must convince the reader both that such a power exists *and* that your character might be brought to face it. Being the One Person Who Can Save Earth is a common fantasy, but its commonness doesn't automatically make it likely or believable.

The character you subject to pressure must be capable of changing in the first place. Television heroes have been stuck in this rut for years; no matter how gut-wrenching the problem this week, at the end of the episode Detective Sergeant McClod solves it, climbs into his car, and drives away to next week's show. Think of how episodes

CHAPTER 5

are rerun in random order, without making a difference; you *can't* do that with the incidents in a real person's life.

Your character may not in fact realize the extent of the change within him; he may not even recognize that he *has* changed. This is a difficult effect to achieve, because the reader must be convinced of the reality of the change, even as the character denies it.

Last chapter we said that the protagonist of a story was the person in pain, the one under stress. Change hurts. People change through the application of pressure. (Sometimes the pressure is too great, and the person breaks; this is the stuff of tragedy, about which more later.)

Of course, not every player, whether in a film, a play, or a story, has a speaking part. SF has a need for stock figures, just as the movies have extras for crowd scenes. But just as the film keeps those extras in the background, out of focus, so the story's stock figures must be kept well back from the action. Even then, they should be drawn from life, not the box of cardboard cutouts.

James Gunn, paraphrasing from E.M. Forster's *Aspects of the Novel,* put it this way: "Flat characters have a single characteristic which does not change throughout the work. Round characters have several characteristics, some of which may be (or seem) contradictory—in the end they are like people: unpredictable, but in a convincing way."

Samuel R. Delany, in *The Jewel-Hinged Jaw,* wrote: "A character in a novel of mine observed that there were three types of action: purposeful, habitual, and gratuitous [or impulsive]. If the writer can show a character involved in a number of actions of all three types, his character will seem more real." Clearly, flat characters are those who are acting out of habit, and occasionally purpose. Round characters do some things from habit (Jeff Castilho "speaking each item out loud just as he'd been trained"), some purposefully (Jeff "took a breath to be sure he kept the irritation out of his voice"), and some on impulse (Jeff "said to the dead microphone, 'You don't have to baby me' "). Sometimes conflict builds on the differences among actions: the narrator of "Global Traveler" out of habit hesitates before reading someone else's notes, starts on impulse to read them anyway, deliberately hides them in her own notes, and flees to the Hawk and Dove to read further.

On the other hand, the nurse and the butler in "Someone Else's House" do not change in the course of the story. The fact that they do remain consistent makes the story work, both by making it possible for "Marian" to make them her allies and highlighting the appearance of "Marian's" inner strength.

We said above that characters must reveal themselves through their behavior: you must *show* your characters in action, not stop to describe them. We know that Castilho has a stringy beard because he saw himself in a mirror—and he did so for a reason that made the story move. "Marian" thinks about her past, and her own slimness, because of what is happening around her. Shakespeare is described as Moriarty sees him—and is only then recognized as the Bard.

Here's another example.

AFRICAN BLUES
by Paula Smith

*Currently a student, a systems analyst,
(with this sale ((a first))) a writer,
and a part-time bum, or so she tells
us, the author claims to have led a
sheltered life, never venturing more
than 12,000 miles away from home.
"African Blues" is the first story
she ever tried to sell, and she is
thinking Real Hard about writing another.*

Musa's cow, Llana, was eight years old, and I did not think she
would be able to calve. But there she was, and she was bearing
another one. It was hard for her; she was quite old. Musa had brought
her in from the savannah when it became obvious she would have
difficulty dropping. He left her at my veterinary barn. "See her
through, Sister Doto," he said, "and I will pay up all I owe." This
for Musa is a major concession.

That is why I was in my barn before dawn with Llana that day.
That was the day the rocket came down over the village. At first it
was only a faraway whistle, high and shrill. I thought it was a bird
and paid it no mind. There were other things to attend to; Llana is
a nasty beast, with a tendency to bite. But then the whistle grew
sharper, very quickly, you see; and Llana shuddered for more reason
than just her unborn calf. Then *bang!* came a crash.

For a moment after the crash it was very quiet; even the hyenas
shut up their morning howling and the dungbirds stopped screech-
ing. Then half the village was awake, hurrying out of their houses
to see what it was. "Llana, you wait for a minute," I said. I wanted
to see what this was, and what it was doing here in Kenya. Besides,
in the barn it was very close; I also needed some air.

It was early morning, and already quite warm. Here on the equator there are certain days when the sun is so bright and hot that it
burns the sky yellow. That is what the people say. The teachers at
the missionary school in Nairobi say it is the dust. Certainly there
is more than enough of it, a lot of dust in the air because it had not
rained in two months. Further, that day the villagers kicked up
more running out into the savannah to find the fallen object. The
sky was already pale with sunrise, and I knew it would not turn
blue that day.

Jama was the first to find it. It was big, bigger than a house. "Is
this one of the whites' spaceships?" he said.

"Yes," I answered. It was indeed a rocket; I had seen several on
the television in the capital. But it did not look like the Americans'

rockets, which are cone-shaped, like our rooftops. This one was circular, round all the way over, like a ball. There were many wires wrapped around it, and a big—parachute, they call it, only it looked more like a huge ship's sail. It was torn.

The rocket was at the deep end of a long rut it had made in the brush. The villagers began to dig it out—who can tell if such a thing might not be valuable?—and I was thinking I must return to Llana. Then Dr. Hunter, the black American who came to our village two years ago, ran up, sweating. He is always sweating. He came here because he wanted to be African; but even African water doesn't stay in him, it always sweats away.

"Don't open it!" he yelled in his Kiswahili, which is very bad. Whenever possible I speak English with him. "We'll notify the authorities first. It might be a Russian capsule."

The villagers looked up, and some moved away. Most moved away. Dr. Hunter is sometimes crazy, and often rude, but he is a smart man. He, too, is educated.

Jama walked up to Dr. Hunter and bowed a little. "Your instructions?" he asked in Kiswahili, for that is the only language he knows. I spoke up, using English, "What authorities should we notify, Dr. Hunter? Brother Jama is ready to do what you suggest."

"Also may I borrow his bicycle," Jama said to me. "It's a long way to Lodwar."

"Oh," said Dr. Hunter, blinking a little. "Authorities . . . well—" He started to count off on his fingers. "Well—the District Commissioner, for one. The mayor of Lodwar, the po—"

I almost jumped out of my skin. The rocket had knocked at us. "Get back!" yelled Dr. Hunter, as if we weren't already scattering. The thumping increased, grew louder, stopped. We waited a moment, holding our breaths. A few of the bolder young men started forward. But they halted, and scuttled back when a section of the rocket opened a bit above the ground. At first the door stuck, grating against the jamb, then it wiggled free, coming all the way open. And from inside the rocket, a man crawled up, leaned out, and fell out of the hatch. A *blue* man.

I must admit I was astounded. He was small, slighter even than a white man. He wore a great deal of padding and a thick-looking round helmet, though there was no visor. We hurried forward to take him away from the rocket, for he just lay there. His face was shaped like a top, very round above—especially wide at the eyes, which were closed—tapering to almost nothing for a chin. Dr. Hunter told us, "Take him to my office."

M'bega, his two sons, and Sulimani picked up the little blue man between them and headed off to Dr. Hunter's very large, very beautiful house. (It has a wooden roof.) The doctor himself followed close

CHAPTER 5

behind them, going, "Sst! sst! careful there."

I stayed behind for a moment, walking around the rocket. The metal radiated warmth, as did the ground around it. Some of the sand had been turned to glass. The sun was fully up now, shimmering on the huge sail. It wasn't cloth, for I could see no weave, although it was like a metal fabric. But it didn't reflect quite like metal. I came back to the opening, intending to close the hatch cover, when I heard a scraping inside the rocket. I didn't know, were there more blue people in there? I was most cautious as I peered in. But it was only M'bega's littlest boy, Faki, who grinned at me from a padded chair. "See what I found, Aunt?" he said, holding up a piece of the metal-like cloth. "It was in here," he said, pointing to a little mesh bag fastened on the side of the chair.

"You come out of there," I said, and leaned in to pull him out. The rocket's—cabin, I suppose you would call it—was very cramped, and it was hot, stifling. There were many more boxes and mesh bags, many things tied to the round walls of the cabin. There were three tiny windows—no, they were television screens—on the curve of the wall before the pilot's chair. I put Faki down outside and shooed him on. Then I looked at the long cloth band I had taken from him. Too big for a headpiece and too narrow for anything else, it was smooth, thick, and quite strong. I pulled out the net bag—it had come from off the side of the chair—and closed the hatch.

Admittedly I dawdled going back to my barn. I was curious; what was this cloth for? Why should the blue man have had it nearest him? Well, something had to be nearest, I supposed. But what were these other things in the mesh bag—two pieces of very soft cloth, not metallic; a length of string; a pencil; a small vial; and a bunch of cotton waste. Strange things, but not strange enough to belong with a blue man.

Well, they were getting dusty in my hand. I put them back into the bag and went on. It was growing hotter, with the horizon shimmering all around in the distance. So flat, the savannah, with nothing but the brush and dust standing on it. But do you know, as I swung that bag while I walked, all the dust in it flew out. None of the articles, but only the dust. I looked inside and all the things were clean. It was quite odd. Do you think Europeans have such things?

I came back to my infirmary, went to see whether all was well with Llana. Ah, the poor old cow! As I approached, she was standing in her stall, shuddering in a labor pain. She strained, twitched all down the length of her hide, then relaxed. "Ah, Llana, poor girl, is it hard when you're old?" I leaned against the wooden slats for a very long time. Llana was well, just that the calf was no closer than before. The sun's rays peeped in from the cracks in the southeast corner, lighting motes in the air. It was dark and still, very quiet, but growing warm even in the shed. The hay smell was thick in the air, too, as thick as the dust outdoors.

Something about the bag's contents—the two kinds of cloth, the pencil, the cotton waste, and the string. And a small vial. It bothered me. I emptied the mesh bag out onto a manger to examine the items. The soft cloth, I found, would stick to itself, and the pencil would cut the string. It would also cut straw in half, but it would not cut my skin. I opened the little bottle, dabbing a bit onto my fingertip. I tasted it—and it was brine! Most unusual.

The silver cloth was a sling; and its edges would hold together, making a sort of small, hollow hammock. It all bothered me. They meant something, I was sure. I felt that. Sometimes, you see, I feel as if I were all the land, that I could hear and smell every thing and every animal that walked across me, that if I could only feel just a little bit more, I should know everything and be perfect. This was the same feeling. If I could only know the why of these curious objects, I felt I should know all about the blue man.

Llana mooed very softly. I gathered the things into the bag—again all the dirt fell out—and noted the time. Forty minutes. Her waters had not yet broken, so it would be a long time yet. I thought, and made up my mind. I would go see the blue man. Maybe that would give me my hint.

Outdoors, the sky was already brass, without a cloud. The dust on the short trail to Dr. Hunter's house was stirred up just by my walking, and it settled over me, turning my arms almost as grey as the old blue jeans I was wearing. The bag I tucked under my belt. As I walked, I tied all the little braids of my hair up into a topknot, wrapping them all with my kerchief. My mother had given me the kerchief last winter, before she died. She had made me come back here to the village when I had completed school in Nairobi.

Dr. Hunter's house had been built years before, even before I was born, by a European, Herr Max. The village people had settled around it because he also had an artesian well drilled. There used to be a garden in back, but Dr. Hunter let it die. It is a shame; it was very beautiful.

I knocked on the wooden door and called, "Hodi?" Nobody answered. Again I called, "Hodi? May I come in?"

Then Dr. Hunter's voice said, "Who is it?"

"It is I, Doto," I said. "May I come in?"

There was a click as he unlatched his door. Opening it, he said, "Ka—uh, karibu, Dota. Is Jama back yet?"

"It is unlikely that he would be," I said, walking inside. "It is a very long way to Lodwar. I have come to see the blue man and ask him about his bag," which I held up. "May I see him?"

CHAPTER 5

He simply looked at me, with sweat of more than heat on his brow. There was a cry from farther within the house, short, sharp, which caused Dr. Hunter to start. "Dota . . . look, the blue man is sick. He must have been injured in that landing. And I sure as Hell—that is, I may be a doctor, but that doesn't mean I necessarily know how to treat blue Martians."

"Oh. Well, I, too, am trained in medical matters. I was schooled at Carleri Veterinary Institute in the capital, and I believe I may already know what is troubling the blue man. I should like to come in." I made to enter his dispensary, but again he stopped me.

"Dota!" he said. "Can't I make you understand? He is an *alien*—who knows what could be wrong with him? He may have hurt organs whose normal functions I couldn't know! The best thing we can do for him is try and get him comfortable until the UN or somebody can get him out of here to better care. Savvy?"

He was gripping my upper arm tightly, his face very close to mine. I do not care for this; it is not respectful. I, too, after all, am educated, perhaps not so much as Dr. Hunter; but even my knowledge of veterinary matters should count for something. And I also had the blue man's bag.

"Dr. Hunter," I said, very calm. "My name is Do*to*. You keep mispronouncing my name, which is not polite. I have come to see the blue man. I have certain things of his from the rocket which he may be needing. Hodi?"

He stared at me for quite a long time. Plainly he was not happy with this situation, but when the high cry came again, he shook himself, growling, "Oh, come on in. But I'm in charge here, understand that. I don't want some back-country witch doctor fouling up interplanetary relations, y'got that?"

"Of course, Dr. Hunter. You would rather do it yourself," I said, as I went into the infirmary.

In there, on the examining table, lay the blue man, awake and looking upward. His padded suit being off, I could see he was blue all over, except for a sort of short brown pelt of hair over his scalp, apparently across his back, and running down the outside of his arms to the back of his hands. He had three fingers on each hand. He was quite thin and slight, like a young boy, with a large round head. I came a little closer and he looked at me.

How do I say it? The eyes—large and round, deep and beautiful, beautiful—like ostrich eyes, like a bowl of water reflecting sunlight. They seemed to be black, though they might have been brown. I have never seen eyes like that; I shall not forget them.

Then I looked away, down to the somewhat swollen abdomen under Dr. Hunter's modesty sheet; and everything, the bag, the belly, the sling, fell into place, as my schoolteacher used to say. "Dr.

CHARACTER 67

Hunter, would you want me to assist you, then?" I said to the American.

"At what?"

"The delivery. The blue man is with child."

Yes, I do say that surprised Dr. Hunter a little bit. For a long moment he gaped at the blue man, his mouth going like a fish's, until the blue man—she—groaned, gripping the sides of the table to help her bear down with the pain of labor. This brought Dr. Hunter back to himself. He snapped at me, "Move over, girl, get me—where's my stethoscope?" He fitted the tips in his ears, put the cup to her belly, muttering, "All the time thought it was a second heart. *Damn!* Sell my soul for a fluoroscope. Such a thing as *too* primitive, Hunter." He flipped out the earpieces and began palpating the abdomen. The blue man looked on, quiet again. "Oh Lord, oh Lord. Doto, you're right. How'd you know?"

I emptied the wonderful bag out onto the cabinet top. "These are the things she had nearest her—this string, to tie the cord; this pencil is a clipper, to cut it; diapers, for herself or the child, as is also the cotton waste, for cleaning and swabbing. And this," I held up the silver cloth, "is a sling to hold the baby across her back. Or chest. It is obvious."

"Obvious, Hell," Dr. Hunter said. I tried to overlook the profanity. "How you know some alien's gonna be placental? She surely isn't mammillary, not with that practically concave chest. Genitals don't even approximate human type. Oh Lord, Lord."

"But," I said to him, "what else could it be? She *does,*" I pointed it out, "have a navel."

He shook his head, his hand wiping his forehead. "Never mind. I'll accept that as a hypothesis." He looked the blue man up and down a moment, then said, "By the way she's acting, birth is imminent. So, yeah, I'll want you to assist me. Go wash up, put on these," handing me a mask, cap, and gown, "and sterilize these." He gave me a forceps, speculum, two scalpels, and several clamps. "Wear these gloves."

He turned away as I balanced all these things in my arms. I already knew that one is supposed to do such things; Dr. Hunter, like all Europeans, is quite peremptory. Oh, I felt—but that doesn't matter. It was at that moment that I looked at the blue man again, at the deep, deep eyes—and Dr. Hunter's rudeness didn't signify. Had the blue man been a person like me, that look would have been a smile, a smile amidst all her pain. I smiled back.

So I did as I had been told, coming back shortly with the instruments piled on Dr. Hunter's steel tray. The doctor had closed the blinds to keep out the flies and dust, and set out several clean glass dishes and test tubes. "For samples," he said. He went to wash up as well.

When he returned, he began by filling his glassware with various of the blue man's excretions. From time to time a few drops of violet-colored blood ran from her birth canal, and nothing we did seemed to stop it. The bag of waters had apparently already ruptured, although Dr. Hunter later said he didn't think there had ever been any. The pains were evident and regular, about ten minutes apart. The blue man grunted with each, holding onto my hand or the table as she bore down during the spasms. Time went on like this.

It was very close in the room, quite extremely warm. Dr. Hunter was sweating. I was sweating—even the blue man had sweat beads about her head and neck. I wiped them away and she spoke some words. They made no sense, but then what do you expect from a foreigner? Dr. Hunter listened to her belly with his stethoscope, poked and prodded, but did little else. He did not try to dilate the birth canal, which I certainly would have done by this time. He wouldn't even allow me to give the blue man some water. "We don't know if her system can tolerate real water—let alone the terrestrial organisms contaminating this stuff. God knows what airborne diseases are already infecting her. And anyway, I don't want her to drink because I sure don't need to load up her bladder right now—if she's even got a bladder." Well, that made sense, so I let the matter go.

As time went by, the sun, in its swing about the building, found a crack between the screen and the window frame. It shone in brightly, falling directly onto the blue man's face. Her eyes seemed very sensitive to our light; she squeezed them shut till I repositioned the blind. "That is the Sun," I said to her. "The Sun. And I am Doto. Do-to." She gazed at me a moment, then said—as nearly as *I* can say it—"Hckvfuhl."

"There!" I said. "That must be her name. Or possibly her country."

Dr. Hunter snorted impolitely. "Me—Man. This—Earth. Sounds more like she's clearing her throat." A moment later, the blue man spasmed again, crying out the loudest she had yet today, and he simply stood there, doing nothing.

I was annoyed. First, at this nasty drip of sweat that had run beneath my mask so I *couldn't* wipe it away; second, at Dr. Hunter. *Mostly* at Dr. Hunter. I said as evenly as I could, "Doctor, she is suffering greatly. There are drugs to relieve pain. Could you not give her a little, just to help?"

Still he did nothing, not even looking at me. Shortly, the blue man's pains ceased.

"Dr. Hunter, I am asking you to help her. Push on her belly, use the forceps, why don't you? Even Juna the midwife would have had this baby born before now. Why, I myself—"

"Oh, shove it!" he yelled at me, while a second pain arose in Hckvfuhl. He turned to me, sweating angrily, and shouted further, "You damn native bitch! What do you know—a horse doctor? This is an alien, do you understand, an *alien.* You don't know—*I* don't know the first thing about her, her physiology, or how it functions. You and your African midwife would have had her dead by now." Yet another cry from the blue man distracted him, and he seemed to sweat even more, if possible. "There is nothing I can do but wait and watch. This may even be normal for her species. I'm not about to kill her by fooling around where I'm ignorant. Just don't you give me any flak, girl." And so he let her cry and cry and cry.

After an hour all the pains had slacked off. That is not right, it doesn't happen with people or cattle. I was alarmed that the child might be dead, but Dr. Hunter still reported hearing the fetal heartbeat. There was still that thin trickle of violet blood which would not be stopped, only slowed. Hckvfuhl moaned often from continuous pain, which was the most frightening of all. The eyes were shut tight.

Eventually it neared sunset. As the sun rimmed the unshaded window on the west side, it grew slightly cooler, quieter as both the insects and the village prepared for nightfall. It comes swiftly here. "I am hungry," I said. Dr. Hunter looked up.

"Mm, yeah, so am I. More than that, I need to take a break; and I bet you do, too. I don't think we better eat anything, we don't have time. But you go ahead. Take five minutes, then be right back."

"All right." I removed my mask and cap, peeled off my gloves. Then, as I suddenly recalled, I put my hand to my cheek, saying, "Llana! Her calf—"

"Doto." Dr. Hunter looked at me wearily. "Screw the cow. This is more important."

Well, Musa might not have agreed with him, but no matter. I took the break—oh, a most welcome relief!—pausing also for a small drink of water at the outdoor pump. It was so cool, so good going down into my belly growling of its hunger. I took a few more gulps and my stomach quieted. The sun was touching the horizon, the sky turning from yellow in the East through blue to red in the West. Tomorrow's would be much the same weather as today's.

I returned to the house and re-dressed, with fresh gloves. As I came into the dispensary, to my utter surprise I saw Dr. Hunter helping the blue man to drink from a glass beaker of water. Hckvfuhl drank it thirstily, making smacking sounds like a child, supported on the American's arm. I leaned against the doorway grinning—I confess it—like a monkey and caught Dr. Hunter's eye. He hunched embarrassedly, then shrugged to indicate the liquid. "Distilled," he said. "Shouldn't do any harm. Anyway, she was thirsty."

CHAPTER 5

"Yes," I agreed, making my face *very* sober, as he carefully laid Hckvfuhl back down. He prepared to go, pulling off his gloves and unfastening his mask, saying, "I think we'll be okay if she just doesn't deliver here. It'll be safer for her in Lodwar—or better yet, Nairobi, or even the U.S. I know you meant well for the alien, but I don't want to force her baby. Do you know what I mean?"

"I think I do," I said. I couldn't help responding to the change in this Westerner. For once he seemed to worry about—how to say it, the *person,* not the "political affiliation." Till now, Dr. Hunter, in trying so hard to be "African," somehow failed to be "Brother Hunter." Then I added, "But you could have been more pleasant about it."

"Oh, excuse me," he said exaggeratedly. "Well, maybe today I haven't done things the way you would have liked, but she *is* still alive, and that's what counts, right? I think we'll just pull this one through, Doto, you and I."

I smiled. "Of course. Was there ever any doubt?"

"None at all." He patted my arm. "Now you be good and make sure the alien stays calm. I'll be going up the road to see if Jama's on the way. Hold the fort till I get back." He winked at me—not respectful, but who could mind now?—and left.

It was beginning to grow dark outside. I peered out past the window blinds at the groundsel trees silhouetted against the twilight sky: short, ugly trees, shaped like a nubby gourd on a stick. The groundsels, and all of the trees, do not grow very tall here, west of Lake Rudolf. There is not much rain.

"Snyagshe." The blue man's word turned me round. She was struggling to sit up, so I helped her. She seemed very tired, and with good reason. The sheet fell away, but it was still too warm to worry about that. Again those lovely eyes shut as she leaned against the wall, squatting on her calves. I sat down opposite her, thinking, how odd it is that the English word "calf" means both baby cow and lower leg. I had gone from the first to the second all in one day. How utterly amazing. My own were excruciatingly tired.

After a bit I stood to light the kerosene lamp. The flame sat steady on its wick in the still air as I replaced the chimney over it. And it was just about then that the blue man cried out.

A lot of blue-tinged liquid was flooding her thighs; I could see her abdomen pulsing, rippling downward. She stood up straight on her knees, her fingers scrabbling for purchase on the wall behind her; found some, evidently. I was there in front of her in a second, pressing downward on her belly with the palm of my hand; maybe it helped. We pushed and strained together, then a little bit of grey head appeared, and more and more, stuttering outward with the pulses. Hckvfuhl was not crying any longer, but her pants were quick and loud. The baby's head was born, but there it halted.

Yet the rippling went on, and Hckvfuhl still strained against the wall. By now it was quite obvious she was placental, so perhaps the cord was restraining the baby? I felt under the child's almost non-existent chin, barely able to fit my fingers into the tiny space; the little one was wedged tight. Indeed, it was the cord, wrapped around the neck, like a noose. I pulled it carefully, it gave slightly; pulled it downward over the child's head and strove to shove it back up into the womb just enough to get the umbilicus over the crown. Over its head, then freed, the child slid out into my hands like a wet seed.

The rest was simple. The baby breathed, the cord was tied, the afterbirth came. I cleaned the child off and Hckvfuhl as well, then carried her into Dr. Hunter's own bedroom to sleep. It was necessary; I wasn't going to allow the blue man to sleep on that mess in the infirmary. She was very light in my arms.

I brought the baby to her, with the lamp and the marvelous mesh bag; and we clothed it. It appeared to be a girl; at least, that's my guess, and it is worth that of anyone else. The baby—hummed, sort of, as we fastened the silver sling around her. It, too, had those beautiful big eyes, open already. Hckvfuhl anointed her little head with the brine from the vial. It was the most beautiful blue baby I have ever seen.

When we were done, I reached for the lamp I had set on the nightstand. Hckvfuhl lay back on the white pillow, watching me. Strange, how those eyes could catch the least ray of light, reflect the lamp like ten lamps in the night. Her hand came up, brushing the back of mine, three blue fingers against my five black ones. "Dto-dto," she said, "Khhon." A moment passed, then I left.

Well, that is what happened the day the rocket landed. Almost as soon as I emerged from the bedroom, Dr. Hunter, Brother Jama, the District Commissioner, and all the official people arrived to take Hckvfuhl to Nairobi; and I never saw her any more. I do understand, though, that she and her daughter are well, wherever they are.

Of course, Dr. Hunter was annoyed at me for not stopping the child's birth—as if I could stop the moon and the stars, too. But he got over it when the newspapers in the capital called him a "Statue of Liberty in the savannah," keeping Hckvfuhl's "fragile spark alight." They printed my name, too.

Oh, and finally, yes, Llana came through without me well enough. Twice as well, in fact; astoundingly, she managed to produce twins. And what do you know, stingy old Musa even did pay up all that he owed.

CHAPTER 5

Concerning how the author came to write "African Blues," she tells us that the plot—extraterrestrial lands in remote spot, gives birth attended only by horse doctor and somewhat snotty medico—had been in her mind for a year and a half before she came to write it.

Then Joan Hunter Holly wrote Ms. Smith and asked for a story for a semi-professional project. The author finished it in three weeks, and recalls that it went down on paper astonishingly easily. She was particularly conscious of the heat imagery (it was July when she wrote it) and an eight-months-pregnant relative of hers. The project never happened, so she sent the story to us.

We asked for a rewrite to make the doctor "more sympathetic" (we felt he was simply too snotty in the original version) and to make the reader a little more conscious that the setting was Africa; neither change affected the story very much.

The author has done a number of amateur stories for various "Star Trek" fan magazines; but this one, she tells us, was perhaps the most easily written story she'd ever done, once she got to it. It was the getting-to-it that was hard.

In this example of first-person narrative, the viewpoint character and protagonist, Doto, never **tells** us that she is proud of her education, generally calm and unexcitable, and a perceptive judge of people around her. (And for her to tell us those things would be quite out of character for the person who has become real to us in this story.) Instead, she **shows** us these things by what she does, by what's important to her, by how she reacts to Dr. Hunter, and especially by the way that she narrates these events. She's not wholly without emotion: the blue baby is the most beautiful blue baby she's ever seen, she's irritated by Hunter's rudeness, and she's pleasantly surprised when Musa pays what he owes after all. But she's calm and reasonable throughout; she never *tells* us that she's the least excited person at the spaceship's side, but the way she describes the scene as well as what she says that she did there brings that information to us much more effectively.

Observe that while Doto never stops and *explains* how she looks on the world, her outlook is decidedly different. She thinks of "the Europeans" as foreigners, and even lumps Dr. Hunter with them. Further, she is someone raised in a small rural community, who went to the city to be educated, but then came back. She is perfectly at home in what is to the reader a strange setting. She has glimpsed our world, but only from the outside.

This kind of perspective is a very important part of characterization, particularly in first person narration, and even more so when the first-person narrator is not from the same background as the reader.

You must ask yourself: What are this character's attitudes? Does she believe in free will or in fate, in progress or stasis, in a responsive universe or an uncaring one? Does she believe that her native culture is the most advanced on Earth, or are other cultures to be learned from?

Now, once you have decided these things, *don't stop and explain them to the reader.* Simply develop a feel for the character's outlook, and try to write from that outlook. To learn how to do this, read books produced by other cultures and eras, no just fiction, but also biographies, travelogues, history, letters: everything from the Venerable Bede to Pliny the Younger to Ben Franklin's *Autobiography* to the sayings of Chuang Tzu to Xenophon's *Anabasis.* Observe the details. What does the author take for granted? What is familiar to him and what is strange? How does he perceive himself? From this you may learn something about creating characters who are *not yourself.* Every professional writer must do this. Many amateurs fail, and their stories have a cast of one.

Note that the author rightly resisted the temptation to have Sister Doto narrate her adventures in dialect, or broken English, or even standard English littered with Kiswahili words. There is a distinctive feel to the way Doto narrates, a feel in the flow of words; but it's very subtle; it doesn't get between the reader and the story.

In the archetypical bad story, on the other hand, the narration is first person, in almost opaque, imitation hillbilly dialect, and the result is both unconvincing and unreadable. It's perfectly true that different people do speak differently. But it takes very little in the way of dialect (of necessity expressed mostly in word contractions, such as "goin' t' th' fact'ry") or unfamiliar idioms to give the flavor of nonstandard speech. To make distinctive dialect work, be accurate (listen to *real* mountain folk, not Beverly Hillbillies), be sparing with it, and be consistent with each speaker's way of talking.

In addition, different people with the same language background will speak a little differently—one tends to say, "Yeah, but . . . ," another to stutter, a third to leave out the subjects of many of his sentences. Again: listen to the way real people do this, use these speech tags sparingly, and be consistent with each speaker. All of this, however, is a way of making your characters sound more real; it is not a substitute for the need to make your players real in other, more important ways.

There is a tendency among some beginners to become over-conscious of the repeated *he said, she said* that peppers extended dialog. Don't worry about it. The readers simply won't notice unless something goes wrong, and you're much more likely to get in trouble by failing to identify who is speaking.

The main reason for using a word other than **said** is when the context of the speech does not or cannot indicate the tone of voice. A whisper, for instance, must usually be identified as such. "Where are you going?" usually takes *he asked,* and "The sun is blowing up!" takes *he yelled* or *she screamed.*

A special case of this is when the content of the speech implies one tone of voice but another is intended. For instance, "Good morning" is usually said in a fairly pleasant, or at least even, tone; if it is actually being delivered in a growl, *he growled* belongs there. On the other hand, "What's *good* about it?" is a growl by implication.

It's all right to insert an occasional adverb—*he said quickly, he said thoughtfully*—if that's the most convenient way of communicating the quickness or thoughtfulness. But it is *not* all right to use an adverb merely to break up the pattern of *he said, she said.* Some people get extreme about this: "he cackled, she snapped, he expostulated." Often this ignores sense: one can *snap* "Shut up!" more or less, but not "Vote Republican!" It is not possible to *hiss* "take that." Eventually words show up that have nothing to do with speech: *"Well," he smirked.* Can you smirk a word? Would you do it in public? James Blish pointed out that writers who compulsively seek out substitutes for "said" are usually neglecting the *content* of their characters' speeches.

The choice of point of view is not so great as it may seem. Basically the choice is of first person ("I") or some kind of limited third person ("he/she"). Second person ("You") is a silly gimmick—is the reader really supposed to believe that *you* are telling *him* about *his* adventure?—and should be avoided. Omniscient third person—in which the imaginary narrator can read all the characters' thoughts and knows all facts past, present, and future—is hard to handle, not least because none of us *is* omniscient. We *can* read our own thoughts, so getting inside one particular character's head (this is what is meant by "limited") is all right; just don't change viewpoint characters too often, or without good reason. Camera eye, in which no one's thoughts can be read, works only if the author is very adept at showing feelings through dialog and gesture.

First person would seem the easiest of all; one just tells the story. Unfortunately, there are several pitfalls. For one thing, our culture does not approve of boasting, and first person often sounds that way—"This is how I saved Earth from the Qwert invasion: . . ."

More important, since stories are about people changing, from what perspective does your narrator speak? Before the change, or after? "Ah, dear reader, had I but known what dread fate awaited me beyond that Stygian stargate . . ." is terrible storytelling—from any point of view.

Stories should be told in the third person, therefore, unless there is a compelling reason to do otherwise. In "African Blues" there is such a reason: to put the reader, as firmly as possible, into Doto's mind in order to show how Dr. Hunter, American-born black man, is coping with the (to him) alien African setting, and on top of that, the extraterrestrial alien blue man as well. This is, then, a conflict of cultures. When Hunter is willing to admit that Doto may be right about giving the alien some water, when he shows concern for the blue man as a person instead of a "political affiliation," then Doto is willing to accept him on her own terms; this resolves the conflict between them. Were the story to be translated to the United States, half the point of it would be lost, and what was left would be a routine visiting-alien story, not worth publishing at all. And were this story not so strong on character—and thoroughly *believable* character at that—the conflict of cultures would simply not be there.

Although Sister Doto is the protagonist and the viewpoint in this story, Dr. Hunter is probably the most familiar (not stereotyped, just closest to most readers' experience) person on stage; it is he who shows some real change throughout the story, beginning to accept Doto as a competent medic in her own right and to accept the blue man as a patient instead of a political problem. Doto changes but little. And it is Musa, the always offstage Musa, who provides a bit of impulsive action at the very end that—to Doto—helps make everything worthwhile.

The next story is told in an entirely different way:

PERCHANCE TO DREAM
by Sally A. Sellers

*This story, Sally Sellers's first sale, is the result
of a writing workshop at the University of
Michigan, headed by Lloyd Biggle, Jr. The
author tells us that she wrote for as long as she
can remember, but wrote only for creative
writing courses while in college. Since
graduation, she worked as a waitress, traveled
in Europe, and worked as a medical
technician in hematology. She now lives with
her family, two cats, and about a hundred
plants, and is a research assistant
at the University of Michigan.*

From the playground came the sound of laughter.

A gusty night wind was sweeping the park, and the light at the edge of the picnic grounds swung crazily. Distorted shadows came and went, rushing past as the wind pushed the light to the end of its arc, then sliding back jerkily.

Again the laughter rang out, and this time Norb identified the creaking sound that accompanied it. Someone was using the swing. Nervously he peered around the swaying branches of the bush, but he saw no one.

He heard a click. Danny had drawn his knife. Hastily Norb fumbled for his own. The slender weapon felt awkward in his hand, even after all the hours of practice.

"It'll be easy," Danny had said. "There's always some jerk in the park after dark—they never learn." Norb shivered and gripped the knife more tightly.

Then he saw them—a young couple walking hand in hand among the trees. Danny chuckled softly, and Norb relaxed somewhat. Danny was right—this would be a cinch.

"You take the girl," Danny whispered.

Norb nodded. All they had to do was wait—the couple was headed right toward them. They were high school kids, no more than fifteen or sixteen, walking slowly with their heads together, whispering and giggling. Norb swallowed and tensed himself.

"Now!" Danny hissed.

They were upon them before the kids had time to react. Danny jerked the boy backward and threw him to the ground. Norb grabbed the back of the girl's collar and held his knife at her throat.

"Okay, just do what we say and nobody gets hurt," snarled Danny. He pointed his knife at the boy's face. "You got a wallet, kid?"

The boy stared in mute terror at the knife. The girl made small whimpering sounds in her throat, and Norb tightened his hold on her collar.

"Come on, come on! Your wallet!"

From somewhere in the shadows, a woman's voice rang out. "Leave them alone!"

Norb whirled as a dark form charged into Danny and sent him sprawling. Oh God, he thought, we've been caught! As the boy leaped to his feet and started to run, Norb made a futile swipe at him with his knife. His grip on the girl must have relaxed, because she jerked free and followed the boy into the woods.

Norb looked from the retreating kids to the two wrestling figures, his hands clenched in indecision. The dark form had Danny pinned to the ground. He was squirming desperately, but he couldn't free himself. "Get her off me!" he cried.

"Jesus!" Norb whispered helplessly. The kids had begun to scream for help. They'd rouse the whole neighborhood.

"Norb!" screamed Danny.

It was a command, and Norb hurled himself onto the woman. Twice he stabbed wildly at her back, but she only grunted and held on more tightly. He struck out again, and this time his knife sank deeply into soft flesh. Spurting blood soaked his hand and sleeve, and he snatched them away in horror.

Danny rolled free. He got to his feet, and the two of them stood looking down at the woman. The knife was buried in the side of her throat.

"Oh my God," whimpered Norb.

"You ass!" cried Danny. "Why didn't you just pull her off? You killed her!"

Norb stood paralyzed, staring down at the knife and the pulsing wound. Fear thickened in his throat, and he felt his stomach constrict. He was going to be sick.

"You better run like hell. You're in for it now."

Danny was gone. Norb wrenched his gaze from the body. On the other side of the playground, the kids were still calling for help. He saw car lights up by the gate, swinging into the park drive.

Norb began to run.

The gush of blood from the wound slowed abruptly and then stopped. The chest heaved several times with great intakes of air. Then it collapsed, and a spasm shook the body. In the smooth motion of a slowly tightening circle, it curled in on itself. The heart gave three great beats, hesitated, pumped once more, and was still.

Norb caught up with Danny at the edge of the woods. They stopped, panting, and looked in the direction of the car. It had come to a stop

CHAPTER 5

by the tennis courts, and, as they watched, the driver cut his motor and turned off his lights.

"This way," whispered Danny. "Come on."

As they headed across the road for the gate, the car's motor suddenly started. Its light came on, and it roared into a U-turn to race after them.

"It's the cops!" Danny yelled. "Split up!"

Norb was too frightened. Desperately he followed Danny, and the pair of them fled through the gate and turned along the street as the patrol car swung around the curve. Then Danny veered off, and Norb followed him through bushes and into a back yard. A dog began yelping somewhere. Danny scaled a fence and dropped into the adjoining back yard, and Norb followed, landing roughly and falling to his knees.

He scrambled to his feet and collided with Danny, who was laughing softly as he watched the patrol car. It had turned around and was headed back into the park.

The heart had not stopped. It was pumping—but only once every six minutes, with a great throb. At each pulse, a pinprick of light danced across the back of the eyelids. The wound attempted to close itself and tightened futilely around the intrusion of steel. A neck muscle twitched. Then another, but the knife remained. The tissue around the blade began contracting minutely, forcing it outward in imperceptible jerks.

Officer Lucas parked near the playground and started into the trees. He could not have said what he was looking for, but neighbors had reported hearing cries for help, and the way those two punks had run told him they'd been up to something. He switched on his flashlight, delineating an overturned litter basket that had spewed paper across the path. The gusting wind tore at it, prying loose one fluttering fragment at a time. Cautiously he walked forward. Gray-brown tree trunks moved in and out of the illumination as he crept on, but he could see nothing else.

He stumbled over an empty beer bottle, kicked it aside, and then stopped uncertainly, pivoting with his light. It revealed nothing but empty picnic tables and cold barbecue grills, and he was about to turn back when his beam picked out the body, curled motionless near a clump of bushes. Lucas ran forward and knelt beside the woman, shining his light on her face.

The throat wound seemed to have stopped bleeding, but if the knife had sliced the jugular vein—he leaned closer to examine the laceration. Belatedly a thought occurred to him, and he reached for the wrist. There was no pulse. He shone his light on the chest, but it was motionless.

Lucas got to his feet and inspected the area hastily. Seeing no obvious clues, he hurried back to the patrol car.

The heart throbbed again, and another pinprick of light jumped behind the woman's eyelids. The tissues in the neck tightened farther as new cells developed, amassed, and forced the blade a fraction of an inch outward. The wounds in the back, shallow and clean, had already closed. The lungs expanded once with a great intake of air. The knife jerked again, tilted precariously, and finally fell to the ground under its own weight. Immediately new tissue raced to fill the open area.

The radio was squawking. Lucas waited for the exchange to end before picking up the mike. "Baker 23."

"Go ahead, Baker 23."

"I'm at Newberry Park, east end, I've got a 409 and request M.E."

"Confirmed, 23."

"Notify the detective on call."

"Clear, 23."

"Ten-four." He hung up the mike and glanced back into the woods. Probably an attempted, rape, he thought. She shouldn't have fought. The lousy punks! Lucas rubbed his forehead fretfully. He should have chased them, damn it. Why hadn't he?

The heart was beating every three minutes now. The throat wound had closed, forming a large ridge under the dried blood. Cells multiplied at fantastic rates, spanning the damaged area with a minute latticework. This filled in as the new cells divided, expanded, and divided again.

Lucas reached for his clipboard and flipped on the interior lights. He glanced into the trees once before he began filling in his report. A voice crackled on the radio, calling another car. His pen scratched haltingly across the paper.

The heart was returning to its normal pace. The ridge on the neck was gone, leaving smooth skin. A jagged pattern of light jerked across the retinas. The fugue was coming to an end. The chest rose, fell, then rose again. A shadow of awareness nudged at consciousness.

The sound of the radio filled the night again, and Lucas turned uneasily, searching the road behind him for approaching headlights. There were none. He glanced at his watch and returned to the report.

CHAPTER 5

She became aware of the familiar prickling sensation in her limbs, plus a strange burning about her throat. She felt herself rising, rising—and suddenly awareness flooded her. Her body jerked, uncurled. Jeanette opened her eyes. Breathing deeply, she blinked until the dark thick line looming over her resolved itself into a tree trunk. Unconsciously her hand began to rub her neck, and she felt dry flakes come off on her fingers.

Wearily she closed her eyes again, trying to remember: Those kids. One had a knife. She was in the park. Then she heard the faint crackle of a police radio. She rolled to her knees, and dizziness swept over her. She could see a light through the trees. *Good God,* she thought, *he's right over there!*

Jeanette rubbed her eyes and looked about her. She was lightheaded, but there was no time to waste. Soon there would be other police—and doctors. She knew. Moving unsteadily, at a crouch, she slipped away into the woods.

Four patrol cars were there when the ambulance arrived. Stuart Crosby, the medical examiner, climbed out slowly and surveyed the scene. He could see half a dozen flashlights in the woods. The photographer sat in the open door of one of the cars, smoking a cigarette.

"Where's the body?" asked Crosby.

The photographer tossed his cigarette away disgustedly. "They can't find it."

"Can't find it? What do you mean?"

"It's not out there. Lucas says it was in the woods, but when Kelaney got here, it was gone."

Puzzled, Crosby turned toward the flashlights. As another gust of wind swept the park, he pulled his light coat more closely about him and started forward resignedly—a tired white-haired man who should have been home in bed.

He could hear Detective Kelaney roaring long before he could see him. "You half-ass! What'd it do, walk away?"

"No, sir!" answered Lucas hotly. "She was definitely dead. She was lying right there, I swear it—and that knife was in her throat, I recognize the handle."

"Yeah? For a throat wound, there's not much blood on it."

"Maybe," said Lucas stubbornly, "but that's where it was, all right."

Crosby halted. He had a moment of disorientation as uneasy memories stirred in the back of his mind. A serious wound, but not much blood . . . a dead body that disappeared. . . .

"Obviously she wasn't dragged," said Kelaney. "Did you by chance, *Officer* Lucas, think to check the pulse? Or were you thinking at all?"

CHARACTER 81

"Yes, sir! Yes, I did! I checked the pulse, and there was nothing! Zero respiration, too. Yes, sir, I did!"

"Then where *is* she?" screamed Kelaney.

Another officer approached timidly. "There's nothing out there, sir. Nothing at all."

"Well, look again," snarled Kelaney.

Crosby moved into the circle of men. The detective was running his hand through his hair in exasperation. Lucas was red-faced and defiant.

Kelaney reached for his notebook. "All right, what did she look like?"

Lucas straightened, eager with facts. "Twenty, twenty-two, Caucasian, dark hair, about five-six, hundred and twenty-five pounds. . . ."

"Scars or distinguishing marks?"

"Yeah, as a matter of fact. There were three moles on her cheek—on her left cheek—all right together, right about here." He put his finger high on his cheekbone, near his eye.

Crosby felt the blood roar in his ears. He stepped forward. "What did you say, Lucas?" he asked hoarsely.

Lucas turned to the old man. "Three moles, doctor, close together, on her cheek."

Crosby turned away, his hands in his pockets. He took a deep breath. He'd always known she'd return some day, and here was the same scene, the same bewildered faces, the same accusations. Three moles on her cheek . . . it had to be.

The wind ruffled his hair, but he no longer noticed its chill. They would find no body. Jeanette was back.

The next morning, Crosby filed a Missing Persons Report. "Send out an APB," he told the sergeant. "We've got to find her."

The sergeant looked mildly surprised. "What's she done?"

"She's a potential suicide. More than potential. I know this woman, and she's going to try to kill herself."

The sergeant reached for the form. "Okay, Doc, if you think it's that important. What's her name?"

Crosby hesitated. "She's probably using an alias. But I can give a description—an exact description."

"Okay," said the sergeant. "Shoot."

The bulletin went out at noon. Crosby spent the remainder of the day visiting motels, but no one remembered checking in a young woman with three moles on her cheek.

Jeanette saw the lights approaching in the distance: two white eyes and, above them, the yellow and red points along the roof that told her this was a truck. She leaned back against the concrete

support of the bridge, hands clenched behind her, and waited.
It had been three nights since the incident in the park. Her shoulders sagged dejectedly at the thought of it. Opportunities like that were everywhere, but she knew that knives weren't going to do it. She'd tried that herself—was it in Cleveland? A painful memory flashed for a moment, of one more failure in the long series of futile attempts—heartbreaking struggles in the wrong cities. But here . . .

She peered around the pillar again. The eyes of the truck were closer now. Here, it could happen. Where it began, it could end. She inched closer to the edge of the support and crouched, alert to the sound of the oncoming truck.

It had rounded the curve and was thundering down the long straightaway before the bridge. Joy surged within her as she grasped its immensity and momentum. Surely this . . . ! Never had she tried it with something so large, with something beyond her control. Yes, surely this would be the time!

Suddenly the white eyes were there, racing under the bridge, the diesels throbbing, roaring down at her. Her head reared in elation. Now!

She leaped an instant too late, and her body was struck by the right fender. The mammoth impact threw her a hundred feet in an arc that spanned the entrance ramp, the guideposts, and a ditch, terminating brutally in the field beyond. The left side of her skull was smashed, her arm was shattered, and four ribs were caved in. The impact of the landing broke her neck.

It was a full quarter of a mile before the white-faced driver gained sufficient control to lumber to a halt. "Sweet Jesus," he whispered. Had he imagined it? He climbed out of the rig and examined the dented fender. Then he ran back to the cab and tried futilely to contact someone by radio who could telephone the police. It was 3 A.M., and all channels seemed dead. Desperately he began backing along the shoulder.

Rushes of energy danced through the tissues. Cells divided furiously, bridging gulfs. Enzymes flowed; catalysts swept through protoplasm: coupling, breaking, then coupling again. Massive reconstruction raged on. The collapsed half of the body shifted imperceptibly.

The truck stopped a hundred feet from the bridge, and the driver leaped out. He clicked on his flashlight and played it frantically over the triangle of thawing soil between the entrance ramp and the expressway. Nothing. He crossed to the ditch and began walking slowly beside it.

Bundles of collagen interlaced; in the matrix, mineral was deposited; cartilage calcified. The ribs had almost knit together and were curved loosely in their original crescent. Muscle fibers united and contracted in taut arches. The head jerked, then jerked again, as it was forced from its slackness into an increasingly firm position. Flexor spasms twitched the limbs as impulses flowed through newly formed neurons. The heart pulsed.

The driver stood helplessly on the shoulder and clicked off the flashlight. It was 3:30, and no cars were in sight. He couldn't find the body. He had finally succeeded in radioing for help, and now all he could do was wait. He stared at the ditch for a moment before moving toward the truck. There *had* been a woman, he was sure. He'd seen her for just an instant before the impact, leaping forward under the headlights. He shuddered and quickened his pace to the cab.

Under the caked blood, the skin was smooth and softly rounded. The heart was pumping her awake: Scratches of light behind the eyelids. Half of her body prickling, burning. . . . A shuddering breath.

Forty-seven minutes after the impact, Jeanette opened her eyes. Slowly she raised her head. That line in the sky . . . the bridge.

She had failed again. Even here. She opened her mouth to moan, but only a rasping sound emerged.

Stuart Crosby swayed as the ambulance rounded a corner and sped down the street. He pressed his knuckles against his mouth and screamed silently at the driver: *God, hurry, I know it's her.*

He had slept little since the night in the park. He had monitored every call, and he knew that this one—a woman in dark clothes, jumping in front of a trucker's rig—this one had to be Jeanette.

It was her. She was trying again. Oh, God, after all these years, she was still trying. How many times, in how many cities, had she fought to die?

They were on the bridge now, and he looked down on the figures silhouetted against the red of the flares. The ambulance swung into the entrance ramp with a final whoop and pulled up behind a patrol car. Crosby had the door open and his foot on the ground before they were completely stopped, and he had to clutch at the door to keep from falling. A pain flashed across his back. He regained his balance and ran toward a deputy who was playing a flashlight along the ditch.

"Did you find her?"

The deputy turned and took an involuntary step away from the

CHAPTER 5

intense, stooped figure. "No, sir, doctor. Not a thing."

Crosby's voice failed him. He stood looking dejectedly down the expressway.

"To tell you the truth," said the deputy, nodding at the semi, "I think that guy had a few too many little white pills. Seeing shadows. There's nothing along here but a dead raccoon. And he's been dead since yesterday."

But Crosby was already moving across the ditch to the field beyond, where deputies swung flashlights in large arcs and a German shepherd was snuffling through the brittle stubble.

Somewhere near here, Jeanette might be lying with a broken body. It was possible, he thought. The damage could have been great, and the healing slow. Or—a chill thought clutched at him. He shook his head. No. She wouldn't have succeeded. She would still be alive, somewhere. If he could just see her, talk to her!

There was a sharp, small bark from the dog. Crosby hurried forward frantically. His foot slipped and he came down hard, scraping skin from his palm. The pain flashed again in his back. He got to his feet and ran toward the circle of deputies.

One of the men was crouched, examining the cold soil. Crosby ran up, panting, and saw that the ground was stained with blood. She'd been here. She'd been here!

He strained to see across the field and finally discerned, on the other side, a road running parallel to the expressway. But there were no cars parked on it. She was gone.

After he returned home, his body forced him to sleep, but his dreams allowed him no rest. He kept seeing a lovely young woman, with three moles on her cheek—a weeping, haunted, frantic woman who cut herself again and again and thrust the mutilated arm before his face for him to watch in amazement as the wounds closed, bonded, and healed to smoothness before his eyes. In minutes.

God, if she would only stop crying, stop pleading with him, stop begging him to find a way to make her die—to use his medical knowledge somehow, in some manner that would end it for her. She wanted to die. She hated herself, hated the body that imprisoned her.

How old was she then? How many years had that youthful body endured without change, without aging? How many decades had she lived before life exhausted her and she longed for the tranquillity of death?

He had never found out. He refused to help her die, and she broke away and fled hysterically into the night. He never saw her again. There followed a series of futile suicide attempts and night crimes with the young woman victim mysteriously missing—and then . . . nothing.

And now she was back. Jeanette!

He found himself sitting up in bed, and he wearily buried his face in his hands. He could still hear the sound of her crying. He had always heard it, in a small corner of his mind, for the last thirty years.

The street sign letters were white on green: HOMER. Jeanette stood for a long while staring at them before she turned to walk slowly along the crumbling sidewalk. A vast ache filled her chest as she beheld the familiar old houses.

The small, neat lawns had been replaced by weeds and litter. Bricks were missing out of most of the front walks. The fence was gone at the Mahews'. Jim Mahew had been so proud the day he brought home his horseless carriage, and she'd been the only one brave enough to ride in it. Her mother had been horrified.

This rambling old home with the boarded-up windows was the Parkers'. The house was dead now. So was her playmate, Billy Parker—the first boy she knew to fight overseas and the first one to die. The little house across the street had been white when old Emma Walters lived there. She had baked sugar cookies for Jeanette, and Jeanette had given her a May basket once, full of violets. She must have died a long time ago. Jeanette's hand clenched. A very long time ago.

The sound of her steps on the decayed sidewalk seemed extraordinarily loud. The street was deserted. There was no movement save that of her own dark figure plodding steadily forward. Here was Cathy Carter's house. Her father had owned the buggywhip factory over in Capville. They'd been best friends. Cathy, who always got her dresses dirty, had teeth missing, cut off her own braids one day. There was that Sunday they'd gotten in trouble for climbing the elm tree—but there was no elm now, only an ugly stump squatting there to remind her of a Sunday that was gone, lost, wiped out forever. She'd heard that Cathy had married a druggist and moved out East somewhere. Jeanette found herself wondering desperately if Cathy had raised any children. Or grandchildren. Or great-grandchildren. Cathy Carter, did you make your little girls wear dresses and braids? Did you let them climb trees? Are you still alive? Or are you gone, too, like everything else that ever meant anything to me?

Her steps faltered, but her own house loomed up ahead to draw her on. It stood waiting, silently watching her approach. It, too, was dead. A new pain filled her when she saw the crumbling porch, saw that the flowerboxes were gone, saw the broken windows and the peeling wallpaper within. A rusted bicycle wheel lay in the weeds that were the front yard, along with a box of rubble and pile of

CHAPTER 5

boards. Tiny pieces of glass crunched sharply beneath her feet. The hedge was gone. So were the boxwood shrubs, the new variety from Boston—her mother had waited for them for so long and finally got them after the war.

She closed her eyes. Her mother had never known. Had died before she realized what she had brought into the world. Before even Jeanette had an inkling of what she was.

A monster. A freak. This body was wrong, horribly wrong. It should not be.

She had run away from this town, left it so that her friends would never know. But still it pulled at her, drawing her back every generation, pushing itself into her thoughts until she could stand it no longer. Then she would come back to stare at the old places that had been her home and the old people who had been her friends. And they didn't recognize her, never suspected, never knew why she seemed so strangely familiar.

Once she had even believed she could live here again. The memory ached within her and she quickened her pace. She could not think of him, could not allow the sound of his name in her mind. Where was he now? Had he ever understood? She had run away that time, too.

She'd had to. He was so good, so generous, but she was grotesque, a vile caprice of nature. She loathed the body.

It was evil. It must be destroyed.

Here, in the city where it was created: where she was born, she would die.

Somehow.

The phone jangled harshly, shattering the silence of the room with such intensity that he jumped and dropped a slide on the floor. He sighed and reached for the receiver. "Crosby."

"Doctor, this is Sergeant Andersen. One of our units spotted a woman fitting the description of your APB on the High Street Bridge."

"Did they get her?" demanded Crosby.

"I dunno yet. They just radioed in. She was over the railing—looked like she was ready to jump. They're trying to get to her now. Thought you'd like to know."

"Right," said Crosby, slamming down the receiver. He reached for his coat as his mind plotted out the fastest route to High Street. Better cut down Fourth, he thought, and up Putnam. The slide crackled sharply under his heel and he looked at it in brief surprise before running out the door.

They've found her, he thought elatedly. *They've got Jeanette! Thank God—I must talk with her, must convince her that she's a miracle. She has the secret of life. The whole human race will be indebted to her. Please, please,* he prayed, *don't let her get away.*

He reached the bridge and saw the squad car up ahead. Gawkers were driving by slowly, staring out of their windows in morbid fascination. Two boys on bicycles had stopped and were peering over the railing. An officer had straddled it and was looking down.

Crosby leaped from the car and ran anxiously to the railing. His heart lifted as he saw another officer, with one arm around the lower railing and a firm grip on Jeanette's wrist. He was coaxing her to take a step up.

"Jeanette!" It was a ragged cry.

"Take it easy, Doc," said the officer straddling the railing. "She's scared."

The woman looked up. She was pale, and the beauty mark on her cheek stood out starkly. The bitter shock sent Crosby reeling backward. For a moment he felt dizzy, and he clutched the rail with trembling fingers. The gray river flowed sullenly beneath him.

It wasn't Jeanette.

"Dear God," he whispered. He finally raised his gaze to the dismal buildings that loomed across the river. Then where was she? She must have tried again. Had she succeeded?

Chief Dolenz clasped, then unclasped his hands. "You've got to slow down, Stu. You're pushing yourself too hard."

Crosby's shoulders sagged a little more, but he did not answer.

"You're like a man possessed," continued the chief. "It's starting to wear you down. Ease up, for god's sake. We'll find her. Why all this fuss over one loony patient? Is it that important, really?"

Crosby lowered his head. He still couldn't speak. The chief looked with puzzlement at the old man, at the small bald spot that was beginning to expand, at the slump of the body, the rumpled sweater, the tremor of the hands as they pressed together. He opened his mouth but could not bring himself to say more.

"Citizens National Bank," the switchboard operator said.

The voice on the line was low and nervous. "I'm gonna tell you this once, and only once. There's a bomb in your bank, see? It's gonna go off in ten minutes. If you don't want nobody hurt, you better get 'em outta there."

The operator felt the blood drain from her face. "Is this a joke?"

"No joke, lady. You got ten minutes. If anybody wants to know, you tell 'em People for a Free Society are starting to take action. Got that?" The line went dead.

She sat motionless for a moment, and then she got unsteadily to her feet. "Mrs. Calkins!" she called. The switchboard buzzed again,

CHAPTER 5

but she ignored it and ran to the manager's desk.

Mrs. Calkins looked up from a customer and frowned icily at her; but when the girl bent and whispered in her ear, the manager got calmly to her feet. "Mr. Davison," she said politely to her customer, "we seem to have a problem in the bank. I believe the safest place to be right now would be out of the building." Turning to the operator, she said coolly, "Notify the police."

Mr. Davison scrambled to his feet and began thrusting papers into his briefcase. The manager strode to the center of the lobby and clapped her hands with authority. "Could I have your attention please! I'm the manager. We are experiencing difficulties in the bank. I would like everyone to move quickly but quietly out of this building and into the street. Please move some distance away."

Faces turned toward her, but no one moved.

"Please," urged Mrs. Calkins. "There is immediate danger if you remain in the building. Your transactions may be completed later. Please leave at once."

People began to drift toward the door. The tellers looked at each other in bewilderment and began locking the money drawers. A heavyset man remained stubbornly at his window. "What about my change?" he demanded.

The operator hung up the phone and ran toward the doorway. "Hurry!" she cried. "There's a bomb!"

"A bomb!"

"She said there's a bomb!"

"Look out!"

"Get outside!"

There was a sudden rush for the door. "Please!" shouted the manager. "There is no need for panic." But her voice was lost in the uproar.

Jeanette sat limply at the bus stop, her hands folded in her lap, her eyes fixed despondently on the blur of passing automobile wheels. The day was oppressively overcast; gray clouds hung heavily over the city. When the chill wind blew her coat open, she made no move to gather it about her.

Behind her, the doors of the bank suddenly burst open, and people began to rush out frantically. The crowd bulged into the street. Brakes squealed; voices babbled excitedly. Jeanette turned and looked dully toward the bank.

There were shouts. Passing pedestrians began to run, and the frenzied flow of people from the bank continued. A woman screamed. Another tripped and nearly fell. Sirens sounded in the distance.

Above the hubbub, Jeanette caught a few clearly spoken words. "Bomb . . . in the bank . . ." She got slowly to her feet and began to edge her way through the crowd.

She had almost reached the door before anyone tried to stop her. A man caught at her sleeve. "You can't go in there, lady. There's a bomb!"

She pulled free, and a fresh surge of pedestrians came between them. The bank doors were closed, now. Everyone was outside and hurrying away. Jeanette pushed doubtfully at the tall glass door, pushed it open farther, and slipped inside. It closed with a hiss, blocking out the growing pandemonium in the street. The lobby seemed warm and friendly, a refuge from the bitterly cold wind.

She turned and looked through the door. A policeman had appeared and the man who had tried to stop her was talking with him and pointing at the bank. Jeanette quickly moved back out of sight. She walked the length of the empty room, picked out a chair for herself, and sat down. The vast, unruffled quiet of the place matched the abiding peace she felt within her.

Outside, the first police car screamed to the curb. An ambulance followed, as the explosion ripped through the building, sending a torrent of bricks and glass and metal onto the pavement.

"Code blue, emergency room." The loudspeaker croaked for the third time as Julius Beamer rounded the corner. Ahead of him he could see a woman being wheeled into room three. An intern, keeping pace with the cart, was pushing on her breastbone at one-second intervals.

Emergency room three was crowded. A nurse stepped aside as he entered and said, "Bomb exploded at the bank." A technician was hooking up the EKG, while a young doctor was forcing a tube down the woman's trachea. A resident had inserted an IV and called for digoxin.

"Okay," said Dr. Beamer to the intern thumping the chest. The intern stepped back, exhausted, and Beamer took over the external cardiac massage. The respirator hissed into life. Beamer pressed down.

There was interference. Excess oxygen was flooding the system. A brief hesitation, and then the body adjusted. Hormones flooded the bloodstream, and the cells began dividing again. The site of the damage was extensive, and vast reconstruction was necessary. The heart pulsed once.

There was a single blip on the EKG, and Beamer grunted. He pushed again. And then again, but the flat high-pitched note continued unchanged. Dr. Channing was at his elbow, waiting to take over, but Beamer ignored him. Julius Beamer did not like failure. He called for the electrodes. A brief burst of electricity flowed into the heart. There was no response. He applied them again.

CHAPTER 5

The reconstruction was being hindered; there was cardiac interference. The body's energies were diverted toward the heart in an effort to keep it from beating. The delicate balance had to be maintained, or the chemicals would be swept away in the bloodstream.

A drop of sweat trickled down Julius Beamer's temple. He called for a needle and injected epinephrine directly into the heart.

Chemical stimulation: hormones activated and countered immediately.

There was no response. The only sounds in the room were the long *hisssssss-click* of the respirator and the eerie unchanging note of the EKG. Dr. Beamer stepped back wearily and shook his head. Then he whirled in disgust and strode out of the room. A resident reached to unplug the EKG.

The interference had stopped. Reconstruction resumed at the primary site of damage.

Rounding the corner, Dr. Beamer heard someone call his name hoarsely, and he turned to see Stuart Crosby stumbling toward him.

"Julius! That woman!"

"Stuart! Hello! What are you—?"

"That woman in the explosion. Where is she?"

"I'm afraid we lost her—couldn't get her heart going. Is she a witness?"

In emergency room three, the respirator hissed to a stop. *The heart pulsed once.* But there was no machine to record it.

In the hallway, Crosby clutched at Dr. Beamer. "No. She's my wife."

Crosby's fists covered his eyes, his knuckles pressing painfully into his forehead. Outside, there was a low rumble of thunder. He swallowed with difficulty and dug his knuckles in deeper, trying to reason. *How can I?* he wondered. *How can I say yes? Jeanette!*

The figure behind him moved slightly and the woman cleared her throat. "Dr. Crosby, I know this is a difficult decision, but we haven't much time." She laid a gentle hand on his shoulder. "We've got forty-three people in this area who desperately need a new kidney. And there are three potential recipients for a heart upstairs—one is an eight-year-old girl. Please. It's a chance for someone else. A whole new life."

Crosby twisted away from her and moved to the window. No, he thought, we haven't much time. In a few minutes, she would get up off that table herself and walk into this room—and then it would be too late. She wanted to die. She had been trying to die for years—how many? Fifty? A hundred? If they took her organs, she *would* die. Not even that marvelous body could sustain the loss of the major organs. All he had to do was say yes. But how could he?

He hadn't even seen her face yet. He could touch her again, talk to her, hold her. After thirty years!

As he looked out the window, a drop of rain splashed against the pane. He thought of the lines of a poem he had memorized twenty years before.

> From too much love of living,
>   From hope and fear set free,
> We thank with brief thanksgiving
>   Whatever gods may be
> That no man lives forever,
> That dead men rise up never;
> That even the weariest river
>   Winds somewhere safe to sea.

The rain began to fall steadily, drumming against the window in a hollow rhythm. There was silence in the room, and for a brief moment, Crosby had the frightening sensation of being totally alone in the world.

A voice within him spoke the painful answer: *Release her. Let her carry the burden no more. She is weary.*

"Dr. Crosby. . . ." The woman's voice was gentle.

"Yes!" he cried. "Do it! Take everything—anything you want. But God, please hurry!" Then he lowered his head into his hands and wept.

Grafton Medical Center was highly efficient. Within minutes, a surgeon was summoned and preparations had begun. The first organs removed were the kidneys. Then the heart. Later, the liver, pancreas, spleen, eyeballs, and thyroid gland were lifted delicately and transferred to special containers just above freezing temperature. Finally, a quantity of bone marrow was removed for use as scaffolding for future production of peripheral blood cellular components.

What had been Jeanette Crosby was wheeled down to the morgue.

The woman's voice was doubtful. "We usually don't allow relatives. You see, once the services are over. . . ."

Stuart Crosby clutched his hat. "There were no services. I only want a few minutes."

The owner of the crematory, a burly, pleasant-looking man, entered the outer office. "Can I do something for you, sir?"

The woman turned to him. "He wanted a little time with the casket, Mr. Gilbert. The one that came over from the hospital this morning."

CHAPTER 5

"Please," Crosby pleaded. "There were no services—I didn't want any, but I just—I didn't realize there'd be no chance to say good-bye. The hospital said she was sent here, and . . . I'm a doctor. Dr. Stuart Crosby. She's my wife. Jeanette Crosby. I didn't think until today that I wanted to. . . ." He trailed off and lowered his head.

The owner hesitated. "We usually don't allow this, doctor. We have no facilities here for paying the last respects."

"I know," mumbled Crosby. "I understand—but just a few minutes—please."

The manager looked at the secretary, then back to the old man. "All right, sir. Just a moment, and I'll see if I can find a room. If you'll wait here, please."

The casket was cream-colored pine. It was unadorned. The lid was already sealed, so he could not see her face. But he knew it would be at peace.

He stood dry-eyed before the casket, his hands clasped in front of him. Outside, the rain that had begun the day before was still drizzling down. He could think of nothing to say to her, and he was only aware of a hollow feeling in his chest. He thought ramblingly of his dog, and how he hadn't made his bed that morning, and about the broken windshield wiper he would have to replace on his car.

Finally he turned and walked from the room, bent over a bit because his back hurt. "Thank you," he said to the owner. Stepping outside into the rain, he very carefully raised his umbrella.

The owner watched him until the car pulled onto the main road. Then he yelled, "Okay, Jack!"

Two men lifted the casket and bore it outside in the rain toward the oven.

Cells divided, differentiated, and divided again. The reconstruction was almost complete. It had taken a long time, almost twenty-four hours. The body had never been challenged to capacity before. Removal of the major organs had caused much difficulty, but regeneration had begun almost at once, and the new tissues were now starting the first stirrings of renewed activity.

The casket slid onto the asbestos bricks with a small scraping noise. The door clanged shut, and there was a dull ring as the bolt was drawn.

There was a flicker of light behind the eyelids, and the new retinas registered it and transmitted it to the brain. The heart pulsed once, and then again. A shuddering breath.

Outside the oven, a hand reached for the switches and set the master timer. The main burner was turned on. Oil under pressure flared and exploded into the chamber.

There was a shadow of awareness for a long moment, and then it was gone.

CHARACTER 93

After thirty minutes, the oven temperature was 900 degrees Fahrenheit. The thing on the table was a third of its original size. The secondary burners flamed on. In another half-hour the temperature had reached 2,000 degrees, and it would stay there for another ninety minutes.

The ashes, larger than usual, had to be mashed to a chalky, brittle dust.

As Dr. Kornbluth began easing off the dressing, she smiled at the young face on the pillow before her.

"Well, well. You're looking perky today, Marie!" she said.

The little girl smiled back with surprising vigor.

"Scissors, please," said Dr. Kornbluth and held out her hand.

Dr. Roeber spoke from the other side of the bed. "Her color is certainly good."

"Yes. I just got the lab report, and so far there's no anemia."

"Has she been given the Prednisone today?"

"Twenty milligrams about an hour ago."

The last dressing was removed, and the two doctors bent over to examine the chest: the chest that was smooth and clean and faintly pink, with no scars, no lumps, no ridges.

"Something's wrong," said Dr. Kornbluth. "Is this a joke, Dr. Roeber?"

The surgeon's voice was frightened. "I don't understand it, not at all."

"Have you the right patient here?" She reached for the identification bracelet around Marie's wrist.

"Of course it's the right patient!" Dr. Roeber's voice rose. "I ought to know who I operated on, shouldn't I?"

"But it isn't possible!" cried Dr. Kornbluth.

The girl spoke up in a high voice. "Is my new heart okay?"

"It's fine, honey," said Dr. Kornbluth. Then she lowered her voice. "This is physiologically impossible! The incision has completely healed, without scar tissue. And in thirty-two hours, doctor? In thirty-two hours?"

Sally Sellers, in response to our inquiry, wrote:

"The best thing that can be said about the story is that it *does* improve somewhat as it goes along. It has half a dozen passages that I now find acceptable, but the rest of it is painfully bad.

"How I came to write it: I had the usual I-don't-have-a-subject problem, and the other people in [Lloyd Biggle's writing] workshop helped by asking the standard questions—what was I interested in, what did I know something about, etc. The group was quite helpful all along the way. They gave me feedback on which parts of the story they thought effective and why, and which parts missed the mark. Some suggestions I used and others I rejected—but the process of rejecting a suggestion I didn't like forced me to think about what I did like and what I did want.

"I can't really remember what changes I made along the way. I do remember rewriting and rewriting certain scenes in an effort to make them more powerful. And realizing that instead of using four scenes to make a point, it was better to use just one or two—and do them better, to use better writing instead of more words. I don't feel that I succeeded, but rather than get off on that again, let me get into Research:

"I used medical reference books to verify my data. I also called every medical student and intern I knew that had ever participated in a blue alert and asked them what their overriding sensations were—and also what the room *sounded* like. Each person gave me a different impression. I meshed them all, threw away the extraneous, and used the rest. (This process would be a little different now, as I subsequently met and married an intern—not only would my phone bills be lower, but I wouldn't have to go around borrowing books from medical students any more.)

"I also visited a crematorium and asked macabre questions to get the details of the death scene. The facts required little embellishment. In addition, my sister is a deputy sheriff, so I was constantly questioning her as to what reasonable police procedures would be. When reasonable procedures wouldn't fit in the plot, I made them semi-reasonable (use reality when it helps; throw it away when it doesn't).

"If I were writing the story now, I would definitely change the beginning, which is awkward and uses characters that never appear again in the story. . . . It's important, of course, to have immediate action, but I would do it some other way. The poem would definitely be out. Also, I would provide more justification for Jeanette's suicide attempts. Reader feedback has told me that not everyone understood why she was always trying to kill herself—I would attempt to clarify her motivation. I would try for more subtle ways of telling the story—the usual 'show, not say' rule.

"All in all, I would make the story better crafted, better written."

Your editors must disagree here; the story is, we feel, the best of the twelve in this book. We think that the writer's critical sense has outrun her formidable writing ability, to the point where it's inhibiting her output.

CHARACTER**95**

This particularly powerful story is told from many points of view. Usually, it is not a good idea to shift viewpoints in a short story, because it tends to destroy the unity that a single viewpoint gives, tends to break the readers' identification with the viewpoint character, and tends to confuse the reader as to what's going on. In this story, the multiple viewpoints are necessary. In addition, there are passages here, which we set in *italic* type, which are told from an omniscient point of view, not from the point of view of any character in the story at all. The scene in the coffin during cremation can hardly be told any other way. Note, however, that each shift in viewpoint is set off by a blank line space; note that the viewpoint character is carefully identified within a sentence or two of each viewpoint change.

The basic story is about Jeanette and Dr. Crosby; the minor characters and their points of view allow the author to introduce those two gradually. It is not necessary to develop each of these minor characters in detail. Had the author done so, the basic story line would be lost in a welter of detail. It is enough to show the two muggers behaving in a believable way—at first stealthy and confident, but panicking when things go awry. Officer Lucas can only be astonished and embarrassed when the "body" disappears—and so on.

Dr. Crosby is the real protagonist here; it is he who can resolve the conflicts of the story, first within himself, then by letting Jeanette die. Note that she never really changes throughout the story. The writer could have gone into those feelings, into *why* Jeanette so desperately wants to die; but that would make a story by itself, with Jeanette as the protagonist. "Perchance to Dream" would be the sequel to that story.

To some extent, we do see Jeanette's motivations. The scene in her old neighborhood is important; the details and incidents here matter to Jeanette, everything from the stump of the elm tree which Jeanette used to climb to the loss of her loved ones as they aged and died. Immortality is so often seen as a curse in science fiction (but what other kind of literature can deal with immortality at all?): if someone is to outlive her contemporaries, forced to move every few years to keep from arousing suspicion, she must either adjust to that peripatetic existence or live in misery, as Jeanette does until the story's end. The idea in "Perchance to Dream" is immortality; this is what the story is about; but all the details of regeneration would fall flat unless expressed in human terms, through human conflicts and resolutions, and ultimately by the characterization of the lead players.

CHAPTER 5

PLOT: THE SHAPE OF
THE STORY

"A whole is that which has beginning, middle, and end."
—*Aristotle,* The Poetics

The plot of a story is the sequence of events that you can synopsize (but make sure you do more than just synopsize it when you write the story!). You know: Macbeth meets three witches, who prophesy that he will become king. Egged on by his wife, he kills the present king and usurps the throne. But it is difficult to hold, and more murders are necessary until Lady Macbeth goes mad with belated guilt and everybody rises in revolt against the tyrant, who has been tricked by vague prophecies. That is a plot. Strictly speaking, it is difficult to have a story without one.

Plot may be defined as a meaningful pattern of events in a story. It answers the question **why?** Usually, the answer is that events proceed as a logical consequence of what happened at the story's outset, but that the flow of events is changed by what the characters do. The plot of the overall story is generally the story of the protagonist; subplots may follow the action of secondary but still important characters. The interplay of these subplots with the story of the protagonist is what gives a story of any complexity its breadth and variety.

Plot is not the same thing as idea. The old, familiar Time Machine is an idea, about which any number of plots may be built. One such is that of H.G. Wells, in which a man of the then-present ventures into the far future and becomes involved with one race of hapless beings against another, malevolent race; another is that of Anne Lear's "Global Traveler," in which some event causes itself to happen.

Sometimes a very short piece can get by as a clever play on words, or as a character sketch, or on mood alone; but a longer work without a plot will be rambling and formless—and in consequence not very interesting. Some contemporary teachers and critics may insist that plot has become obsolete, and that today character is the only thing. We disagree. We feel that characters are not interesting purely of themselves but for the situations—the plots—surrounding them. Sir Thomas More would doubtless have been a man for all seasons born at another time, in another place; but it was the thought and motion of his time that gave him his particular place in history. How many people of equally strong convictions have passed by silently, for want of a King Henry to oppose?

Human characters do not merely settle into shapes; they are formed by the pressure of events.

The plot may *be* the development of the characters, the events forming a pattern that illustrates how they became the people they are—a novel of this type is called a *Bildungsroman*—but this is far different from having no plot at all. Conflict and resolution (for example, the hero approaching life with preconceived ideas and failing) are still present. While many contemporary novels are indeed rambling and formless, they tend to attract brief critical attention and then vanish. Asimov's *Foundation Triology*, on the other hand, has been continuously in print since 1951—and need we even mention the works of H.G. Wells and Jules Verne?

Human beings seem to desire an imposed order on the events in a story. Sharon Webb's Theory: **Reading is a vicarious experience in which, for a short time, order can be perceived in existence; the reader can thereby hope for order in his or her own life rather than futility and chaos.**

Whatever the reader's perceptions, plot has worked since the Epic of Gilgamesh, which is as old as history gets, and it will work for you.

The archetypal plotline is built up like this:

1. Situation. The protagonist encounters a difficulty. Fiction has been described as "interesting people in difficulties"; your protagonist must be someone, or something, the reader can care about. Caring is far from automatic; how many people turn the newspaper page without reading because the story concerns people in another country, or state, or even across town? You must work for reader concern and identification with your characters.

2. Complication. The situation forces the protagonist to do something about it. This may be moral, social, or physical force; but if it does not believably move the protagonist to action, either the difficulty or the protagonist is wrong for the story.

As complication increases (called "rising action") the efforts of the protagonist do not solve the problem; in fact, they worsen it. There may also be an antagonist; a character, a natural process, or both, that adds to the difficulty. (Keep in mind, however, that antagonists have motivations too; they do not complicate the protagonist's life for the fun of it.)

3. Climax. Finally the problem becomes unendurable; the protagonist must solve it or be broken by it. (Exactly what the Ultimate Threat is depends on the story. It should not be so large that the reader cannot comprehend it, or the protagonist cannot reasonably face it. This is a fault of so many world-saving space operas. Nor should the threat be trivial. Ideally it will be something the reader fears personally, so that she or he feels the same anxieties as the protagonist.)

At this point the characters make the crucial decision of the story. The decision must be required by the characters' personalities and the surrounding events; for maximum effect it should also be somewhat unexpected, surprising the reader *while still being absolutely logical.* If you cannot do both, do without surprise and maintain logic.

4. Resolution. Now the problem unwinds, based on the climactic action—*never* through some outside agency introduced on the spot. Likewise, the problem resolved must be the main problem, not some secondary one.

The protagonist may fail or succeed, or some of both, but *something* must happen, or there is no resolution. The story may end tragically, comically, or somewhere in between—but again, there must be an ending.

Resolution ("falling action") should be as swift as possible without causing confusion in the reader; the single pull of a string that unravels the complex knot of preceding events, as Raymond Chandler said.

5. Anticlimax. Everything that comes after the climax is "anticlimax." This should be as brief as possible; the best technique is to eliminate it entirely by fusing the climax and resolution together, because every word that comes after the resolution blunts its point and dribbles away its drama.

Never have characters moralizing or making speeches after the main action has ended. Shakespeare sometimes had to do this, because his stage had no curtains and there had to be some excuse to cart away the dead bodies. *You* can drop the curtain, and should.

These elements may not always appear in this order; for example, a bit of complication, or even of the climax, may appear before the situation is fully set up, to "hook" the reader's interest with action. While this narrative hook is usually a good idea, remember that any attempt to upset the natural order of story elements requires both greater skill on the writer's part and greater consideration from the reader, who must be willing to accumulate the pieces of the story and assemble them. We cannot overstate that the story is for the reader's pleasure, not exhaustion; nor is it a mere showcase for the writer's assumed cleverness.

Sometimes the original problem is made irrelevant by the developments in the story. In "A Simple Outside Job," the original problem, for Jeff to show himself able to take care of himself on Titan, is only partly solved. The second problem, how to get out of the ice, is solved. And—as in the real world—life goes on and there's trouble with the methane compressors. In "The Global Traveler," the identity of the Third Murderer is solved, but we're left with the self-sustaining paradox: who wrote the lines that Moriarty *remembered* the very *first* time anyone ever spoke them? And in "Someone Else's House," the protagonist never does discover her real identity, being distracted by the more pressing task of staying alive and getting in control of the situation. One cannot simply abandon the original problem, however; it must be either resolved or else superseded by something of greater importance.

Above all a plot must be *logical*. If what resolves the story violates the story's original premises, the reader will feel cheated, and rightly so. Note that the extra oxygen bottle is mentioned by paragraph five of "A Simple Outside Job," and remember Jeanette's fixation on self-destruction was too great to be plausibly overcome in "Perchance to Dream." If the oxygen bottle had *not* been mentioned early on, if Jeanette had been merely *talked* out of her fixation, then all credibility would have been lost. People do change; their changes make the important core of any substantial story; but, alas!, they don't change very much, either in real life or in convincing stories.

Almost as important: a plot must not be *mechanical*. If there are too many lucky coincidences and if the villain conveniently has a nervous breakdown just as the hero stumbles across the shield that will protect the world from the extra-cosmic menaces, and if the heroine finds the hidden atomic bomb because she happens to be telepathic, telekinetic, clairvoyant, and good with a dowsing rod—well, the readers will see you're pulling strings all too obviously. The events in a story should flow as they do in real life, save that the writer edits out most of those that aren't important to the story. (If *everything* that happens is crucially important, the story will be wonderfully economical of words, but it'll be unrealistic. Just as there are false clues in a mystery story, in other tales there should be at least some irrelevant details—but not many.)

What about coincidences? Aristotle wrote, in *The Poetics:* **A likely impossibility is always preferable to an unconvincing possibility.** Mark Twain put the same idea another way: **Truth *is* stranger than Fiction, but it is because Fiction is obliged to stick to possibilities; Truth isn't.** Yes, some pretty fantastic ones happen in real life, but coincidences are of limited value in fiction.

The long arm of coincidence may be used to drag the protagonist into the action—you know, this farmboy buys a couple of used robots and ends up fighting the Empire. In this book, a researcher in the Folger Library finds a letter; a spaceship lands near an African woman's barn. But notice that none of these are pure bolts from the blue; everyone has a reason for being where they are. The robots are looking for someone nearby; given the letter tucked in the pamphlet, *some*one (with an interest in murderers) would in time find it; the "blue man" needs help and lands near human dwellings.

Similarly, characters may show up largely by accident—most fantasy heroes seem to acquire their sidekicks this way, usually during a brawl that distracts the reader from the coincidence in the foreground. (And just as often the "accident" turns out to be no accident at all, but part of a greater plan revealed at the story's end.)

The point is that coincidence is usable as a plot element, provided it isn't too pure—provided the reader does not see you, like a prompter in an amateur play, feeding forgotten lines and props to the stammering, empty-handed cast.

There is one place where coincidences never belong: in the story's resolution. This is known as *deus ex machina* (literally "god from a machine") after a contraption of the ancient theatre that made an actor dressed as a deity appear on stage. At the same time they were doing this, Aristotle was complaining that it was dramatically unsatisfying. More recently, it has become known as "bringing on the cavalry," after a device of the Western movie that made actors on horses appear in the nick of time. We doubt that Aristotle would approve.

Similarly, the reader is willing to accept Moriarty's arriving on the stage of the Globe Theatre—he had to land *somewhere*, after all—but the editor asked for a rewrite to remove the additional coincidence that Moriarty had also landed—quite by chance—in the midst of the historical event upon which the play was based.

Once upon a time, there were plot-machines. You can build one yourself: list half a dozen heroic names for your heroic hero. List half a dozen different heroic descriptions. List as many initial menaces, from plague through mad scientists to anthropophagic aliens. List further complications. List secondary characters (set of names and set of descriptions for each). List various climaxes . . . and so on. Then, to construct a "plot" one need only take a name from the first list, a description from the second list . . . and so on until a whole story is plotted out. Yards and yards of predictable pulp fiction were turned out this way, science fiction not excepted; the Captain Future stories always included a superscientist hero, plus a robot and an android, and of course a beautiful woman. The hero had to be captured and escape three times. . . .

Sounds pretty bad—and it was. Do not—repeat *not*—plot your sto-

PLOT   **101**

ries this way. Instead, set up your characters and conflicts, then see where their natures take the story. If you make your characters sufficiently real to you, then you'll find it almost impossible to make them act out of character. If your characters aren't real to you, they won't be real to your readers. Again: characters show their natures by what they *do* and how they *change;* you must show them in action.

Many manuscripts are rejected because the plot lacks an adequate resolution. Like this:

> "Aha," the computer sneered, its vacuum tubes flashing menacingly. "I'm going to take over the world, and there's nothing you humans can do to stop me!"
> "What are we going to do now, Professor?" moaned Harvey Smeedlop.
> "God only knows," intoned Professor Snaxlefrax, "and he isn't telling."
>
> THE END (?)

If your story ends as limply as this, you probably never got beyond step **2**, or at best step **3**; and steps **4** and **5** are wholly lacking. Perhaps the characters did something that allowed the computer to take over; this might be an unexpected twist, but it's a long way from the end of the story.

If you add the following lines—

> "I've an idea!" Harvey scintillated. Moving quickly, he pulled the computer's plug.
> The world was saved.
>
> THE END (!)

—you have an ending, but no step **4**; no climax. No improvement, either.

We couldn't resist making this horrible example doubly horrible by adding some overblown speech-tags: a sneer, a moan, an intonation, and a scintillation, not to mention a menacing flash. Do they sound silly? Indeed they do. That's the point; avoid fancy speech-tags.

The last thing a plot must do is be "validated," in Algis Budrys's term. Simply put, validating events are those that show the story is truly over, that no more plot twists are forthcoming. The classic example is the final cinematic embrace between Errol Flynn and Olivia de Havilland (Bogart and Bacall, Roy and Trigger, whoever). The winning of the heroine, whatever it may say about the status of women in film, proves that the obstacles of black-hatted villain, fire, flood, and storm have been overcome once and for all.

Budrys points out that the common story complaint, "The ending is weak," often means that the ending is inadequately validated. Suppose you're a nice young Wookiee who's just helped save the Rebellion from a fate a whole lot like death. What do the Rebels do? Nothing! They don't even give you a medal. . . .

Those medals are a validation. So is a kiss from the Princess. So is a punch line, which tells you that this *is* the end, simply from its shock value.

As Budrys puts it, "Since the classic seven-step plot's middle section consists of nothing but seeming solutions followed by crushing reversals, on a rising scale, there is some danger that the reader will not accept even an apparently overwhelming victory as the sixth step. That is the reason for the swift delivery of validation—Step Seven. The on-screen destruction of the Death Star is not a validation. An off-stage voice shouting, 'There goes the Death Star,' begins a process of validation which, in the specific case of *Star Wars,* goes on to fully exploit the satisfactions possible to a properly staged anticlimax."

To return to our specimen stories, "Someone Else's House" could have ended right after the business conference; the "mystery" was "solved," and "Marian" knew the truth about her situation. As "Marian" broods about her future, if any, we fade to black. . . . And that's a terrible ending. The reader would quite rightly have asked, *"Now* what? What's she going to *do?* What are *they* going to do to her?"

Some amateurs think that finishing the story is the reader's responsibility. They are dead wrong. The reader is already giving you valuable time and attention. The least you can do in return is to finish your job properly.

Now, two plot-centered stories, both with endings:

SCRAP FROM THE NOTEBOOKS
OF JOHANN WOLFGANG VON GOETHE
by K. W. MacAnn

*Mr. MacAnn tells us that, at 24, he is
an instructor at a private high school
in Chicago and a free lance copywriter
for an advertising agency. In addition
to the usual sports, he raises (and
sometimes buries) tropical fish.*

*This story, for all its fantasy trappings,
still fits Dr. Asimov's definition of SF.
We know this sounds defensive–but–
well, read the story and enjoy, enjoy.*

Faust and Mephistopheles entered the tavern and shed their
heavy overcoats. The barmaid needed only to look once at Faust's
expression before she scurried off to get him a brandy. Mephisto
helped the good doctor into a chair. Faust slumped down, his face
the color of dead ash.

When the barmaid returned and fed Faust his drink, Mephisto
sank into the opposite seat and ordered ale. By the time the ale was
being served Faust finally drew words from his brandy-hoarse
throat. "My God, Mephisto, the horrors! Nothing you said prepared
me for what I saw."

The barmaid set down Mephisto's tankard and went off, giving
Faust a last, concerned look.

"Are you better?" Mephisto asked.

Faust nodded. "My God! To have seen Hell! Incredible, the ugliness—so many people in torment! It's more than the human soul
can bear." He reached into his pocket and withdrew a scroll, the
wording etched in browned blood. "Our agreement states that you
will take me to see the future after Hell. Let me compose myself and
we can go."

"Oh my!" Mephisto said. "Was I supposed to take you to Hell *first?*"

TANK
by Francis E. Izzo

Mr. Izzo is 27; he lives in the seaport town of Rowayton CT with his wife, Cheryl. Although his work has appeared in Playboy, Time, House Beautiful, *and* Western Horseman, *the present story is his first sale. That, he hastens to explain, is because he's an advertising copywriter, and he's written ads for everything from baby bottles to Scotch. He also skis, bicycles, and (obviously) plays electronic games; currently he's also working on what he hopes will be his second fiction sale.*

Davis slammed the flipper and watched the steel ball go skittering up toward the 500 target.

"Go, baby!"

Five hundred more points and it would be free game time.

The ball kissed the target, but lacked the strength to register on the scoreboard.

"Hell!"

It wobbled back down the slope, heading for the flipper again.

This time he tensed his body, ran through some unconscious calculations, and pushed the flipper hard, while lifting the underbelly of the machine with a practiced jerk.

"TILT," sneered the box.

He looked away in disgust. In the arcade, he could hear the music of the pinball jockeys: bells and buzzers, whirs and clicks, thuds and springing noises.

He knew every machine in the place and had won on most.

As he walked up the aisle, which was covered with cigarette butts and soda stains, he passed his favorite machines. Reno Gambler. Rodeo Roundup. One-Eyed Joker. The quarters jingled in his jeans as he headed into the next aisle, where the new electronic machines were blinking.

"Transistorized ripoffs," he thought, contemptuously.

He could remember when the first came out. The Pong games and the Hockey games were first. Good for a few laughs. But you needed a partner to play, and there were few if any who could match Davis.

Then after the Pong games came the fancy electronics. Indy 500, where a computerized track weaved in and out, throwing obstacles at your speeding car. It took him five hours and 15 dollars to get that one down. Now he could drive it in his sleep.

Then there was Submarine. It had a periscope to sight enemy ships on a screen. The ships came at him at different speeds, so he was constantly forced to readjust his range. It took some judgment, but nothing too difficult.

He had it figured out in an hour.

It all led him to one conclusion: a computer hooked to a TV screen couldn't do what those simple steel pinballs could. It couldn't provide him with an infinite variety of challenge. The electronics always had a pattern.

He simply couldn't understand what drew the people to the electronic screens. But they were there day after day in increasing numbers, plugged into the *blip blip bleep* of the cathode tubes.

They were the suckers: the men in business suits out for a plug-in thrill. They'd drink their beer and have ridiculous contests. And not one of them could score a free game on the simplest pinball in the place.

Davis pulled alongside one man going into a hairpin turn at LeMans.

A dull explosion came from the speaker as the man's car ran into a wall. He tried pathetically to wheel it around and three other cars struck him. He spun the wheel the other way and got hit again. His car was bouncing back and forth like a shooting-gallery duck.

"Give it the gas," muttered Davis.

"Pardon?"

"When you get hit like that, just give it the gas and hold the wheel straight until you get clear."

"Oh . . . yeah . . . thanks, kid," said the man, sliding another quarter into the slot, then quickly driving off an embankment, through a moat, and into an oncoming car.

Davis turned, annoyed, and kept walking, letting the continuous explosions from LeMans fade into the general noise of the arcade.

Whatever turns you on.

But for him, it was time to go back to Lady Luck. That pinball had been giving him a lot of trouble lately. It had a particularly treacherous combination of holes, targets, and bumpers that kept his senses spinning with every roll.

On his way back up the electronic alley, Davis noticed something new.

There was a booth with a seat and a screen. On the front it lacked the psychedelic paint of most of the games. No lights flashing. Simply painted dull green with the word **Tank** printed in block letters on the entrance.

Fresh meat. A new game to master, then throw away to the uncultured palates of the amateurs.

He climbed into the booth, slightly nervous in anticipation of

CHAPTER 6

breaking in a brand-new machine.

He looked for the directions. They weren't in sight. Neither was the coin slot. They were probably still setting this one up.

It looked a little different from the other electronic sets. With a small slit screen, similar to the kind on a real tank, it had a panel of control wheels and levers marked with elevation marks, and many other controls he had never seen on a game before.

Davis ran his fingers over the seat. Leather, and quite worn for a new machine. There was a pungent odor in the booth, a kind of locker-room smell.

The controls looked sophisticated. He imagined that this game might turn out to be some fun, once they set it up.

Just as he was leaving to return to the pinballs, he noticed one of the control levers had some writing on it.

It said, "ON."

When he pulled it, the door to the booth closed. A light was activated above his head. A sign flashed, "FASTEN SEAT BELT."

Not bad.

Davis reached across the seat and pulled up a heavy leather strap across his waist. It tightened and firmly planted him in his seat.

Another light went on.

"PLACE HEADGEAR."

Directly above his head there was a leather headpiece dangling from a wire.

Nice effects, he thought, putting on the headgear. The light flicked off, then another one came on. It was a bright, piercing blue button that glowed with the word "START."

When he pushed it, three things happened: an engine started rumbling and shaking his seat, the screen lit up in full color *(color!)* and his booth started to move. Or at least it seemed to move.

Quickly he felt for gas and brake and found them in a comfortable spot on the floor. His hands went instinctively for the steering wheel. It was a bit like one of the old tanks he'd studied in basic training.

The rumbling in the booth increased as he pushed the gas pedal. Soon it was almost deafening.

On the screen, there was an open field, bouncing up and down to the movements of his booth.

Okay, he thought, *if they call this game* **Tank** *I should be seeing some tanks one of these days.*

He was not disappointed. A thick green object appeared on his screen, from behind a break of trees.

It looked like a German Tiger, the kind used in World War II. Very realistic in detail. They probably picked up some war footage, then synchronized it to the game computer.

The Tiger was heading straight for him, sending puffs of blue smoke from its cannon.

Not only could he see shells firing, he could hear them and feel their impact vibrations coming up from under his seat. His seat was shaking so much, he could hardly keep his hands on the wheel.

Blindly, he reached for the stick in front of him and jammed the button on top.

The force of what came next threw him deep into his seat. It was the recoil from his own cannon fire.

Through the screen he could see his shell break the ground, far to the left of the oncoming tank.

He flipped some levers, trying to adjust his range. When he fired again, his shell headed in the correct direction, but fell about fifty yards short. The explosion sent a hot wave into his booth.

By now, shells from the enemy tank were closing in on him. With his right hand, he spun his wheel in evasive moves. With his left hand, he readjusted his range, and fired his third shell.

The result was a tremendous explosion, followed by silence.

Mud and dirt were splattered on his screen, but in the clearing he could see the Tiger in flames in front of him. Black smoke poured from it and he noticed the thick smell of burning oil in his booth.

How does this thing keep score, he wondered, waiting for some points to register on his screen.

All he saw was the same burning carcass.

Davis was quite pleased with the result of his first encounter. The movements of the enemy tank appeared quite unprogrammed and unpredictable.

He turned his wheel slowly, scanning the field for signs of other tanks.

There were none. However, there was a small troop of infantry, some carrying anti-tank weapons.

The hot button to his left looked good, so he fingered it and heard a flat *rat-tat-tat*. On his screen, half the infantry fell to the ground for cover, the other half fell in pieces. He gunned his motor and headed straight for them, losing them under his field of vision.

Somewhere far away he heard the unmistakable sound of a human scream, and felt a slight jostling under his seat.

Before he had a chance to reorient himself, another tank appeared on the screen. It was much larger than the first one, but seemed to have the same purpose in mind. By its look, it was one of the heavy tanks the Germans introduced late in the war. If this game followed history, his American tank was at a distinct disadvantage. He wasn't sure he liked playing a game with a handicap.

Before he could ponder much longer on this, a thunderous roar shook his booth, sending his head forward into the jutting controls.

Blood. There was blood on the controls, and a thin trail of it worming down from a gash over his eye.

Totally confused, Davis decided to run.

He spotted a dirt road into the woods and headed down it, feeling the hot breath of the enemy tank on his back.

He followed the road at full throttle, with the ground opening up around him from the attacking shells.

It was an incredibly rough ride. He had all he could do to keep his tank out of the trees. Sooner or later he knew he would have to stop, turn and fight, or he would lose some points.

Up ahead there was a large farmhouse. His senses were slowly coming back after that last blast. Blood was caked on his hands and sweat poured down his front and back. The plan was this: he would duck behind the farmhouse, turn immediately, and face his enemy head on. Another violent blast put an end to those plans. His entire booth rattled and let out a great grinding noise.

The scenery on his screen stood still.

He stomped on the gas, but it stayed still. Must have lost a tread, he thought. Turn and fight now, or lose this round.

His heart pounding in his ears, he threw his body behind the wheel that sent his turret moving. What he saw next was this: the barrel of the other tank, aimed dead center on his screen. Instantly he fired.

What took place next, he could not see. The first explosion knocked him unconscious. The second explosion was his shell catching his attacker in a vital spot, sending up a flash of burning fuel.

There was fire all around him when he regained consciousness. His head was bleeding again, his lungs burned from the hot smoke in his booth. Davis grabbed for the seat belt, but it was jammed. The heat was becoming unbearable.

Suddenly he heard an odd scraping noise coming from over his head.

He looked up, his eyes tearing profusely from the smoke. The sound of metal giving way rang through his ears, and sunlight burned through a momentary hole over his head.

Something fell in, then the crack of sunlight was shut off.

He recognized it and was instantly sick.

Grenade.

He was clawing frantically at the seat straps when it went off with a dull thud.

There was no explosion. No impact. No flash. Just a single piece of cardboard issued from the metal casing of the grenade.

And it said, neatly printed in block letters,

"GAME OVER."

$\mathbf{O}$n the genesis of "Scrap. . . ," Kevin McAnn writes:

"I very deliberately set out to write a short-short SF story after some friends had pointed out that *Asimov's* was partial to them. I had no idea what the story would be like; I just wanted to write a short-short story. For research, I read over Asimov's and Conklin's *50 Short Science Fiction Tales* to get an idea of how a short-short is structured. I decided that a short-short is essentially a 'joke' story—that is, a buildup followed by a punch-line.

"One problem was characterization. With so little space, characters become secondary. I decided to solve the characterization problem by lifting characters who already existed. At this point I began musing on Goethe's *Faust* for no other reason than the fact that I keep a copy handy. I've always been fascinated by Faust and Mephisto, so they naturally came to mind.

"From this point on, the story was easy. Actually, it wrote itself. I connected Faust and Mephisto with the film of Marlowe's *Dr. Faustus* that had been on TV the week before. One of the more interesting points in the play was the agreement Mephisto and Faust reached that Mephisto would take Faust through Hell. Once I'd established the background, it was a logical (for me) transition from Hell to the Future. At the time, I was busy with other things; the story simply appeared in my mind. I went to the typewriter and typed up the first draft.

"Afterward, I rewrote it a few times, but lightly, because I've always felt that a short-short has a certain life of its own. It has to be a self-contained unit; it has to say everything in as few words as possible. Like a poem, a short-short can't be tampered with too much, once it reaches a certain logical point. So, in answer to your question about whether or not I'd change anything, the answer is no. If I were to touch a word I'd wind up changing the entire story, and no doubt for the worse.

"I've had some exposure to people who want to write SF stories, and most of them have a pessimistic attitude. They expect rejection slips. On my part, I never for a minute believed that *Asimov's* would take the story, since it was offbeat by traditional SF standards. But a friend suggested that I send it in and it *was* accepted. For me that ended the myth that SF magazines don't read their slush piles. Today I'm convinced you simply have to know your art and apply yourself to it (which is hardly as easy as it sounds).

"I should point out that most of what I came up with was 'subconsciously' written. One thing I've learned in the advertising business is that you can absorb just so much information—but then the imagination has to handle the rest of the job. You simply can't force good ideas to appear; they have to come up of themselves."

CHAPTER 6

Frank Izzo writes of his story, "Tank":

"As far as I can see, there weren't a whole lot of early versions of 'Tank.' The idea is pretty straightforward, and the execution was quite clear in my mind from the start. The idea: that electronic games might someday proceed to a point of such sophistication that they would appear and feel real. The execution: that a man would play a game called **Tank,** based loosely on an existing game, and that he would lose himself in the authenticity of the game to such an extent that he would fear for his life.

"In my first version of 'Tank' I had no real ending in mind. I worked the story around a character named Davis, who had no real definition to his personality. Yet.

"The story progressed in my next draft, to include the development of Davis's character as a pinball purist. At this point, I still had only a working ending, one that I didn't like and planned to improve. One day—I can remember it quite well—I was reworking some passages of 'Tank' when it came to me: Davis thinks this game is real, but is it? What if he were to actually be killed? How would a game kill him?

"This is when I thought of the hand grenade sequence. If Davis were actually killed, what a sardonic twist for a machine to deliver the death sentence: GAME OVER. And if Davis were not killed, what a sense of humor the machine must have been programmed with. Was he killed or not? I'll never tell. I've gotten letters and phone calls asking me. I say, 'What do *you* think?' I know what *I* think.

"Was I being ambiguous? Yes. Did I intend it? Yes, again.

"Once I had my ending, it was only a matter of a couple more trips through the typewriter before I'd built suspense to where I wanted it. At this time, I also took a trip to my library to do some research on World War II tanks, for authenticity. This complemented my already good knowledge of electronic games. (I've spent a considerable number of hours and quarters on them.)

"Next, I packaged my finished manuscript and sent it off to you, as I had done with perhaps four or five previous short stories (some of which, I might add, were science fiction). The rest, of course, you know. Except for some kind and sparing editorial comments, the writing of 'Tank' was over. All that was left was to read it for the first time. In print. And when I finally did read it in print, it was almost as if I were reading it for the first time. Could I have written this? It's better than I thought. In most places. But there are some things I would change.

"I'd flesh out Davis's character even further. I'd rework the language, try to build even more suspense. But then again, I'm so busy these days rewriting my unpublished works, I think I'll reconsider and say I'd leave 'Tank' just the way it is, perfect in every way. (As

Dr. Asimov has often indicated, modesty is not a trait highly prized by writers.)"

Does "Scrap . . ." have a plot at all? Yes; it has a plot of a very special kind. This is an example of the short-short story, an exceptionally difficult form.

Remember that a plot need not proceed through physical action. Many stories do not; the *Foundation Trilogy* does not, for example. A short-short proceeds through the unfolding of an idea. Every word is important. Description must be at a minimum. Scene and characters must be set immediately, in the first line if at all possible, as here. Then the idea comes forth, with just enough revealed in each line for the snap ending to have its effect. In this story, the revelation is at the last possible place, in the very last word of the story, at which point the story doesn't quite turn into science fiction, but does shift its focus to science-fictional concerns. You can't put a ghost in a spaceship and call the story science fiction, but when the story is about the future, or perceptions of the future, it becomes of interest to science-fiction readers.

Pacing is the speed of events. Usually, this varies through a story, with the fastest pace at the climax. But since a plot doesn't have to proceed through physical action, stories need not be paced in only that way. Many detective stories, for example, are paced by the discovery of clues and by how rapidly the detective reaches his conclusions. "Scrap . . ." is also paced by the appearance of ideas. First there is the deal with Mephisto and the setting of the scene. Considering how short the story is, this is slow pacing. The description of what Faust believes to be Hell is rapid, then—**bang!**—the final revelation is upon us.

"Tank" is paced by physical events, which pile on more and more quickly toward the end. An unusual feature of this story is that the reader has been told—several times, in fact—that the battle is a simulation, but both point-of-view character and reader become so caught up in the action that they've forgotten this when the denouement arrives. (We're not sure we agree with the author's claim that the ending is ambiguous; *we* were sure that Davis survived.)

The story is a marvelous example of playing fair with the reader, carefully warning the reader of the key fact—here, that it's all a game—and then catching the reader by surprise at the end. It's just the opposite of what we call a "tomato surprise" ending, which is one in which the writer achieves surprise by cheating.

There are several classic tomato surprises which editors see over and over: the one about the evil, horrid aliens that turn out in the last paragraph to be humans from Earth; the converse, in which what the reader assumes to be human characters are revealed in the last paragraph to be giant lobsters or worse—but you get the general idea. All depend on withholding from the reader essential facts that would be instantly obvious to whatever viewpoint is used in the story. Were we able to see the scene (and one of the signs of good writing is that we can see the scene in our mind's eye), we would instantly know the "aliens" were Earthmen or that the giant lobsters (or worse) were indeed just that. Then, of course, there would be no story—because there wasn't one in the first place, only a weak, very dumb joke.

Lots of stories like this show up on television, apparently because their producers think they're clever. Science-fiction editors and readers do not. But then, Hollywood produces a lot of other idiotic things, like giant-insect movies.

So: don't write tomato surprise stories, and you'll save everyone a lot of trouble. You can and should write stories in which there is a surprise at the end, such as "Tank" or "Perchance to Dream," or—for that matter—the *Foundation Trilogy*. But the surprise must be one which the reader has a chance to figure out beforehand. There is a vast difference between withholding basic information which should be obvious to the point of view from the outset and revealing some startling new development which the characters cannot legitimately be expected to know but *could* figure out or at most guess. Note that while the short-short story must have a "punch line" at the end, it need *not* be comic.

The next few paragraphs are suggested for mature audiences: we're going to talk about sex. ("About time!" you say? Well, read on.)

A number of people who wouldn't think of sticking in a blaster fight or an aircar chase just to pad out the action feel compelled to provide at least one instance of sexual activity among their characters.

We are not going to discuss "taboos." If you seriously believe that the SF magazines are confined by a whalebone-corset censorship, that nobody in modern science fiction ever says or thinks or does anything less than respectable, you are suffering from underexposure and had better do some more reading in the field before coming back to writing.

It is one of the most fundamental elements of plot construction that every scene must have a reason for being; it must move the plot forward, it must tell us something crucial. And rarely is it necessary to tell the reader that Character **X** is capable of lust. All normal post-adolescent humans are, just as all normal people are capable of controlling their sexual feelings. (Aha! Another source of conflicts!)

Mystery (and occasionally SF) writer Donald Westlake has said that detailed bedroom scenes are really rather useless. If you've been there, you don't need to be told—and if you haven't, you're not going to be able to write the scene anyway.

Here is an exercise—a gimmick, really—one that may produce some bad scenes, but will get you thinking in the right direction.

Start by concentrating not on the upcoming action but the next strong *emotion* you want to induce in the reader. Is the scene supposed to amuse? Frighten? Merely inform? (Uh-oh, false start. This isn't a lecture. What's this scene doing here?)

Now, what's the conflicting emotion? Is there an element of dire straits in the comic character's predicament? Is the atmosphere of terror offset by the protagonist's determination to press on?

When you have these intersecting emotions firmly fixed in your mind, and welded tight to the proper characters—*then* write your action. It may not take the direction you had expected: the characters are thinking and acting, not dancing like puppets to the pull of plot-strings.

Once you get the hang of this, you can work on the relationship of motivations to actions. Try strong contrasts—what in the graphic arts are called "figure-ground reversals." For instance, a scene of great stress set in a quiet coffee shop, or of total calm on the deck of a foundering ship. (Notice how heavily the current batch of horror novels depends on this one device: terror in the nursery, the amusement park, the supermarket, *et cetera*.) If despite our comments you are determined to toss in a sex scene, make it earn its keep. Induce some strong feeling other than the immediately obvious one: rage, fear, hysterical giggling.

Again, this may produce some truly terrible scenes. Your instincts are not perfect and never will be. Characters do not always choose the most dramatically correct action.

This is all right. Do not be afraid of misfires; instead, learn to recognize and calmly correct them.

Success in writing is something you cannot have without first wanting it very much. Because of this powerful emotional drive, a story, some words written on paper, is invested with a psychic charge it does not really deserve. The next story you write is not going to make or destroy your career by itself, no matter how good or bad it may be. Fear of mistakes can freeze a story unfinished, and no one ever bought a story that did not get out of the typewriter.

BACKGROUND: SETS, PROPS, AND SOUND EFFECTS

"Merely corroborative detail, intended to give artistic verisimilitude to an otherwise bald and unconvincing narrative."
—*The Lord High Poo-Bah, in* The Mikado

Where and when does the story happen?

That's background. Every story has at least one. Some have many; for every character in a tale has a past, a set of places and events that brought that person to the point at which the story begins—and determines how he or she will react to the events about to unfold, and the place they will unfold *in*.

Even if the action takes place in that cliché with chairs, the spaceport bar, that action is still shaped by what's going on outside. Is the planet long-settled? Or is the spaceport the only inhabited spot in a vast wilderness? Is that wilderness explored but empty? Unexplored and full of Scatterer-knows-what critters? The author need not give explicit answers to any of these questions, and *should* not, unless an explicit answer is vital to the story—but the answers must be known, for the characters must know if they're going to live there. Consider this detail: is there another bar in town? That will affect everything from the clientele to the prices, and so must be thought through, even if it's never mentioned and never directly matters.

Where does this corroborative detail come from? The same places story ideas do. Asked if a certain element in one of his stories was autobiographical, one of the present authors replied, "All fiction is a mixture of autobiography, reportage, and lies. In well-constructed fiction the three blend without a seam."

Autobiography is the most powerful of the three, and the most difficult. "This is true, it happened to me," is a potent authority. However, in fiction, truth is not always good enough. (Remember the Twain quote in Chapter 6, about Truth being stranger than Fiction.)

More important, an incident that happened to you had the specific effects it did because of the person you are. This is so with fictional characters, too. So the fictionalized incident must be presented in a context that will be understandable to people other than yourself, and interesting to them as well. It is all too easy to skirt around the hard details of such an event (especially if it was painful or uncomfortable) or to grind one's personal axe too loudly.

Straight reportage is easier and safer; after all, you're just relating the facts. (Personal observations that did not affect you directly can be classed as reportage.) The main hazards are lecturing and over-detailing; remember, you're writing fiction, not encyclopedia entries.

When the truth is exhausted, one must lie. Being able to lie effectively is probably an innate talent (?), but there are some guidelines to follow:

Include as much of the truth as you can; make the actual falsehood as small and inconspicuous as possible. Use the old magician's technique of misdirection. If the reader has been made desperately concerned that Oberon Starsmith get to the pirate stronghold around Spica, he'll care less that Starsmith's stardrive breaks a couple of physical laws on the way.

Learn what you can lie about, and what you cannot. You can call pretty much any assemblage of plumbing and wire a faster-than-light drive, and the readers (who, we assume, have been convinced of the need for such a gadget) will play along. But fraudulently built human relationships are like mismated gears in a drive train—there will be a great deal of noise and motion, but the transmission will be erratic at best and the whole thing is doomed to break down.

Many stories have backgrounds that are unreasonably small and uniform; we call this the Kent County Syndrome. Real planets are vast, enormous places. Mars—fairly small as such things go—has a surface about as big as all the continents of Earth put together, with a correspondingly big variation in topography and climate. While it's possible for an ocean-covered planet whose land area is limited to islands to have a uniform climate, anything that has as much land as Earth will have at least as much variation as Earth does, from poles to equator; and most planets will probably have even more. Some fictional planets—usually unpublished ones—have the feel that they are no bigger and no more varied than, say, Kent County, Delaware. A planet that is all rolling, grassy hills or all jungle is simply not to be believed. (It is possible, of course, to make an otherwise unbelievable uniformity of climate or topography into your story's one, permissible, independent wonder; but you'll then have to justify that wonder in some or other plausible way.)

Consider Poul Anderson's Rule: **A planet is a *world*, likely to be as diversified both physically and socially as Earth.**

Sure, it does simplify your story to have explorers from Earth land at random on a distant planet, stroll to the nearest village, and there find that the mayor also happens to be the head of the planetary government. But it simply Does Not Convince—unless *that* (instead of the uniformity of climate, as above) turns out to be the central mystery of the story, which—when revealed—will turn out to have been obvious all along from the clues carefully laid out along the way.

But your story may be set on Earth in the future. Remember John W. Campbell's Observation: **The future doesn't happen one at a time.** The biologist, Garrett Hardin, has generalized this even further into a Rule of almost universal applicability: **You can never do merely one thing.** Consequently, our world a century hence could be almost as alien as another planet; each change triggers countless others. The development of the automobile depended not only on the invention of the internal combustion engine, but also on the discovery of extensive oil fields, as well as the invention of the pneumatic tire and the assembly line. The automobile, once established, replaced not only the horse-and-buggy, but also the streetcar and the passenger train. Its acceptance caused the paving, in the United States alone, of an area almost the size of Connecticut; and eventually made a lot of camel-drivers into millionaires. The future will depend on many such chains of developments. And even if the future brings a decline into barbarism, that won't happen one thing at a time either.

Nor will a future dark age follow some past example from history point-by-point. The Saxon invasions of England, complete with Aurelius Ambrosius and the battle of Badon Hill, will not transplant convincingly into your barbarian future. It would be far more interesting, not to mention believable if done right, to work out what a real post-technological barbarism would be like. There is no precedent for such a thing—yet.

But remember that the future, dark age or not, won't be uniform. A global Los Angeles freeway with extra tailfins wasn't credible even before the oil started running out. Simply setting a story 100 years in the future, let alone 1,000 or 10,000, will do extraordinary, unexpected things to a host of background details. Consider how much has changed since 1880, remembering the technological explosion of those years. Consider the changes since A.D. 980—and how the whole period from A.D. 700 to A.D. 1350 is blurred into the "Middle Ages." And there are no written records at all beyond 4000 B.C.

And isn't our immediate future beginning to shift again? Right now, the prediction of a homogenous "global village" brought about by rapid travel is giving way to the idea of heterogenous communities linked by almost-instantaneous communications.

SF is like historical fiction in that both are set in backgrounds that the reader himself has not experienced. In both cases, the writer must bring to life a milieu which exists mostly in his own imagination (since none of us have visited Augustan Rome, your idea of it, ours, and Robert Graves's exist separately in our imaginations, even if all of these are based on research). The writer of historical romances has an advantage: his reader probably knows what a chariot is, that the Moon rises in the East, that Africa is south of Italy, *und so weiter*. The science-fiction writer is starting with a blank tape. He faces problems unique to this genre: he must get much, *much* more background into his story than any other kind of fiction writer. The reader must be brought into the scene quickly, and the writer doesn't have time to lecture, even if he could afford to.

Lecturing is one of the deadly sins of unpublished authors. Until they get over it, they'll probably stay unpublished. Stopping a story to lecture (or worse, to deliver a sermon) will kill that story deader than a Vegan sandsplat.

Years ago, science-fiction writers lectured, in the style of the utopian writers of the nineteenth century. Sometimes they moved a man from their present to the future so he could have all the wonderful technology explained to him. Sometimes the people of the future would tell each other at great length what they already knew about that future (their own present) for the reader's benefit.

Your future, to be convincing, interesting, and salable, must be *lived in;* the inhabitants should take it for granted. They won't stop to lecture each other about what they already know, like how streetcars work, what a blank tape is, or even the mortality of Vegan sandsplats. They already know—and to a surprising extent, your reader will, too, just by picking up words and ideas in context, just as you did a few lines back when you decided that Vegan sandsplats are proverbial for being dead, or a few lines before that, when you figured out that *und so weiter* probably means "and so forth" in German.

One of the most famous lines in science fiction is this:

The door dilated.

It's from Robert A. Heinlein's *Beyond This Horizon.* Critics cite that line because in it, using just three words, Heinlein sets us firmly into the future. Today, doors swing or slide; they do not dilate like the iris of a camera or an eye. By that one detail we are suddenly out of the present. This is far more effective than any amount of lecture. Heinlein's characters don't stop to explain the mechanics of such a device to one another; they just use it. Here are a few more examples:

> I am an old man now, but I can still see Helen as Dave unpacked her, and still hear him gasp as he looked her over.

This is from Lester del Rey's "Helen O'Loy"; yes, Helen is a robot. Or:

> The drizzle sifted from leaden skies, like smoke drifting through the bare-branched trees. It softened the hedges and hazed the outlines of the buildings and blotted out the distance. It glinted on the metallic skins of the silent robots and silvered the shoulders of the three humans. . . .

So begins Clifford Simak's "Huddling Place." The place is Earth, robots imply an advanced future, but hedges and buildings and the drizzle tell the reader a lot hasn't changed. Another:

> The coupe with the fishhooks welded to the fender shouldered up over the curb like the nose of a nightmare.

This first sentence of Fritz Leiber's "Coming Attraction" not only puts the reader into the story's time and place, it also captures the mood of the frightening future shown there. All of these, however, begin with what's *seen*. And to be effective, the writer must appeal to more than one of the senses—like this:

> The place stank. A queer, mingled stench that only the ice-buried cabins of an Antarctic camp know, compounded of reeking human sweat, and the heavy, fish-oil stench of melted seal blubber. . . . Yet, somehow, through all that reek of human beings and their associates—dogs, machines, and cooking—came another taint. It was a queer, neck-ruffling thing, a faintest suggestion of an odor alien among the smells of industry and life. And it was a lifesmell. But it came from the thing that lay bound with cord and tarpaulin on the table, dripping slowly, methodically onto the heavy planks, dank and gaunt under the unshielded glare of the electric light.

Notice how the writer, John W. Campbell, grabs the reader by the nose, then the ears (". . . dripping slowly, methodically . . ."), and then—only then—makes a direct appeal to the eyes. And when they start to unwrap that slowly thawing thing, the reader's *there*. Compare the first few paragraphs of Sellers's "Perchance to Dream"—laughter, the creaking of a swing, gusting wind—and the awkward feel of a knife in a hand. Simply put: appeal to as many of the senses as you can, whenever you want to put the reader into the story. At the same time, integrate the salient details into the story without stopping to lecture. All successful writers know this, else they'd not be published.

You are writing a *story*, not a travelog. You can't stop to explain and describe every wonder in the future, on another world, or whatever. You are not (let us hope) writing a treatise on the perfect or the perfectly awful society, which is what those Victorian lecturers were doing. You can't stop to explain and describe every wonder of your tale; you must get on with the story, and show the wonders as part of your characters' environment. The door dilated so that Hamilton Felix could step through it to see the Director. The creaking swing drew to it the youth with the knife. And that odor alien leads directly to what was dripping—slowly—as the expedition's biologist pulled back the tarpaulin; the story's in motion, and it's only paragraph three.

A caution here: just as a few words can set the scene almost anywhere in space and time, that very flexibility can trip up writer and reader. Consider an entirely different sentence:

Her world exploded.

Without a context, this is hopelessly ambiguous. Is she feeling emotional shock because her beloved has said 'No'? Or is she a woman who owns a planet which has suffered a mishap? Or . . . As Delany points out, the writer must watch for unintended double meanings in SF with much more care than in mainstream, contemporary stories, where there are few wonders and fewer surprises. If your interstellar empire styles itself "The Solar Republic," you can call its citizens "Republicans"; but expect an unintended giggle every so often.

Theodore Sturgeon once made an Observation which is true of all fiction, but because of the special nature of science fiction, is particularly important here: **When you are writing a scene, imagine yourself there.** Suppose you are walking across a room. Describe only those things which you would naturally notice. If, for example, the room is dark, you might notice the table you bumped into. If a bomb explodes at this moment, you are not likely to notice the holograms on the walls, so don't describe them. Essentially, present details in order of being noticed, from coarse to fine.

The SF reader is intelligent enough to realize that strange details *mean something*. He expects them to. You must write so that they do. Irrelevant details are like false clues in a mystery story; they are at least distracting, and often confusing. The reader expects details to be there for a reason, and is rightfully upset to find that they are not. Just as all the clues must be present in a formal whodunit, all the significant details must be stated in science fiction.

At the same time, it's important not to confuse the *then whats* with a new *what if*. Years ago, E.E. Smith, Isaac Asimov, and others developed the Galaxy-spanning interstellar civilization as a *what if;* now, decades later, such futures are so familiar that one can be laid down as a background without elaborate justification or explanation. *Star Wars* did just that, and no one even blinked.

And against this background, you may set your wonder: something strange even to these truly cosmopolitan people. For example:

THE TRYOUTS
by Barry B. Longyear

Mr. Longyear once edited an underground magazine, followed by ghostwriting and running a printing company. Now thirty-five, he lives in Maine, with the world's most understanding woman, his wife, and writes. This story is his first science-fiction sale.

The stranger sat crosslegged on the sand, staring at the vent from which the natural fire of the planet Momus illuminated the small wayside depression on the road to Tarzak. His black hood was pulled forward, leaving only twin dancing flames reflected from unblinking eyes as evidence of a face. As a light breeze rose from the desert, bringing the heavy smell of sulphur from the fire, a portly figure dressed in gray robe and apron stepped between the rocks into the firelight. He raised his hand and motioned toward a place near the flames.

"The fire is free," answered the black-hooded stranger. The newcomer squatted next to the flames, pulled a wad of dough from his pack and placed it on a rock close to the fire. In moments the sweet smell of cobit bread drove the odor of sulphur from the depression.

"Care you for some cobit, stranger?"

"For half, two movills. No more."

"Two? Why, it would distress me no more to hand out my bread for nothing."

"In which case, I would gladly take all."

"Three."

"Two."

The man in gray broke the cobit and handed half to the black-robed stranger, who handed back two copper beads. The bargaining hadn't been in earnest; only enough to satisfy custom.

Finishing his cobit first, the one in gray tapped himself on his chest. "I am Aarel the mason. Have you news?" Aarel jingled his money pouch. The one in black shook his head. "But, you wear the newsteller's black."

"True, Aarel, but I am an apprentice only. However, my master will be along directly."

"What fortune! A master newsteller at the fire! Is he known?"
"No."

Aarel shrugged. "I am not one to discourage youth. Is this his first news?"

"No, but only small ones until now. His news tonight will play Tarzak, he thinks."

Aarel raised an eyebrow. "Tarzak? I hope his is the enthusiasm of experience rather than youth."

"My very words, Aarel."

They sat in silence watching the flames until two other men, wearing the tan robes of merchants, entered the circle of firelight.

"Ho, Aarel!" called the taller of the two.

"Parak," the mason answered; then, nodding at Parak's companion, "Jum."

Parak pointed at the fire. "It costs nothing; join us," said Aarel.

The merchants squatted close to the flames, each placing wads of cobit dough on the hot rocks. After some social bargaining and exchange, the four travelers sat munching cobit. Parak produced a wine flask, they bargained further, then passed around the flask while Parak pocketed his movills.

"It has been a weary trek from the Deeplands." He cocked his head toward the black-robed stranger and asked Aarel, "Has he news?"

"His master has news he believes will play Tarzak, and he should be here soon."

"Tarzak, eh?" Parak rubbed his hands together in anticipation. "Has the apprentice introduced it?"

"No."

At that moment they all turned to see another black-hooded figure enter the firelight and gesture toward the flames. "No copper for the flames, newsteller," said Parak. "Are you the master of this apprentice?"

"Yes. I am Boosthit of the Farransetti newstellers." Boosthit seated himself by the flames and cooked cobit, which, after rapid and impatient bargaining, was quickly gulped by the eager travelers. The master newsteller finished his cobit and brushed the crumbs from his robe. Turning to the travelers, he asked, "Is news to your liking tonight?"

Aarel squinted and tossed his purse in the air and caught it. "I can meet a good price for good news, Boosthit. But, I admit, your name is unfamiliar to me. We get few Farransetti this way."

"I agree," said Parak. "Could you tell us a little about it to enable us to judge the fairness of your price?"

Boosthit held up his hand, palm outward, and shook his head. "The Farransetti do not introduce."

"Why so?" asked Jum.

"We believe small glimpses of the whole are devoid of the grace of logical construction."

Aarel shrugged and held up his palms. "How, then, do we judge the price?"

"What would you pay for excellent news?" The mason and the two merchants thought deeply.

"Twenty movills," answered Aarel, "but only for excellent news."

"I would pay twenty-five," said Parak. "That is a fair price in Tarzak for excellent."

"I agree," said Jum, "twenty-five."

Aarel wagged a finger at the merchants. "But, friends, we are not in Tarzak. Do we not deserve credit for trudging out here on the road to hear Boosthit's news?"

Parak smiled. "You are a bandit, Aarel. The newsteller has trudged just as far to tell us the news, and we would be on the road in any event."

Aarel shrugged. "Very well; twenty-five movills."

Boosthit nodded. "Hear me then. I will give my news at that price in advance, but no money back."

"But, what if . . . ?"

"I must finish my offer, Aarel. Twenty-five movills apiece in advance, or hold onto your coppers and pay me double that price at the conclusion of my news if you judge it to be excellent."

Aarel's mouth opened in amazement. "It is an honor to meet a newsteller capable of making such an offer." Parak and Jum nodded in agreement. "We will hold our coppers."

Boosthit arranged his robe, closed his eyes and began. "This news is of Lord Ashly Allenby, special ambassador to Momus from the Ninth Quadrant Federation of Habitable Planets. His mission: one of grave importance to his government, and to the people of Momus. His journey: one of great heroics and high comedy."

"A peculiar opening," said Aarel, "but it captures the attention. The hint of serious events relating to Momus is the true hook, am I correct?"

"I agree, Aarel," said Parak, "and what could it be that interests the Federation in Momus? We have no trade for them, and we refuse to serve them. What could Lord Allenby's mission be? Jum?"

"It is the promise of comedy that intrigues me, but, nonetheless, the opening captures the attention. I had heard the Farransetti were experimenting with openings devoid of prayers and tributes, and many think this radical. But, having heard such an opening tonight, I approve."

Boosthit waited a moment, then continued. "On Earth, the ancient parent planet, high within the tall, gleaming spires of the Federation complex, Lord Allenby was called to meet with the Council of Seven.

" 'Allenby,' said the council president, 'you are made special ambassador to Momus, with all of the rights and privileges of an ambassador of the first rank.'

" 'I am most honored,' replied Allenby. Lord Allenby stood fair

CHAPTER 7

tall as he accepted his charge, his pleasant features composed and dignified, his uniform uncluttered and tasteful."

Jum held up a hand. "Boosthit, is that the extent of the hero's description?"

"Yes."

Aarel scratched his chin. "We are used to lengthier descriptions. Is there a reason for this brevity?"

"Perhaps," Parak interrupted, "it is to let us fill in the description ourselves. Would a mistaken image affect the truth of your news, Boosthit?"

"No."

Aarel frowned. "That is radical, no doubt." He closed his eyes. "But, I can see an image. Yes, I can see him."

"And I," said Jum.

"And I," said Parak.

Boosthit cleared his throat. "Allenby was confused, since a planet of Momus's stature hardly rates an ambassador of the first rank." Aarel, Parak, and Jum nodded.

"This is true," said Parak. "What could the Council of Seven have in mind to make such an appointment?" Aarel and Jum shook their heads.

"Allenby asked the reason for this," continued Boosthit, "and this is the president's answer: 'Momus lies just upon the boundary of the Ninth and Tenth quadrants. In actuality, it is closer to the main population centers of the Tenth than it is to ours. We have learned that the Tenth Quadrant Federation plans to occupy Momus to use as a forward base from which to launch their invasion of the entire Ninth Quadrant.' "

Aarel, Parak, and Jum gasped.

"But Momus has no defense against a military force," said Parak.

"This is grave indeed," said Aarel.

"But," said Jum, "what, then, could the mission be?"

"Lord Allenby asked this question, also," said Boosthit. "The president told Allenby that his mission was to establish relations between the Ninth Federation and Momus for the purpose of mutual defense against the coming invasion."

"A worthy mission," remarked Aarel. "I think sufficient to motivate the hero. What do you say, Parak?"

"It would appear so. Do you agree, Jum?"

Jum rubbed the bridge of his nose. "Allenby is only told of the threat. In the actuality, not the telling, is the real threat, and, therefore, sufficient motivation. I shall reserve judgment."

BACKGROUND 125

Boosthit waited until it was silent enough to hear the hissing of the flames. "Lord Allenby could not prepare for his mission; there was no time. He had to make all possible speed to Momus to warn us of the threat, which was difficult since there are no regular routes to Momus. A Federation cruiser brought Allenby as far as the Capella system, but had to turn back because of power problems. Stranded on Capella's fifth planet, awaiting passage on a freighter reported to be heading in this direction, Lord Allenby's baggage was stolen, as well as his money and his Federation transportation pass."

Aarel shook his head. "All he could do, then, would be to wait for the return of the Federation cruiser, is this not true?"

"It would appear so," answered Parak. "A sad day for Momus, except there's something wrong. Jum?"

"Indeed there is, Parak. Such news would be pointless and futile. No newsteller, Farransetti or otherwise, would bother with such a tale, much less inflict us with it. Perhaps the hero is made of stern stuff and will complete his mission?"

"But how?" Parak shook his head. "He cannot travel without money or his pass."

Boosthit smiled. "Lord Allenby, not the kind to be defeated by chance circumstance, set himself the task of continuing his journey. At the Federation consulate, he demanded transportation; but the consul, in turn, required verification of Allenby's mission before he would authorize the release of a ship or money. Allenby was furious, since it would take many weeks for verification to come from Earth; but the consul was within his rights and could not be swayed.

"Allenby haunted the spaceport, the consulate and even exporting establishments trying to get transportation, but was unsuccessful until he caught wind of an opening on a freighter for a cargo handler. Selling his uniform and medals, he purchased ordinary clothing and secured able-bodied spacer papers from the Federation consulate. Then he signed on with the *Starwind,* which was scheduled to pass near Momus on its way to trade with the Tenth Quadrant."

"I think I see his plan," said Aarel. "It is daring, but it is also dishonest."

Parak shook his head. "The mission outweighs the act, Aarel. Besides, the Federation would pay for the stolen lifeboat, would it not?"

"Perhaps. What say you, Jum?"

"I will relent on the motivation; I think it is sufficient."

Boosthit leaned toward the fire, spreading his arms. "As you guessed, Lord Allenby took a lifeboat from the freighter as it passed abreast of Momus, but the range was not ideal. After covering the distance, establishing an orbit for pickup was out of the question. He decided to break atmosphere and go for a hard landing as soon as he arrived. To do otherwise would cost both his life and the mission, as he was low on air.

"He had hoped to assume manual control after achieving flight, in order to put down near a large city, but he lost consciousness before reaching our outer atmosphere. As chance would have it, however, the boat's automatic system put Allenby down near Kuumic on the edge of the Great Desert. He wandered the desert for two days until he chanced to meet Garok the cobit gatherer."

"Hah!" Aarel exclaimed. "I know Garok—the thief."

"I have heard of him," said Parak. "A spirited bargainer, Garok."

"Allenby said to Garok, 'Say, fellow, can you point me in the direction of Tarzak?' " Boosthit smiled and suppressed a chuckle. "Garok tapped his purse and said, 'What is this information worth to you, stranger?'

"Allenby, coming from a rich world where such information is as free as the fire, was very confused. 'You demand payment for such a thing? Absurd!'

"Garok began walking away, but thinking better of it, came back and explained. 'What I say now, stranger, has no value to me and I let you have it for free. I know where Tarzak lies, and you do not.'

" 'So much,' said Allenby, 'could be deduced from my question.'

" 'That's why it is of no value. But, the direction of Tarzak is of value to you, is it not?'

" 'Of course.'

" 'Then, it is of value to me.' Again, Garok tapped his purse. Lord Allenby had little left over from the sale of his uniform, and he felt in his pocket for the scraps of paper they use for money."

Aarel grabbed his ribs and laughed until he gasped for air. Parak and Jum shook their heads and chuckled.

"Allenby held out one of the scraps at Garok, who took it and examined it closely. 'What is this?'

" 'Money. That's what you wanted, isn't it?'

"Garok handed the scrap back, and said, 'Stranger, how long have you been in the desert? The paper itself might have a value, except for its being covered with ink.' Garok opened his purse and brought forth a single movill. 'This is money, stranger.'

" 'Well, then, fellow, where can I get my money converted into yours?' Garok tapped his purse. Allenby was perplexed. 'You would charge for that information, too?'

" 'Is the information of value?'

" 'Yes, but. . . .' Garok kept tapping his purse. As he turned to leave, Allenby had one remaining try. 'Tell me, fellow, would you accept something of value in exchange for the information?'

" 'Barter?'

" 'Yes.'

BACKGROUND   **127**

"Garok rubbed his chin, then fingered a fold of Lord Allenby's utility suit. 'This would do.'

"Allenby was outraged. 'Not that! I landed here in a ship's lifeboat. Would that have value to you?' And, Garok was interested. The boat's fuel and supplies were exhausted, and the ship itself was inoperable, but the furnishings were intact as well as the wiring and other materials. Garok made an offer of one hundred movills, and Allenby accepted."

Aarel snorted. "I said Garok was a thief; I wouldn't have parted with it for less than four hundred. Parak?"

"I was thinking the same thing, although my price would have been higher. Jum, does this make our hero a fool?"

"I think not. The boat had served its purpose and no longer had any value to Lord Allenby. Besides, if I was stuck in Kuumic and didn't know the direction to Tarzak, I might have taken even a lesser amount."

Aarel and Parak pondered Jum's remarks, then nodded.

"Garok counted out a hundred movills," continued Boosthit, "and handed them to Allenby. Allenby took two of the coppers and handed them back to Garok. 'Now, can you tell me the way to Tarzak?' Garok pointed the direction and reached into his own purse to pay for Allenby's information concerning the location of the lifeboat.

" 'Where is the lifeboat, stranger?' Allenby didn't notice Garok's hand in his purse, and he truthfully pointed the way to the lifeboat. Garok assumed, since no payment was demanded, that the information was worthless. Therefore, he turned in the opposite direction and struck out to find and take possession of his new purchase. It is said that Garok still wanders Momus looking for his lifeboat, and if he maintains his direction, he will eventually find it."

"No more, Boosthit," gasped Aarel. Parak and Jum rolled in the sand laughing. "No more! Let us rest!"

After more cobit and wine, Aarel rose to present and resolve a complicated stonecutting problem in pantomime, followed by Parak's mummery of a wedding ceremony he had supplied with gifts at a price that drew admiration from the travelers. Jum recited a comic poem concerning his efforts to marry the daughter of a cheese merchant. Exchanges were made, and silence settled around the fire as they waited expectantly for Boosthit to continue his news.

"Lord Allenby's journey to Tarzak was one of privation and hardship, not knowing that fat cobit roots just under his feet slept, waiting to be milked. Instead, he visited the fires along the road, buying cobit from other travelers, until he ran out of movills."

"Boosthit, had this Allenby no act?" Parak frowned and shook his head. "Had he nothing of value?"

"He had the news of his mission, Parak; but this he kept to himself."

"Why?" asked Aarel.

"Why, indeed?" asked Jum.

"It is curious, but it is the custom among Allenby's people to play information of that sort only before governments. He was waiting until reaching Tarzak," Boosthit laughed, "to play it before *our* government!" The travelers laughed and shook their heads. "Yes, it was not until he hired himself out to a priest as a beast of burden in exchange for cobit and information that he learned Momus has no government."

"A sorry fellow," said Aarel, chuckling.

Parak nodded. "Yes, and can such a character be the hero around which excellent news transpires? I fear for your fee, Boosthit."

Jum held up his hand. "You are too hasty, Parak. Think; would any of us do better, or as well, on ancient Earth, Allenby's planet? As Boosthit said, the information is for no charge, but I have heard that the fire is not! Would we appear any less foolish if someone asked us coppers for fire?"

"But, Jum, is it not part of the diplomat's skill to be versed on where he is sent?"

"Only recall Boosthit's opening, Parak." Jum closed his eyes. "In the second part covering Allenby's trip to Momus: 'Lord Allenby could not prepare for his mission; there was no time.' "

"Ah, yes," said Parak, "I stand corrected."

"And I," agreed Aarel.

Boosthit nodded and smiled. "Allenby carried the priest's pack and paraphernalia, and the the priest told him of our freedom. From the priest, and from other travelers along the road, he learned that for Momus as a planet to agree to something, half of each town must petition for a meeting, then half of all the towns must vote and agree, for this is the law.

"Allenby remarked to the priest, 'Momus doesn't have many laws, does it?'

" 'Only one,' answered the priest, 'which is our law for making laws. It suffices.'

"Lord Allenby, coming from a planet which has millions of laws, was perplexed. 'If Momus needed a new law,' he asked the priest, 'how would one go about it?'

" 'To move the people in each town to petition for a meeting, the law must be something the people want. Before they can want it, they must be aware of it.'

"Allenby nodded at this wisdom, and said, 'Since I have yet to see so much as a wheeled vehicle in my travels on Momus, I don't suppose the planet sports anything resembling mass broadcasting media.'

Boosthit laughed with the other travelers. " 'Ever since the first settlers of Momus were stranded here, we have communicated with art,' said the priest to Allenby. 'It was many, many Earth years before the skies of Momus saw another starship; and by then we were numerous, satisfied with our lot and with our customs.'

" 'And mass media, I take it, is not art.'

" 'I suppose it could have been,' answered the priest, 'except no one knew how to build a radio. In any event, it was not their way.'

"Allenby's doubts concerning the success of his mission grew. 'The original settlers of Momus,' he said to the priest. 'What were their occupations?'

" 'Why, there were many. Acrobats, mimes, storytellers, clowns, razzle-dazzle operators. . . .'

" 'It was a circus ship?'

" 'Not just a circus ship,' answered the priest, 'but O'Hara's Greatest Shows, the finest collection of artists and games in the entire quadrant.' "

Boosthit allowed the travelers a moment of silent prayer. When they raised their heads, Aarel rubbed his chin and thought deeply. "I do not understand, Boosthit, why the hero needs a new law. It would seem sufficient for the Ninth Federation to occupy Momus itself without fanfare. This would serve their objective, and we would be powerless to stop them."

"And," said Parak, "once Momus learned of the threat from the Tenth Quadrant, we would not object."

"The law does seem unnecessary," Jum concluded.

Boosthit held up his hands. "It is complicated, friends, but I shall explain. There is the Great Law of the Ninth Federation, which is actually a collection of many laws. It decrees that the protection of the federation cannot be extended to a planet that has not asked for it. Because of our one law for making laws, Momus is considered a governed society. If the Ninth Federation occupied Momus without our consent, the Tenth Federation would consider that an invasion, because of *their* laws. This, too, would violate even greater laws that govern all the quadrants. . . ."

Parak held his hands over his ears. "It is clear to me why our ancestors chose to remain on Momus!"

"That is true," Aarel agreed. "Would it not be easier for the Ninth and Tenth Quadrants to change their laws?"

"Impossible," answered Jum. "The objectives of the two quadrants differ. They could not agree. Boosthit, this means that the hero must resolve his mission with the laws that already exist?"

"That is true."

"Which also means he must move the people of Momus to pass

another law."

"True, as well, Jum. Allenby asked the priest how this could be done, and the priest told him to wait. 'We will sit at the fire this night, and you shall see how. I have heard a newsteller, Lett of the Dofstaffl, will entertain.'

"That night, Lord Allenby saw the work of his first newsteller. Lett performed well and fattened his purse. Afterward, Allenby asked the priest, 'Is this how the news is communicated?'

" 'Yes.'

" 'Doesn't it strike you as a trifle inefficient?'

" 'Bah! Art is not to be judged by efficiency!'

" 'But, what if there were news that should be communicated to all of the people quickly?'

" 'You weary me with your endless questions! What kind of news could it be that would be of such immediacy?'

" 'I have such news,' answered Allenby, 'would you listen to it?'

"The priest took his things from Allenby. 'Stranger,' he said, 'your price of endless answers to endless questions to carry my things is high enough. But, to sit and listen to a frustrated newsteller? You take me for a fool!' With that, the priest left Allenby by the fire and hurried off into the night."

Aarel looked into the fire and frowned. "I see the hero's problem, Boosthit, for even I would have acted as did the priest. I would not have listened."

"Nor I," said Parak. "Even though he had news of importance, I would not have listened."

Jum rubbed his hands together, then pointed at his fellow travelers. "The hero is the thing of importance here. Lord Allenby, an ambassador of the first rank, is reduced to a beast of burden in an attempt at accomplishing his mission. Will he continue his struggle to bring his news to the people of Momus; or will he be defeated, letting Momus fall to the evil designs of the Tenth Federation?" They turned toward Boosthit and saw that he had pulled his hood over his eyes. Bowing their heads, they moaned softly.

"For three nights, Lord Allenby stayed at the fire, trying to tell his news, meeting with failure with each new group of travelers. After failing on the fourth night, Allenby was defeated. He bartered his wedding ring for a card trick from a wandering magician, and using this he kept himself in movills until he reached Tarzak, where he planned to find transportation to Earth.

"While awaiting the rare ship that comes to Momus, Allenby purchased two more card tricks and an illusion. With these he paid for his town lodgings, meals, and clothing, and began saving for his passage back to Earth. It was during this period that Lord Allenby chanced to hear of Vyson of the Dofstaffl newstellers, playing his news at the Great Square in Tarzak." Boosthit removed the hood from his eyes.

Aarel smiled. "Will the great Vyson inspire Allenby?"

"I heard Vyson play the burning of Tarzak years ago," said Parak. "I was inspired to petition in the town to form the fire company."

"Yes," said Jum. "I heard just an apprentice licensed to repeat Vyson's news, and was inspired to petition for a fire company in my own town of Miira. Yes, that was good news."

"Indeed," said Boosthit, "Allenby was inspired, but not by Vyson's news, which concerned the second eruption of the Arcadia Volcano. What caught Allenby's attention was the number of newstellers and apprentice newstellers among the listeners. After Vyson finished, the newstellers gathered around to bid for licenses to repeat his news. I was among those attempting to get through the listeners in order to bid, when I was stopped by Lord Allenby.

" 'Unhand me, trickster,' I said, for he wore the black and scarlet of the magicians. 'I must get to the bidding.' He released me, but try as I might, I could not get close to Vyson before he closed the bidding. Times had not gone well with me and I was desperate for news that I could take on the road. With this opportunity lost, I turned to look for the trickster to vent my anger. I found him standing behind me. 'See what you've done? News that played in Tarzak, but I can't repeat it because you made me miss the bidding.'

"Allenby pointed at the newstellers clustered around Vyson. 'They will repeat Vyson's news?'

" 'Of course.'

" 'But the people of Tarzak have already heard it.'

" 'They won't repeat it in Tarzak, fool. They will take it on the road and play it in other towns. Some newstellers will issue second licenses to unknown and apprentice newstellers. In days, Arcadia's eruption will be all over Momus.'

" 'Can't you get one of those second licenses?'

"I admit I was exasperated with this nitwit trickster, and told him so, for even children know there are no coppers in a second license. 'I am a master newsteller, trickster. I do not second license, nor do I pick up fireside gossip and play it for news. My news must have played Tarzak!'

" 'News that plays Tarzak will spread, then?'

" 'Of course. You tire me; go away.'

"Allenby stood there a moment, watching the clamor of newstellers running off with their new licenses, then he turned back to him. 'Newsteller,' he said, 'how much would you charge to hear my story—a story that will play Tarzak, if done properly?'

"I laughed. 'Trickster, there are not enough coppers on Momus to entice me to endure your amateur efforts.' He tossed his purse at me, and when I caught it, I could feel the weight of over five hundred movills in it. As I said, I had been on desperate times. 'Very well,' I said, tucking the purse into my belt, 'but be brief.'

"Allenby told me his tale, and it was raw, clumsy and presented in bad order. But, I saw in it the potential for greatness—possibly news that would play Tarzak.

" 'Can you play this in Tarzak now?' he asked me.

" 'Of course not. It must be worked on, polished, and then taken on the road to see how it plays. If we do well on the road, then we may try Tarzak.' Allenby rubbed his eyes, sighed, and nodded."

Aarel, his eyes wide, turned toward the apprentice newsteller. "But, then . . ."

"Yes, friends," said Boosthit, "I would like to present Lord Ashly Allenby, special ambassador to Momus from the Ninth Quadrant Federation of Habitable Planets."

The apprentice stood and pushed the robe back from his face. "Oh, excellent, Boosthit!" Aarel exclaimed.

"Yes, excellent, indeed!" said Parak. Allenby turned to Jum.

"And you?"

"Oh, yes. Excellent; most excellent."

Allenby reached within his newsteller's robe and withdrew an empty sack. "In which case, friends, that will be fifty coppers apiece."

As they trudged through the dark on the road toward Tarzak, Allenby said to Boosthit, "We were judged excellent and brought twice the price. I think we are ready for Tarzak. I don't see why we should play any more fires."

"There are still a few things that need to be worked out, Allenby. Your escape in the lifeboat was too easily guessed. I'll have to rework that."

"Humph!" They walked along in silence for a piece, then Allenby spoke. "Boosthit."

"Yes?"

"Since we will be on the road a bit longer, perhaps there is something we could do about my presentation as a comic character. Don't you think if the news were a little more serious . . ."

"Bah!" Boosthit strode ahead, raising angry puffs of dust from the road. "Everybody wants to be a critic," he shouted at the night. "Everybody!"

Of the genesis of "The Tryouts," Barry Longyear wrote us:

"For many months before making this, my first sale, a picture would form in my head at odd moments: a fire, with a black-hooded stranger sitting on the sand looking at the flames. I knew it was a setting I would put into a story, but I didn't know how, and I certainly didn't know when. I had no interest in short fiction at all, having concentrated my efforts on books. Meticulously I would plan my stories to the last detail, then in longhand I would write, using the transcription process for revision. Nothing sold. Since those who can't do, teach, I began making periodic visits to a local school to talk to a friend's sixth-grade class about writing. At one point I took every story that every member of the class had written during the quarter, then spent the next two weeks analyzing each piece and writing a letter to the author explaining what was wrong.

"In the process of explaining the parts of a story so many times, I learned them myself. Then another idea occurred to me. What of a society where news was conveyed by word of mouth through 'news-tellers.' But it would not be a simple recounting of events; the news-teller would have to tell the news in accordance with the form of a structured story: hook, backfill, buildup, dark moment, and resolution. Then I forgot about it. It simply didn't seem meaty enough to form the basis of a story.

"Some weeks later, watching the 'Dick Cavett Show,' someone on the program made the remark, 'Everybody wants to be a critic.' That brought it all together: what about a society where everyone *was* a critic? Put that together with my newsteller idea and the hooded stranger sitting before the fire. . . .

"I 'felt' I had a story. I had no idea what the story was going to be about when I sat down to write. All I knew was that a newsteller was to come to the fire that evening, and the black-hooded stranger figured in somehow. This was the first story I did straight onto the typewriter, and I don't remember planning a thing, nor do I recall anything of the writing process. The entire story was in my fingers, and I let them do the work while I sat back and enjoyed the tale. I wrote it at one sitting, corrected some of the grosser spelling errors, then mailed it off the same afternoon. And that is how I write now: I feed information to myself; kick ideas around; visualize scenes, settings, situations, and characters—and then something starts pounding on the back of my head and I begin writing. It sounds silly, but it works.

"The story was published as written, except for changing the word 'rent' to 'vent' in the first line and adding 'planet' to 'Momus' in the second. Rereading the piece now, it's almost as though someone else wrote it, and I can't think of a thing I would change. The piece could

CHAPTER 7

probably use more in the way of description and characterization if it could be done without making the story drag. But to do that I would have to take a cold, clinical look at the people I've created; and I could never do that to friends."

"The Tryouts" is a marvelous collection of techniques for integrating story with background. An excellent way to show a wholly new society is to start with a very small part of it. The writer of contemporary-setting—mainstream—fiction can put down: "He was riding in a taxi," and at once the reader knows the background. The SF writer has a formidable task; he too must introduce the reader to his background and do it quickly. Unless the reader finds out *when* and *where* the action is happening, he well may not read beyond the first scene.

In this example, the stranger sitting on the sand appears in the first line. In the second, we are told directly (never sacrifice clarity in an attempt to be subtle or to save words—be quick, precise, and blunt if need be in presenting essential data) that the scene is on the planet Momus. By the end of the first sentence of the story, the reader has been firmly placed on the planet Momus, at a sandy location where natural gas burns over vents in the ground.

The man in gray arrives by the third sentence. Longyear has not stopped to lecture; the story is well under way in the first paragraph.

The great advantage in starting with two people sitting by a lightly traveled road is that the reader can get his bearings without being overwhelmed by detail. Now that we, the reader, have a foothold on Momus, we are ready to learn more about it.

"The fire is free," the black-hooded man says. This by itself doesn't mean much to us, but by the time we're off the first page, we know that virtually everything else costs. It is also obvious—from context, not from explanation—that "movills" are the medium of exchange. It would be awkward to explain more; instead, the information comes on its own, in a natural flow. When the newcomer introduces himself as a mason and remarks that the other wears the black of a "newsteller," another important detail has been unobtrusively planted: the society of Momus is divided into guilds—yes, very much so, for there are masters and apprentices.

And this is still the first page! Look at how much information we have received, without the pace of the story being halted even once. Had Longyear started this story with a lecture on Moman history and customs, the story would have been less interesting, would have failed to catch the editor's attention quickly, and probably would never have been published in that lecture format. Catching the editor's attention quickly is important because he must judge stories by how well—and quickly—they will catch the attention of his readers. It is entirely true that: **A story receives the amount of attention it demands.** So is Rear Admiral Pinney's Observation: **If you don't get a reader's attention in the first paragraph, the rest of your message is lost.**

As you read this story, you will find passages which, taken out of context, seem to be lecture or synopsis. But "The Tryouts" is more complicated in structure than most short stories are. The adventures of Allenby don't make up the plot; the *telling* of those adventures does. It's an ingenious way to present both Allenby's experiences *and* Moman customs in a single, short story. From the standpoint of the Moman audience to the newsteller's performance, the most interesting setting of the story is the beginning, the—for them—off-planet portion. From the viewpoint of the person reading "The Tryouts," the most interesting setting is Momus.

Had "The Tryouts" been written from Allenby's point of view, and presented in the order that things happened to him, it would have worked far less well, for the really interesting setting—Momus—would not have come on stage until well into the story. Instead, Longyear has built a story within a story—each starting at a point which is of interest to *that* story's audience, and both merging into a single narrative at the end. Thus, even though this story is a first sale for its author, it is far more sophisticated in structure and technique than many stories by the biggest names in the field forty years ago, before Heinlein and others solved the problem of presenting background without stopping to lecture.

Note that the act of telling Allenby's adventures becomes *action:* the newsteller performs; the audience criticizes and comments, interacting in a meaningful way. Longyear is *showing* us the Moman way of spreading the news, complete with the storytelling elements of introduction, buildup, crisis, and so on, just as he shows us Moman bargaining. But not a detail is wasted; both bargaining and newstelling are integral to the resolution of the story.

The story could not have happened this way anywhere *but* Momus. This, in the end, is the test of a background: if the events of the story could have turned out in just the same way in a less exotic setting, then that exotic background hasn't been made an essential part of the story, and the characters in the story aren't interacting with the background as they should. If a story has a science-fiction background but neither its characters nor the events in the story are basically any different than they would be if the cast and the plot line were moved, for example, to Dodge City in the 1870s, then the story's not really SF; it's what H.L. Gold first labeled a "Bat Durston," and most SF markets won't touch it.

Note too that the story could not have happened this way if the past history of Momus were substantially different—if the planet had been settled by a wrecked spaceship carrying, say, a party of construction engineers, or space marines, or even a traveling, Gilbert & Sullivan operetta company, instead of a circus. For that matter, if the length of time between the wreck of the circus spaceship and Allenby's arrival were a couple of generations longer—or shorter—than Longyear assumes for this story, things would have turned out somewhat differently.

Background, then, is more than "merely corroborative details"; it's an essential, integral part of any good SF story. The background is much like an iceberg: there's a lot more there than shows. You—and your cast of characters—must know what's happening offstage, must know what happened before the action begins in *this* story. You must know these details, but you mustn't tell a word more about them than the action of the story requires along the way. Don't feel that you are throwing away the ideas you do not put in this time. No creative effort with real results is wasted; no thought with survival value is lost.

SCIENCE: THE ART OF KNOWING

"Now my suspicion is that the Universe is not only queerer than we suppose, but queerer than we can suppose."

—*J.B.S. Haldane*

"Natural laws have no pity."

—*Lazarus Long*

"Half of being smart is knowing what you're dumb at."

—*Solomon Short*

While you don't have to be a scientist to write science fiction, whatever science there is in a story must be convincing.

Does that seem to be a contradiction? It isn't. The reason is that science fiction is not fiction about science; instead, it's fiction about *people* who are *affected* by science. The focus is less on how science works, more on what it does to people, and most of all on how people respond. Fifty years ago, Hugo Gernsback said that the purpose of science fiction was to teach science. That idea, still known as the Gernsback Delusion, just isn't so. (Certainly one *can* learn some science from SF—but that's not its *purpose*.)

You must get your science *right* whenever you are in the realm of what is presently known. You simply cannot tell the readers that electricity is mysterious, or that space is pervaded by the Luminiferous Æther, or that uranium can be poured from a bottle, or that asteroids have breathable atmospheres—and get them to believe you. The standard mistake made by movie and TV directors who don't understand SF is to think that scientific mistakes don't matter, that the audience can't tell the difference and wouldn't care if it could. As an SF writer, you must have more respect for your readers than that, for those readers are extraordinarily diverse and well-informed people indeed.

You must not, out of your own ignorance, contradict what is known to be known. Editors see many stories about, for instance, cloning, by authors who clearly have no idea what the word means. Cloning is not an unknown procedure, nor is it a magic spell for making copies of people. *Someone* knows what cloning is all about; biologists do, and some of them read SF. If you don't know, it's your fault, not theirs. Likewise, you can't write of the steaming jungles of Venus, or a temperate "twilight zone" on Mercury; astronomers know better.

Robert Heinlein has called SF based on such faulty information "wooden nickel" SF, comparing this kind of story with a historical novel in which King Henry VIII of England is made the son of Elizabeth I. Very few readers will put up with that kind of sloppiness, and SF readers are more particular than most. Many still play what is called "The Game"; picking out scientific howlers, and letting the editors and authors know where they slipped.

Frederik Pohl printed a Rule on his rejection slips when he was editor of *Galaxy* and *If* in the 1960s: **Learn your science from science books, not other people's science fiction stories.** While much of the science in SF is correct, you can't be *sure*. Someone might have slipped up, or the writer might have introduced a deliberate mistake for plot reasons and you missed the clarification later, or the science on which the story rests may have been outdated by later discoveries. (That's what happened to the twilight zone of Mercury. When it was discovered that Mercury did, after all, rotate, there could be no twilight band and one could no longer set one's outpost there.)

As an extension of Pohl's Rule, never, *never* get your science from filmed or televised SF. While there have been some notable exceptions, most of what makes it to the screen is either Buck-Rogers nonsense or pure drivel of the Von Däniken variety. Television documentaries are another matter—though again, watch out for "Space Chariots" or "Bermuda Triangle" hogwash—but science journals such as *Scientific American* and *Science 81*, and the more technical magazines like *Science* and *Nature,* are better by far.

And you *don't* have to be a scientist; you don't have to know *everything.* Darrell Schweitzer's Other Rule: **If you don't know it, don't say it.** Find the gaps in your knowledge, and educate yourself to fill them as best you can. Beyond that, don't go out on a limb—or into orbit—without some kind of support. If you don't know what cloning is, don't write a story about it until you do. If you don't know what tachyons are, don't get involved in the details of "tachyon motors" to power your starships. Readers would rather be told nothing than to have their intelligence insulted by being told things they know are wrong.

SCIENCE

Gordon R. Dickson has said that when a trained reader spots a small, but accurate, detail—a surgeon, for instance, who sees your fictional surgeon reach for the right size of suture silk—that reader is more likely to assume that details outside his field are also correct. Conversely, if that familiar detail is wrong, the reader may assume that the author generally doesn't know what he is doing.

And when you go to a science book, study *real* science, not pop- or pseudo-science. While they do their best to keep open minds, SF editors are usually hostile to the standard crackpot theories. So are SF readers. These theories are seldom as imaginative as real SF, though they sometimes resemble it; and they tend to collapse under rational examination. Chariots from outer space, the Bermuda Triangle, Velikovskianism, Dianetics, close encounters of various kinds—these are not science, they are irrationalism. It *is* useful to read books such as Martin Gardner's *Fads and Fallacies in the Name of Science*, L. Sprague de Camp's *The Ragged Edge of Science*, and Lawrence D. Kusche's *Bermuda Triangle Mystery—Solved*, to learn how pseudoscience operates. You might even be able to get a story out of some such piece of bunkum, but most of the supermarket-rack revelations are too old to be much use—and unless you handle it *very* carefully, your readers are likely to say, "Oh, not *that* again!" and drop the story.

The reason for putting real science into science fiction is to make the story convincing. This is why you must be so careful with scientific facts and accepted theories. If you make an elementary mistake with these, your reader will not trust you. And if the reader won't willingly suspend disbelief for the really fantastic premise upon which the story is built, then all is lost.

But what if, for dramatic purposes, it becomes necessary to contradict some generally known scientific fact? First, *try* to make the story fit the real universe. Perhaps a story that requires a small planet with a breathable atmosphere can be moved from Mars—which we know does not have such an atmosphere—to another planet that does. Perhaps the story would work on Mars if you gave your cast of characters lightweight space suits. Second, shift the contradiction from what we know isn't so to what we don't know *yet*. If a story requires spaceships that can travel faster than the speed of light, which we know to be impossible now, then shift the story to the future, when some imaginary (but plausible) scientific development has made faster-than-light travel a commonplace thing. Third, if neither re-plotting the story nor assuming future discoveries works, then meet the contradiction head-on, presenting the reader with a statement so audaciously untrue that the reader will go along with the concept out of bemused curiosity. If you need, for your story, a flat Earth with edges that unwary travelers can fall off, go ahead and create one, using a minimum of explanation and fuss; then get on with it. Basi-

CHAPTER 8

cally, the reader will go along with—will suspend disbelief about—almost any *one* outrageous assumption so long as it's made clear that *you* know better, that you know the reader does too, and that there are no more independent wonders waiting to "surprise" (and irritate) him.

Of these three techniques, the most common in SF is the second: the contradiction with known facts is explained away by future developments, future discoveries, whole new sciences. This does *not* mean throwing all present knowledge out the airlock, nor simply inventing a Magic Whatsit that solves all plot problems. Norman Spinrad offers some rules for the Rubber—imaginary—Sciences:

1. **Be internally consistent, no matter how much or how little you explain.**
2. **Any fake fact must be planted in the reader's mind early in the story, well before it surfaces as a means to resolve an important problem.**
3. **Know when to *stop* explaining.**
4. **Pay attention to how *real* science evolves.**   (Spinrad's entire essay, in *The Craft of Science Fiction* [see Bibliography] is well worth your time.)

In essence, you play fair with the reader, build up the background logically from a minimum of independent assumptions, and concentrate *not* on those assumptions themselves but on how their consequences interact with people's lives.

In the chapter on backgrounds we suggested that you misdirect, like a magician whose left hand palms the ace while all eyes are on his right. If the faster-than-light drive in your story is there solely to get Oberon Starsmith from Earth to Lalande 21189 in eight hours flat, don't overplay the gadget, even if it is a wonderfully baroque piece of engineering. If you were writing a private-eye story set in San Francisco, your hero wouldn't stop to explain the grip mechanism of the Powell and Hyde Street cable car; he'd grab the rail and get aboard. We invoke Jonathan Milos's Jaded Muttering: **The universe is full of astonishing and marvelous things, but you'd never know it to live there.**

In the *Foundation Trilogy*, Asimov's characters generally take the "science" of psychohistory for granted, and Asimov never explains exactly how it works. (If he could, he wouldn't be writing SF; he'd be collecting Nobel prizes.) There's no need for his characters to lecture each other on how psychohistory works; they, and the reader, are interested in what psychohistory is doing to those characters and their society.

However, psychohistory is not merely a catch phrase. We are told that it is a mathematical procedure, and we see Hari Seldon work out a prediction on his pocket computer. This is much more solid-seeming than for Seldon merely to think a moment and utter a prophecy.

For the purpose of a story, you may assume that sometime in the future scientists discover the principle of predicting the future, or traveling faster-than-light, or living forever. However, since you haven't *really* solved those problems, it would be foolish for you to explain your solution in minute detail. You *can* show your solution in action, and how it links with the real knowledge of here-and-now; for example, how your immortality process is rooted in real cellular biology. It is also perfectly permissible for a character to *not know* something (do you know what goes on inside your liquid-crystal wristwatch?). Don't, however, use that ignorance as an excuse for another character to say, "Well, stupid, the frammistat is grommished by . . ." and lecture for a page or three.

Jargon and gadgets are very powerful tools, used in moderation. It's easy to overdo it. As Ben Bova said, a story which begins, "The jumpship warped out of hyperspace ten parsecs from Procyon IV," is opaque to anyone who has not read a lot of SF. "Warping" and "hyperspace" are common SF terms, but they are still invented words which must be defined in context for each story. "Parsec" is a real word, and "Procyon" is the name of a real star, but not everyone knows that. It is daunting but true that, in SF, practically no word has meaning out of context. (Is a **ship** sea-, space-, or star- ? Does a **tavern** serve alcohol, pills, or electrical brain stimulation?)

The reader must be firmly assured that *you* know what your words mean. Remember that spaceport-bar scene in *Star Wars: A New Hope,* where Han Solo claims that he made "the Kessel run in under twelve parsecs." But a parsec is a unit of distance, not of time; it's like boasting that you swam the English Channel in under 20 miles. Now, *if* you know this yourself and if you assume that George Lucas did too when he wrote the scene (and the "Oh, come *on* now" expression on Obi-Wan's face supports this), then the scene makes sense: Solo is trying to dazzle the farm boy and the old man with ridiculous boasts, and Obi-Wan doesn't believe a word of it. The problem is that those who didn't know what a parsec is missed the point for one reason; and those who *did,* but didn't believe that Lucas knew, missed the point for another reason.

If you attempt to make such a point in your story, you should be a little more explicit; the reader must *know* that you are kidding. Often, there is just no substitute for being obvious; don't overestimate what the reader already knows, while at the same time, don't underestimate the reader's ability to figure things out when the data have been given—as, in the present example, by using "parsec" as a measure of distance a couple of scenes earlier on.

The other Rubber Science trap is giving imaginary solutions to

CHAPTER 8

imaginary problems. This was a staple of old-time space opera: the ship carrying the medicine to combat the Piffle Plague develops a squitch in the wave intolerator, and as time ticks away the hero invents a Rothman wave-bridge out of garbage bags, an interferometer, and some old McGovern buttons. All is saved. Big deal; the problem was imaginary and so was the solution. On the other hand, Heinlein's story "Sky Lift" *is* about a ship carrying plague vaccine; however, the problem is not an imaginary short in an imaginary space inverter but the real effects of high acceleration on human beings, and the solution is not a magic invention but a tragic personal sacrifice.

In many ways, fantasy is very similar to SF; both deal with the universe of the imagination. In other ways they are totally different. Many authors and critics will argue until Hell freezes over that science fiction is really a specialized form of fantasy, or vice versa, or that both should really be labeled "speculative fiction." Others point out that, according to Dante, Hell froze over a long time ago, and that there is a distinct difference between the SF and fantasy audiences. From a practical standpoint, the fiction markets *do* make a distinction, even if they cannot always explain it very precisely, and you need to know what kind of story should go to what market. For this, labels are useful.

Generally, **fantasy** describes stories with elements known to be impossible; **science fiction,** stories with elements that *might* be possible. By convention and long usage, stories which treat magic *as* magic, which involve supernatural forces, or which are built around gods and ghosts and the like are classed as fantasy. Again by custom, stories based on scientific-sounding premises or on scientific-sounding rationalizations of otherwise magical phenomena are classed as SF, along with time machines, faster-than-light travel, and space piracy. Thus, if your character gets the power to read minds by prayer or by selling his soul to the Devil, the story that includes him is fantasy. But if your character calls his power to read minds "telepathy" and gets that power from a mutation or a complicated machine, your story is SF. In a sense, then, fantasy is fiction built on aspects of mythology and religion, taken—like mythology and religion—on faith; science fiction is built on scientific rationalization.

This lack of a scientific rationalization doesn't make fantasy easier to write than SF; quite the contrary. Fantasy which takes one fantastic premise and then treats the results with rigorous, convincing logic requires very careful attention to internal consistency, early disclosure of anything fantastic that will be used in the story's resolution, and just enough explanation to keep the story moving. Such fantasy has all the difficulties of SF—or, for that matter, the formal detective story—without the built-in believability that non-fantasies have.

SCIENCE 143

Less rationalized fantasy, such as the supernatural horror story (which for contrast and verisimilitude is often set in the present and in a familiar setting, as was *Dracula* for the English readers of the 1890s) and the imaginary world or myth-making fantasy (e.g., *The Lord of the Rings*), does not appeal to reason in the same way that science fiction does. It follows some of the same rules, such as the need for internal consistency, plot logic, and emotionally believable characters to serve as ties to reality; but it affects the reader in a wholly different way and is created by a different kind of imagining. Ursula Le Guin, in her essay, "From Elfland to Poughkeepsie," summed fantasy up like this:

> . . . its affinity is not with daydreams, but with dream. It is a different approach to reality, an alternative technique for apprehending and coping with existence. It is not antirational, but pararational; not realistic but surrealistic, superrealistic, a heightening of reality. In Freud's terminology, it employs primary, not secondary process thinking. It employs archetypes. . . . Fantasy is nearer to poetry, to mysticism, and to insanity than naturalistic fiction.

A fantasy may be more aesthetic than speculative. It may derive from an image, or some personification of fear, as in supernatural horror fiction. The "pathetic fallacy" of poetry, the idea that inanimate things have awareness and feelings, may make perfectly good fantasy if treated in terms of human existence, as it is in an animistic religion.

Samuel R. Delany has pointed out that in SF, words take on new meanings. "She turned on her left side," suggests she has insomnia in realistic fiction, but in SF she may be activating circuits in the machine half of her body. The same principle gives somewhat different results in fantasy. Freed from the need for rationalization (as the half-mechanical woman requires) and working more directly from the subconscious ("primary process thinking"), the elements of fantasy stories are often literalized metaphors. "The shadow of his pride" is a somewhat purple metaphor in realistic fiction and in SF, but it is a basic plot idea in Le Guin's fantasy novel *A Wizard of Earthsea*.

SF makes metaphors literal as well, but does so in a different fashion. To illustrate the difference: "The edge of the world" is merely a cliché in mainstream fiction. In SF it must refer to some kind of constructed world, like an orbital habitat or Larry Niven's Ringworld (which has an edge with a thousand-mile-high wall to hold the atmosphere in). In fantasy, Lord Dunsany wrote of the clearly defined edge of the Earth, beyond which there is only a starry abyss, and at the brink of which are towns with magical inhabitants. A marvelous image, which has nothing to do with rational construction but everything to do with the aesthetic construct, is that all the houses at the Edge of the World have windows on the Earthward side only, looking out over the Fields We Know.

The story that follows *is* science fiction, for its handling of a classic fantasy theme is wholly rational; it is, therefore, an illustration of how the scientific approach divides SF from Fantasy.

BORN AGAIN
by Sharon N. Farber

A native of northern California, the author is 25 and a perpetual student (currently in chemistry). She raises apples and horses—one of the mares is due to foal and looks like the Goodyear blimp. This is her first SF sale, but she has sold a few short pieces to other markets in the past.

ABSTRACT. The historical condition vampirism is found to be caused by a microörganism which revamps the host's physiology and metabolism through negentropic processes. Evolution of the organism is conjectured and potential uses of the discovery suggested.

TITLE. Haematophagic Adaptation in Homo Nosferatus, with Notes Upon the Geographical Distribution of Supergene-moderated Mimicking Morphs in Homo Lycanthropus.

I'd forgotten the pitch black of a country road at night. Overhead, between the aisles of trees, you can see the stars; but otherwise it's the same as being blind. Totally different from the hospital where I'd just completed my residency, an oasis of fluorescent light in an urban jungle. You couldn't walk down the best lit streets in safety there. It felt good to be home, even just for a short vacation.

I walked by the feel of the asphalt under my feet. At the bend there'd be an almost subliminal glimmer of starlight on the mailbox at the foot of the drive to my family's farm. The halo of an approaching car rounded the bend, illuminating the road. I discovered I was standing directly in the center, and moved to the side of the road. Headlights washed over me. I shut my eyes to keep my night-sight.

The car hung a sharp left into the driveway of the old Riggen place, and stopped.

City-conditioned nerves made my heart pound faster.

The car door swung open, the overhead lighting up a seated man in his late twenties. He had dark hair and a bushy moustache.

"Are you lost?" he asked.

"No, I'm close enough to home to call the dog."

He chuckled, and his smile turned him handsome. "Don't be so paranoid. Hmmm . . . you must be the Sangers' famous daughter who went to the Big City to become a doctor."

"Guilty as accused. And you must be the Mad Scientist renting the Riggen spread."

"No, I'm just a humble master's in microbiology. Kevin Marlowe. My boss Auger is the mad scientist."

"*The* Auger?"

He flashed another grin. "Ah. Why don't you come to tea tomorrow, Doctor, and see."

AUTHORS. Alastair Auger, Ph.D.
Kevin Marlowe, M.A.
Mae Sanger, M.D.
Asterisk. Funded by a grant from the Institute for the Study of Esoterica.

INTRODUCTION. Recent advances in medicine have necessitated differentiating between clinical death, or cessation of heartbeat, and biological, or brain death. The distinction has been further complicated by the increasing use of heroic life support methodology.

History reports rare cases in which clinical death was not followed by biological death, but was maintained in status. The affected undead individuals were called Nosferati, or vampires. The authors' investigation of this phenomenon has led to the discovery of a causative microorganism, Pseudobacteria augeria.

"Dr. Sanger, Dr. Auger."

"Charmed." The great Professor Alastair Auger smiled down at me. He was tall, gray-haired but with dark eyebrows, somewhat out of shape, a couple of decades older than Marlowe and I. He had the clipped words, riveting eyes, and radiating intellect of the perfect lecturer.

He continued, "At last we meet someone in this semi-civilized intellectual backwash who at least aspires to the level of pseudoscience."

"You must come by sometime and see my herb-and-rattle collection," I replied.

He raised an eyebrow. "I understand that you've heard of me."

"Sure. Everyone knows about Professor Auger, brilliant—"

He preened.

"But nuts."

Auger said, "You see, Kevin? She has retained the delightful candor of the local rednecks, untempered by her exposure to the hypocritical milieu of higher education. She'll do fine."

My turn to raise an eyebrow.

The doorbell rang. Marlowe looked out the window and groaned. "Hell. It's Weems."

I followed his gaze. Leaning on the bell was a small ferret-faced man, with a gray suit and a loud tie.

Auger grimaced with pain and clutched his abdomen for a few seconds, then recovered. "I'll get rid of him. Take her on a tour of the lab."

METHODS AND MATERIALS. The Pseudobacteria augeria *was stored in isotonic saline solution kept at 37°C, at which temperature it is inactive. Titers of inactive P.* augeria *were injected into host animals, which were then sacrificed. After a critical period, depending on the number of injected pseudobacteria and the generations (Graph 1) necessary to achieve the species specific ratio of pseudobacteria/kg body weight (Table A), the dead host animal was reanimated. The mean latency was three days. The dotted line indicates the threshold number of primary infecting pseudobacteria necessary to replicate sufficient progeny in order to reanimate the body before irreversible decay occurs. In vivo, a number of vampiric attacks or "bites," ensuring a large founding colony, would increase chances of postmortem revivification.*

"Vampires?" I repeated, petting a white rabbit. "Come on, we did that one in med school. Funniest gag since Arlo left a piece of his cadaver in a confessional."

I looked around the lab, believing my eyes as little as Marlowe's story. They'd turned an old farm house into a modern-day Castle Frankenstein. Cages of lab animals faced a small computer, nestled amongst the centrifuges, particle counters, electron microscope, and spectrometers. Automatic stirrers clacked away in the background.

Marlowe handed me a stethoscope. "First, assure yourself that it works."

I put it over my fifth rib and heard a reassuring *lub dub lub dub.* "I'm alive."

"Try the rabbit."

No heartbeat.

I stared at it, snuffling in my hands. Marlowe put out a saucer of what looked like blood. The fluffy little bunny tore free of my hold, dove at the bowl, and began lapping up the red liquid.

"Okay, I believe you. How? I mean, its brain is obviously getting oxygenated or it wouldn't be hopping around. But how does the blood circulate if the heart's not pumping?"

"We're not sure." He waved at a garbage can. There was a former rabbit inside.

"Were you dissecting it or dicing it?"

"Auger's a biochemist, and me . . . well, neither of us can even carve a roast."

"I see. You need someone who feels at home with a scalpel, right? Look, this is my first real vacation in seven years, and I have a job that starts Back East in a month. . . ."

Weems and Auger entered the lab.

"I am certain, Mr. Weems, that even you will notice that we have not had recourse to the pawnshop," Auger said, gesturing expansively.

Weems pointed to a coffee mug sitting on the infrared spectrometer. "Is that any way to treat the Foundation's equip— Who's she?"

"Our new associate," Auger said.

Weems looked at me contemptuously.

"You wanna see my credentials?"

He sneered. "I think I see them."

I said, "You boys just got yourselves a surgeon."

The progressive effect of vampirism upon host physiology was studied in rats. One group was injected with a threshold number of P. augeria, sacrificed, and placed in an incubation chamber held at 15°C to hasten replication. Ninety-seven percent of the infected rats reanimated between 54 and 73 hours post-mortem. Specimens were sacrificed at intervals of 0, 6, 12, 24, etc., hours post-revivification, and the gross anatomy, pathology, and serology studied.

Another group of control rats was injected with normal saline, sacrificed, and placed in the 15°C incubation chamber. These underwent classical necrotic decay, and were disposed of on the sixth day.

"Whew. Smells like a charnel house," Marlowe said. "How do you stand it?"

"It's obvious you never worked in an inner-city clinic, Kevin. Or lived on a farm." I pointed to the rat I had pinned open on the table and was dissecting under red light.

"See that? They may not be using the heart as a pump, but it's still the crossroads of the circulatory system. That must be why the old stake-in-the-heart routine works."

"Only as a temporary measure," Marlowe said. "The microörganisms seem able to repair tissue. Remember, the classical method of killing vampires is staking, followed closely by decapitation or burning."

"Mmm. Stake, season well with garlic, and place in a hot oven until thoroughly cooked. Look at those little buggies move."

"Please do not call my *Pseudobacteria augeria* 'buggies'," Auger said, walking in on us. He was good at that.

"Oh, you'll want to see this, sir," Marlowe said, handing the taller man an electronmicrograph.

"Beautiful!"

I stood on tiptoe to see. The micrograph showed the bug, with its bacteria-like lack of a nucleus, its amoeba-like pseudopods and irregular cellular borders, and its just-plain-weird ribosome clusters and endoplasmic reticulum, plus some things not even Marlowe could identify. There was a smooth, anucleate disc attached to the outer membrane.

"Wow! That's got an erythrocyte hooked on!"

"I let them settle out instead of centrifuging," Marlowe said proudly. "The spinning must dislodge the red blood cells from the surface."

"Well, that explains how the blood is transported," I said. Auger lifted his eyebrow slightly, to signify intellectual condescension.

We heard a car drive up.

"Hell and damn!" Auger said. "It must be Weems again." He scowled and left the room.

"How about seeing the movie in town tonight, Mae?" Marlowe suggested.

"We've seen it, twice, unless you mean the new Disney over South-County."

"Lord, what a dull area. How do you stand it?"

"Well, in three weeks—when I'm in a Manhattan emergency room and up to my ears in blood—I'll cherish these nice quiet memories. Why don't we take a day off and drive down to the city—"

"*Idiot!*"

Outside in the garden, Professor Auger was shouting. We heard Weems shouting back. Marlowe and I ran out.

"It's revoked," Weems was yelling. The little man had ducked behind his car for protection. Auger looked mad enough to throttle him. His face was livid, and he was breathing as if he'd just run the four-minute mile. I didn't even want to imagine what his blood pressure was up to.

"Calm down, you'll give yourself a stroke," I said.

Weems turned to us triumphantly. "The Foundation's revoked the grant. We'll want a total accounting."

"You bastard!" Auger bellowed, and lunged across the car at Weems. He halted in mid-stride, a confused expression on his face, grabbed his stomach, and collapsed.

I leapt over and began examining him. He was pale and breathing rapidly, with a weak, racing pulse. Shock.

"Is it a heart attack?" Weems asked. The little rodent sounded happy.

Marlowe knelt on the other side. "What can I do?" he asked. I ripped open Auger's shirt and felt his abdomen. It was hot, pink and firm. Internal hemorrhage.

"Oh, Christ." I reached inside his pants and felt for the femoral pulse. There was none. "Well, that's it. Damn." I realized I was crying.

Auger stopped breathing, and Marlowe began mouth-to-mouth

CHAPTER 8

resuscitation. I reached to the neck and felt for the carotid pulse. It fluttered weakly and then faded.

"It's no use, Kevin. He's dead."

Weems chortled gleefully, jumped in his car, and sped up the driveway in reverse. Marlowe began external heart massage, anxiously doing it 'way too fast.

I pulled him off and shook his shoulders. "Stop it, Kevin. It won't help. Remember those stomach pains he had? It was an aneurysm, a weakness in the wall of his abdominal aorta. It burst, Kevin; he's bled to death internally. CPR won't help, dammit, nothing can."

"Ambulance, call a—"

"Listen. Even if they could get here within a half-hour, it wouldn't do any good. Look, Kevin, five minutes ago, if I'd had him on the table in a fully equipped operating room, with a good team, we could have tried a DeBakey graft. But the chances of saving him would have been maybe five percent."

Marlowe stood and stared down at the body. Then he turned and ran inside the house, leaving me with the corpse. Dead, Auger was devoid of charisma. His features were bloodless white; he looked like a horror waxwork. I closed his mouth and rearranged the clothes to give him more dignity.

Marlowe returned with a huge cardiac syringe and a bottle of milky liquid.

"You're crazy."

"It would work, Mae. We can bring him back. I centrifuged them down to a concentrate. There are enough pseudobacteria here to repair the damage and reanimate him almost immediately."

The implications were terrifying. Vampire rabbits were bizarre enough, but he was preparing to do it to a human being.

"You can save his life! Come on, do it."

Typical Marlowe, always leaving the decisions to someone else. I filled the syringe and plunged the six-inch needle deep into the blood-distended abdomen. Marlowe looked ill, and turned away. It was hard work pushing in the fluid. I pulled the needle out, and a small amount of blood welled up through the puncture. Two more syringes full and the bottle was empty.

We carried the body into the lab and packed it in ice to lower the body temperature quicker. Marlowe went away to vomit. I brewed some coffee and added a stiff jolt of medicinal Scotch.

"Here's to a fellow future inmate of Sing Sing," I toasted Marlowe.

Half an hour later we were feeling no pain.

"We'll have to buy him a black cape," I was saying. "Lessons in Transylvanian diction, too."

"I vant to suck your blood," Marlowe said, and leapt on me. We collapsed on the floor together, laughing.

The doorbell rang. Weems had returned with a sheriff's deputy. "Hey, Fred!"

"Uh, hi, Mae. Long time no see." The deputy looked embarrassed.

"We went to high school together," I announced to no one in particular.

"Sorry to have to disturb you, but this guy says you've got a stiff here."

Marlowe giggled from the floor. "A body? I don't see anybody." He adopted a stern voice. "The only thing dead around here is the night life in town."

Weems piped up with, "They're drunk."

"Brilliant, Weems, an astonishing deduction," I cried.

"They've hidden the body! Alastair Auger was dead. She even said so." He pointed at me accusatorily.

"Remove your finger."

The deputy stepped between us. "Uh, I'm sorry, Mae, uh, Doc, but I have to make a report."

"Professor Auger's not feeling well, Fred; he shouldn't be disturbed. Hey, you can believe me when I say he's alive. I'm a doctor. We're trained to know these things."

"They're faking. I won't leave until I see Auger's body."

"Yes, it is awe-inspiring. But I'm afraid you're just not my type, Weems."

Weems's face blanched at the sight of Auger, leaning in the doorway to the lab, and smiling malevolently at us all. He was glistening from the ice, and was wearing a towel.

"She's done something to him," Weems stuttered. "He was dead."

The deputy took Weems's elbow and propelled the little man out the door. "Sorry, Mae, Professors—" He headed for the patrol car, saying, "Okay, mister, there's a little matter of making false reports."

Marlowe laughed hysterically.

"If you hadn't woken up right then," I said, "you'd have woken up in the county morgue."

Auger said, "If you'll excuse me, this light is most unpleasant and I'm starving."

I offered to fetch him a pint of blood.

"Yes, please, Doctor. I'm finding myself uncomfortably attracted to your neck."

RESULTS AND DISCUSSION. The vampire is traditionally considered a body occupied by a demon. We may now modify that picture to encompass a mammal, dead in that its heart does not beat and its body temperature is abnormally, indeed fatally, low, but still functioning as an organism due to the presence of a colony of symbiotes.

CHAPTER 8

The pseudobacteria function as metabolizers and as transporters of oxygen, nutrients, and wastes, functions assumed in uninfected organisms by the circulatory and digestive systems. P. augeria is a weak infective agent, requiring the special environment found after death, and susceptible to most common antibacterial drugs. Folklore documents the vampire's aversion to garlic, a mild antibiotic.

The host physiology undergoes changes which seem to eliminate unnecessary systems and increase efficiency for vampiric adaptations. These changes appear to be progressive, but must await long-term studies.

The first major change is the atrophy of the digestive tract. Nutrients pass directly from the stomach to the blood-stream, with the concurrent necessity that only isotonic solutions be ingested, to avoid the osmotic destruction of the blood cells. As the only isotonic solution available in nature is blood, the vampire's fluid intake has traditionally been in this form. An external blood source is also necessary for other reasons. Because blood transport is pseudobacterial rather than hydrostatic, and hence much slower, the body requires more red cells than can be produced by the host's bone marrow.

"All the great men are dead—myself, for instance."

"Breathe in," I replied.

Marlowe walked in, saw us, and blushed. The longer I knew Kevin, the more I realized how anal retentive he could be.

"Am I interrupting?"

"Yes," Auger said. When he spoke, I could see his sharp canine teeth.

"No. Pass me that, yeah, the sphygmomanometer. You don't realize what a pleasure it is to have a patient who doesn't complain about the stethoscope being cold."

I joked as I put on the blood pressure cuff, trying to hide the creepy feeling Auger gave me. Intellectually, I knew he was the same man I'd met a week before, but emotionally I had problems relating to a patient with a current body tempoerature of 30°C—midway between what it should be, and the temperature of the room. And because of the vagaries of his circulation, even in the warmest room Auger's hands felt like he'd been out in a snowstorm without his mittens.

"Must we do this again?" Auger winced as I pumped up the cuff. I nodded, and listened with the stethoscope. I just couldn't get used to the fact that his heart didn't beat, and that he had no blood pressure.

"No diastolic, no systolic," I said. "Sir, your b.p.'s holding steady at zero over zero."

"Ah, normal," Auger said, reaching for his shirt. "Enough time wasted. Shall we return to the lab?"

He hated medical exams (and, I was convinced, doctors as well). I argued in vain for the opportunity to take him to a hospital and run some *real* tests on him: X-rays, metabolic studies, EEGs. . . .

"It's three in the morning," Marlowe complained. "I need some coffee."

"Can't get used to working graveyard shift?"

He acknowledged my joke with a weak smile. This nocturnal living was tough to get used to. Auger had acquired the vampiric dislike of daylight. Another thing that needed more study: was it because of the temperature, or the infrared radiation? In any case, my parents seemed to think my new hours were the result of an affair with Kevin Marlowe, and this made things fairly uncomfortable on the home front.

Auger accepted a cup of coffee, and stirred in a spoonful of salt, to make it osmotically similar to blood.

"There aren't enough metabolites and nutrients in the blood you drink to sustain you, Professor. Where the hell do you get your energy?"

"It's a negentropic process, similar to the one which allows my *Pseudobacteria augeria* to be dormant over 35°, while ordinary enzymatic processes become accelerated," he told me. "How much calculus have you had, Dr. Sanger?"

"Two semesters."

"You'd need at least four to understand. Hadn't we better return to work?"

As human populations grew, they tended to eliminate competing species, creating a niche for a predator. It may be possible to remutate Pseudobacteria augeria *to its hypothetical ancestor,* P. lycanthropica, *which could survive at normal body temperature and changed its hosts into carnivorous animals. The body type was probably mediated by a supergene complex similar in principle to those found in butterfly mimicry, resulting in discrete morphs with a lack of intermediate types. Examination of the literature suggests the morph adopted was that of the major natural predator of the geographical area, leading to werewolves in Northern Europe, were-bears in Scandinavia, and were-tigers in India. Some cases have been reported of werewolves becoming vampires after death, suggesting either concurrent infection, or evolution in progress.*

I was driving back from town when I saw police cars lined up along the road. I slowed up and yelled out the window.

"Need a doctor?"

My deputy friend Fred flagged me in behind a patrol car. "Re-

member the wimp who accused the big guy of being dead?"
He led me through a swarm of cops, down the gully to the creek.
Weems lay with his arm dangling in the creek. His wrist had been slashed, and he had bled to death.

"Not much blood," I finally commented. "It usually gets all over when someone exsanguinates."

"Washed away downstream," the sheriff said. "They always have to come on my territory to kill themselves. How long would you say he's been dead?"

The body was cold. Rigor mortis was complete but not yet passing off. I estimated twenty hours, maybe less allowing for the cold.

"Damned suicides," the sheriff muttered.

"Big goddamn nuisance." I agreed, and we all stood around for a few minutes swapping gross-out stories.

Then I sped home, parked the car, and walked over to the lab. It was dusk when I arrived.

Marlowe was in an elated mood. "We've started on the last draft of the article. We'll submit simultaneously to *Science* and *Nature*. Well, Mae, start working up an appetite because I hear they have great food at the Nobel awards."

I stomped past him to Auger's bedroom. Auger was lying on his bed, absolutely straight, like a corpse already laid out. As I stood there, clenching my fists, he awoke and sat up.

"Well, Dr. Sanger. To what do I owe the honor of—"

"You killed him."

"Whom?"

Oh, he could be suave.

"You were clever making it look like suicide. The cops have swallowed it."

He gave me his most charming smile, not realizing how his long teeth spoiled the effect. "I had no alternative. The man was our enemy. He convinced the Foundation to revoke our funding."

"His death won't get the grant back, Auger. You just killed him out of spite."

He laid a cold hand on my arm. "Calm down. By next week we'll all be famous. You won't have to take that cheap job in New York. You'll be the most pre-eminent witchdoctor in America."

"You're making me sick." I wrenched my arm away and walked out. "Good-bye, Kevin. It was swell while it lasted. Leave my name off the article. I want to forget that any of this happened."

Marlowe had a hurt-little-boy look on his face. "But you can't just leave."

"Watch me," I muttered.

It was pitch black already, but I'd walked it a dozen times. When my feet felt asphalt instead of gravel, I turned right and headed uphill. A passing car lit up the road, and I moved to the side. The tail-lights dwindled in the distance, and in their faint afterglow I saw a tall figure come from the driveway.

Auger.

Following me.

Then it was black again. I saw two eyes, shining like a deer's, only red. They were all I could see: the stars above, the two red eyes. They stared right at me, the nightsight of the predator.

Auger spoke softly, his voice carrying in the stillness.

"It won't hurt. You know you want it."

I panicked and started running, going by the sound of my feet on the blacktop, my hands outstretched as I ran blind. My heart was pounding with fear and cold sweat poured down my body, but the supercharge of adrenalin kept me going.

I saw the glimmer of light on the mailbox. I could turn down the driveway, run the quarter-mile to my home. Home, light, safety. . . .

Something cut off the glow of the mailbox; and I knew it was Auger, in front of me now, blocking the driveway. Six feet above the ground, two red eyes.

I swerved and plunged into the forest. Branches whipped against my face and caught in my clothes and hair. I tripped and fell in the stream, got up and kept running.

Hands caught me from behind and pulled me against a body, invisible in the dark. I was conscious of an inhumanly strong grip, and a coat smelling of wool and chemicals. I started pounding and flailing, but he ignored my blows.

He caught my hands and held them in one ice-like hand.

"Don't fight it," he whispered. "You'll enjoy it."

I felt his breath on my neck, and tried to scream, but I couldn't. I was too scared.

This can't be happening to me, I thought. *Not me.*

The bite was sharp and painful, followed by a warm sensation as my blood welled up through the punctures. I started struggling again, but he was oblivious to everything but the blood he was greedily sucking in.

My mind went clinical on me. *Two pints equals fifteen percent blood volume. Moderate shock will set in.* I could feel the symptoms start. *He's killing me.*

My knees gave out and I sank to the ground, Auger still drinking from my left jugular. Over the roaring in my ears I could hear my gasping breath and the vampire's gross panting and slobbering. I was too weak to fight any more. The summer constellations gazed down uncaring, and became part of a light show as lack of oxygen brought hallucinations, and a strange feeling of euphoria.

The dying started to feel good.

CHAPTER 8

CONCLUSIONS. Throughout history the vampire has been maligned as a villain and demon. Now that the etiology of the condition is understood, there is no reason why the vampire cannot take his place as a functioning member of society. With prescription availability of blood, the disease will be limited to present victims. Under these conditions it need not even be classified as contagious.

I woke up under an oak tree. A spider had used my left arm to anchor its web, and earwigs were nesting in my hair.

"Ohhh. I must have tied one on good," I groaned, and pulled myself into a sitting position, leaning against the oak. I felt like hell. Weak, cold, splitting headache, and hungry. Never so hungry in all my life. The feeling of hunger seemed to fill every inch of my body.

Absently, I put two fingers to my wrist to take my pulse.

There was none.

I reached up to check the carotid. Every movement hurt.

My heart wasn't beating.

I withdrew my hand and stared at my fingers. They were pale: dead white.

I was dead. I was a vampire. I tongued my canines and felt their new sharpness.

Auger did this to me. I remembered it all, and felt nauseated.

He'd be in the lab.

And blood. They had blood there. Whole refrigerators full. Rabbit blood. Rat blood.

Human blood.

The new moon is still a sliver in the sky, but I can see in the dark now. A deer crosses my path and freezes in terror until I pass. As I approach the house I can hear Marlowe typing the article. The damned article.

It will even be possible, through a controlled infection of Pseudobacteria augeria, *to conquer death, allowing us to revive and preserve indefinitely great minds and*

"Kevin. Get me some blood. Quick, before I bite you."

I clutch at a chair to control myself. When I look down, I see that my new vampiric strength has crushed the hard plastic.

Marlowe tremulously hands me a liter of O-negative. I gulp it down. It's cold, cramping my stomach.

"More."

It takes six liters before I can look at Marlowe without wanting to attack him. Then I clean up some, comb my hair, cover my filthy clothes with a lab coat, and slip a filled syringe into the pocket.

"Where is he, Kevin?"

"You're alive, Mae, that's what counts. Let's not—"

"He sucked me damn near dry. Where is he?"

"It didn't hurt you. He said it wouldn't—"

I grab his arm, and he flinches at the touch. "Feel it, Kevin, dead flesh. Is a Nobel going to keep either of us warm at night?"

"Add this to the conclusion, Kevin: 'Where there is no longer any death, murder must be redefined.' Welcome back, Dr. Sanger."

Auger stands in the lab doorway. I realize that I'm shaking.

He can't hurt me now, I repeat over and over. But I want to flee. Or else cry.

"Refrigerated blood is nothing. Wait until you've drunk warm, pulsing, living blood."

"Shut up," I whisper.

"And the power. The strength. You've always admired strength. You'll enjoy being a vampire, Dr. Sanger."

"No. No, I won't become power-crazy. I won't kill. I'm trained to save, to heal . . . I won't be like you!"

He laughs.

"Biology isn't destiny!" I scream.

He laughs more. I almost don't blame him.

"I thought we'd give you a chance. All right, Kevin, stake her."

I spin around. Marlowe has a wooden stake and a mallet, but he's vacillating, as usual. I pick him up and toss him to the floor before Auger.

Auger curses and snatches up the stake.

"Am I to assume this won't hurt either?" I asked.

"I've always admired the late doctor's resilient sense of humor," he says.

I pull the syringe from my pocket, duck in close, ram it into his side and push the plunger.

"Admire that—twenty cc of tetracycline."

He roars and throws a table at me. I duck, and it crashes into a shelf of chemicals.

"You're cured, Auger. I've killed those little bugs, the ones that are keeping you alive."

He picks up a 200-pound spectrometer and tosses it at me. It bowls me into the cages, liberating a half-dozen specimens. Vampire rabbits scurry about underfoot. I get up and dust myself off.

"Temper, temper. That's Foundation equipment."

Marlowe watches dumbfounded as Auger throws the gas chromatograph at me. It shatters on the floor, sparks igniting the spilled chemicals. A brisk fire begins, punctuated by explosions of bottled reagents.

Auger closes in and grabs me, but this time I push him back, pick

CHAPTER 8

up the wooden stake, and shove it into his heart.

He looks surprised.

"Why me?" he asks, and dies again.

"Kevin. Come on. The place is burning up."

"Get away from me," he yells. "Don't touch me, vampire!" He pulls, open his shirt to show a cross on a chain.

"Don't be stupid, Kevin."

The fire has reached the chemical stockroom. I run for the window, and plunge through in a cloud of glass. The lab behind me explodes.

Marlowe's screams die out.

Charred paper blows away as heated air rushes out the shattered windows. The plastic on the typewriter melts and runs, laying bare the sparking wires inside. The metal letters writhe and bend and wrap around each other, and then melt into an indistinguishable lump.

I go home and clean up, and get back in time to watch the firemen. Not much is left of the old farmhouse.

"I'm a physician. Can I help?"

"They're beyond help, Mae." The fire chief remembers me from 4H. "Think you could identify the bodies?"

They've covered them with yellow plastic blankets, two gross, body-shaped chunks of charred meat. The fire chief looks at me sympathetically.

"I guess their own mothers wouldn't know them . . . you're pale, Mae. Johnny, you better walk her home."

A husky young fireman takes my arm and steers me up the path, away from the lights and smoke.

"They were scientists?" he asks. "What were they doing in there?"

"Working on things man was not meant to know," I say. He doesn't recognize the quote.

I stare sideways at my escort.

He's young and strong and healthy.

He won't miss a pint at all.

The author reports that she wrote "Born Again" for Drew Mendelson's science-fiction writing class at Sonoma State College.

"It was a chance to write a strong, violent, perverse story in which the woman wins. (I was the only woman in Drew's class. Another student's stories had managed to make me uncomfortable, and I thought it only polite to reciprocate.)

"The scientific aspects of vampirism grew from daydreams during a biology lecture (though a bacterial basis was first postulated in *House of Dracula*). I wrote the article excerpts first (in the style of the stodgiest journals), then tried to structure the exposition so it flowed with or around the article. For mood I drew on experiences as an ambulance attendant, talks with victims of violence, and the feel of living in a redwood forrest.

"I read the second draft to the class, tightened and typed it, and sent it off. It bounced right back from *F&SF* and *Analog*, before I thought to try the 'new mag.' The editor there asked for revisions, specifically that I remove the short, present-tense introduction that established the rest as flashback and killed any suspense. (I kept the switch back to present tense at the ending.) The story is better as revised; but for the sake of history, this is the original beginning:

> Crashing through the woods, heading for the faint staccato sound of typing, and I'm three days dead. I'm remembering the first casualty I ever saw, a man hideously mutilated in a motorcycle accident, with blood spurting two feet in the air and pooling on the asphalt.
>
> I remember, but now I want to bathe in the fountain and let the hot blood trickle down my throat.
>
> And what I'm wishing makes me hate myself.
>
> Heading for the sound of typing. . . .

"It continues, then, with the abstract.

"If I were writing the story now it would probably be essentially the same, aside from word substitutions and some new ideas on vampiric physiology. I'd definitely replace Auger's dying "Why me?" and change some naïve comments about scientific publishing. And I might try to solve Sanger's problems without the comic book fight, though I did enjoy vicariously trashing a lab (I had four chemistry classes that semester)."

The story works because it is science fiction; without the science, there's nothing but melodramatics about the biters and the bitten. The rationalization gives the traditional vampire an entirely new aspect. And as for *how* Sharon Farber made the story seem plausible . . .

First, she made it *feel* like science. Her characters behave like scientists. The desires to have one's name on an important paper and to get a research grant are common among scientists. There are many scientific paraphernalia in the story. The laboratory is convincing as a laboratory, without the glowing coils and bubbling vats of horror movies.

More important, the expository sections are indeed "in the style of the stodgiest journals." Real articles written by scientists for other scientists are exactly like this imitation; each begins with an abstract, then describes experimental methods, and lists results.

The author even thought out the story in a scientific way. The first step was to devise a natural explanation for a vampire. She did: bacteria. This is her permissible, independent wonder for the story. "*Pseudobacteria augeria*" is the premise for the story; everything else grows out of this initial idea: the explanations of how it repairs tissue, circulates blood, and so on.

As submitted, the story contained one logical lapse. After telling the reader that it takes two days for a corpse to be reanimated, the author reanimated Dr. Auger in the time it took Weems to run for the sheriff and return. At the editor's suggestion, the author added the detail that Dr. Auger was given an exceptionally large dose so that the bacteria acted more quickly. The explanation, of course, is wholly arbitrary; but it reassures the reader that the author thought of the problem too and isn't just being sloppy.

The story intersects with real science. Sharon Farber does know something about medicine and anatomy, and she uses that knowledge to take the reader on into wholly imaginary phenomena while retaining an air of scientific plausibility throughout.

TRAGEDY AND FUTILITY: WAS MACBETH FRAMED?

"Tragedy, however, is an imitation not only of a complete action, but also of incidents arousing pity and fear. Such incidents have the very greatest effect on the mind when they occur unexpectedly and at the same time in consequence of one another; there is more of the marvelous in them than if they happened of themselves or by mere chance."

—*Aristotle,* The Poetics

When a parked truck slips its brake and rolls over a small child, the newspapers will call the result a "tragedy." Reporters say that events are tragic when they mean that they are unfortunate and sad. This may be fine in journalism, but in literature the word *tragedy* has a much more specific meaning. Tragedy today may not follow the strict rules of ancient Greek theater, where tragedy meant a form as particular to the drama as the sonnet is to poetry; but it still means some kind of plot in which the protagonist meets his downfall through some incorrect, *but voluntary*, choice.

We thus exclude two kinds of stories: those in which the character is simply crushed by an unbearable weight of uncontrollable events, and those in which the protagonist chooses to simply give up. A tragic figure is a sympathetic character who comes to a bad end because of an inherent flaw in his nature which leads to the fateful decision or action.

The destruction of the tragic figure may be cruel, but it must be just; and to be just, the terrible fate must arise from within the character's nature. Tragedy is often about Men Who Learn Better—but who learn too late; thus Othello, Lear, Macbeth. (But not Romeo, who never learns—which may explain why Romeo and Juliet is not one of the "great tragedies.") In the course of the story, the tragic figure may become more (or less) sympathetic; for a tragedy, like any other work of fiction, must have some degree of character change in order to rise above the level of an anecdote.

Equally important: *in a tragedy, there must be conflict.* Indeed, tragedy must have more conflict, and that conflict on a more serious level, than stories that are not tragedies. "Born Again" could have been written as a tragedy if the protagonist hadn't come to terms with her vampirism. "Perchance to Dream" is a tragedy, for the immortal woman is never able to accept her immortality and struggles to die, while her husband struggles within himself until he decides to let her die.

These stories are about something beyond death and disaster, and gloom and doom by themselves do not constitute tragedy. They rarely make for a publishable story.

We—like many editors before us—have discovered that all too many beginning writers do not understand the difference between tragedy and futility. A *futile* story ends meaninglessly or arbitrarily, often because an author doesn't know what to do next. Killing all your characters off is not an acceptable solution when you've written your-self into a corner. If the conflicts in a plot have not been resolved by the time everybody dies, the story was aborted, not concluded; quite the opposite of *Hamlet,* in which all the loose ends have been tied up in the final scene.

Shakespeare's *Macbeth* is a tragedy: Macbeth, a heroic nobleman, meets three witches who tell him that he will be king one day. His tragic flaw is ambition. Normally, he controls this; but with what he believes to be infallible assurance of his success, he succumbs to temp-tation and murders the reigning king. If Macbeth had his way, the story would end there. But the witches (not to mention the author) have other ideas. Macbeth has to kill again and again to keep his crown. Ultimately, he becomes a grim tyrant, practically wading in gore, who no longer sees any course but to carry the matter to its grisly conclusion. And he does. Birnam Wood shows up on the castle doorstep, Macduff explains the circumstances of his birth, and Mac-beth loses his crown and the head it rested so uneasily on.

In a tragedy, though the hero has no choice at the *end,* he does (or did) at the *beginning.* Whether knowingly or not, through some de-liberate act—inspired by his tragic character flaw—he sets the train of events into motion; once the decision is made, the story rolls on to its inevitable end—and the protagonist's.

In a futile story, on the other hand, there is never any choice; the protagonist is either swamped by irresistible forces or simply gives up. To answer our title question, no, Macbeth was not framed. "He done it."

We hesitate to be dogmatic about philosophical points, but if you don't believe in at least some degree of free will, your fiction isn't likely to be very entertaining.

John W. Campbell frequently rejected stories with the comment, "You've stated a problem, now solve it!" Ben Bova of *Omni* does not like stories—all too common in the slushpile—in which the characters moan of the injustice of the universe, roll over, and die. We don't care for tales like that either. Neither do any science-fiction editors—because the readers hate them most of all. SF readers also dislike the anti-intellectual, antiscientific bias of the statement: "It is beyond all human power to cope with." History is full of insoluble problems, like small-pox, that proved soluble once effort was applied; and SF readers know it.

Many young writers go through a period of having just discovered that justice in this world is about as reliable as the Easter Bunny—and wanting to tell the rest of us about it. So they put this depressing discovery into their stories, and they write of little else. These young writers are terribly, terribly sincere; and their stories are terribly, terribly unpublishable. The message—that the world is unfair—is something the rest of us already know, and know we must live with—and the purpose of fiction is *not* to belabor the obvious.

Thus we get the story in which a spaceship is hit by a meteorite, and the characters sweat out the tale making repairs and suffering hardships—only to be wiped out on the last page by a bigger meteorite. This isn't irony, and it certainly isn't sophisticated. It's stupid and pointless. No one would pay to read it, let alone publish it.

As if the facts of injustice were not grim enough, a number of amateurs make nature malevolent as well: the world is out to *get* their characters, and one can practically hear the sadistic laughter of the gods as another mortal succumbs.

Well, we don't want to argue theology, but the truth is that the laws of nature—of physics, chemistry, and so forth—are not cruel. They are cold and absolutely unforgiving, but they will not break you unless you break them first, and the breaking will not be done with gloating or chuckling (or *even smiling*, as Dunsany once wrote).

And then there are stories that stop, rather than ending when the basic problems are resolved. In "The Tryouts," Barry Longyear comments on this, when Lord Allenby's baggage and transportation pass are stolen, apparently aborting his mission right at the beginning:

> Aarel shook his head. "All he could do, then, would be to wait for the return of the Federation cruiser, is this not true?"
> "It would appear so," answered Parak. "A sad day for Momus, except there's something wrong. Jum?"
> "Indeed there is, Parak. Such news would be pointless and futile. No newsteller, Farransetti or otherwise, would bother

with such a tale, much less inflict us with it. . . ."

If "The Tryouts" had been a futile story, Allenby would never have reached Momus, and there would be nothing to prevent the enemy from conquering the planet and wiping out the population. With little else but scenes of death and destruction, there would have been no conflict, no character development, and in the end—no story.

There is a fairly common belief among amateur writers that the purpose of tragedy is to create the most powerful feeling of pain and sorrow possible. This is not quite right. The climax is not the greatest agony but its relief: the point at which the suffering finally stops. This may not be a happy event; it may be Macbeth's head rolling in the heather. The feeling we are after is called *catharsis:* a releasing of the pent-up strong emotions.

The story that follows is about a thoroughly depressing, painful situation, but it did get published. Take a look.

HEAL THE SICK, RAISE THE DEAD
by Steve Perry

Mr. Perry tells us that he is 29, married, with two children. During his yearning-to-be-a-writer-someday-when-I-have-time period, he has been a lifeguard, a swimming teacher, an aluminum-salesman-&-fork-lift-operator, a private investigator, a kung-fu instructor, and a male nurse. Currently, he's working at a family medical clinic as a Physician's Assistant—sort of half-nurse, half-doctor, half-technician, and general flunky. The writer lives with his family in the bayous of Louisiana; this story is his first sale.

After I finished attaching the last of the electrodes to the body, I looked at the girl, making it into a question with my raised eyebrows. She nodded, her thin-and-young face very pale. I turned back to my instruments—all the connections seemed to be correct—so I punched the power switch. The body gave a small, convulsive twitch; there was the smell of burned hair, then . . . nothing.

"Sometimes it takes a while," I said. Anything important usually does. I thought about my own decision. Soon, I'd likely be lying on a table like the one I now stood next to.

She nodded again, and I wanted to tell her that, in this case, it might take longer than a while—it might well take forever.

Despite the cryo-table and the holding-embalm, six days was a long time, a hell of a long time. I didn't know of any case ever brought back over a week or eight days, and anything over five days was usually good enough to make the medical journals.

The girl stood by the body, her slight frame tense and trembling. Her fingers were knitted together, the knuckles white and bloodless. Small beads of sweat stood out on her upper lip and neck, despite the hard chill of the crematorium. Her eyes never left the inert form of the dead boy.

I mostly watched my instruments, lost in my own thoughts. It was cold, and I always got cramps from standing too long when it was cold. I moved about, shifting from one leg to the other, to keep the circulation going. The smell of burnt hair was rivaled by that of stale death; there were over a thousand bodies lying on tables around us.

There was nothing yet to see on the scopes. The EEG was flat, the ECG straight-lined. Total Systems Output was nil, and enzymes were dormant. The polyvital injection/infusion was running well, despite the collapsed state of the blood vessels, but six days was still six days.

I glanced at the lifeless body, and tried to see myself there. I couldn't picture it, being dead. I wondered again how much that had to do with the whole business.

I'd figured her for a grafter this morning when she first came in. But the spiderweb skintight she wore was revealing enough to show that she had no obvious scars from prior surgery. No matter how good a medic is, there is always something—a discoloration here, a stretchmark there. She was clean, like a baby.

She had high, small breasts and a thin, leggy body. Her feet were covered with clear spray-on slippers. There was an odor of some musky perfume about her that was pleasant enough, and I figured that she was maybe fifteen.

No graft marks, so today might be her first time. The latest was to have the little finger of the right hand replaced with a live coral snake. Deadly, but who cared? It was novel—this month. Last big fad had everyone wearing raccoon tails for crotch cover. Next month, who could tell?

"What can I do for you?" I asked, giving her my best professional medic smile. I wondered if I had any snakes left in the cryo-tank—business had been good this month.

"I want a Reconstruct," she blurted, her voice a high quaver.

Reconstruct? Damn! So much for my *augenblick* diagnosis of neo-phyte grafter! I tried to hide my surprise with a question. "How old are you?"

She hesitated for a second. "Thirteen—almost fourteen!"

Missed again. I'd thought fifteen generous, but thirteen? That was much too young to be asking for a Reconstruct. Legally, anyway. Not that too many people paid a hell of a lot of attention to the laws these days.

"Who's this package you want defrosted? Parent?"

She shook her head, and looked down at the floor.

"Sibling?"

She brought her eyes up to meet mine. "Pronger," she said softly.

Well. She didn't look thirteen, and I supposed that if they were big enough, they were old enough. I looked at her small-and-slim body, and sighed. They were maturing earlier all the time, those that were left. When I was young, they'd have put you under the jail and left you there for sleeping with a girl that age. Except that a mob would probably have dragged you out and hanged you from the nearest tree in short order.

I sighed again. When I was young. That was so long ago, it seemed like a million years.

Maybe I was getting senile, living in the past, I thought. Sure, senile at fifty-four.

That was young, fifty-four. If you wanted to bother, you could figure on three times that age before you died, given the state of modern medicine. If you wanted to bother. Hardly anybody did. I mean, what for? I was one of the oldest people I knew—maybe one of the oldest, period.

I pulled myself back to the girl. "When did he terminate?"

"Last Friday."

Today was Thursday. That irritated me! Damn people who held off until the last minute! What did they expect, miracles? "Waited kind of long, didn't you?"

"I was . . . afraid." It was a whimper, a plea.

Go on, I scolded myself, *make the little girl cry.*

"How old was he?"

"Fourteen."

Another child. "How'd he die? Accident?"

She took a deep breath, and said it with a rush. "Self 'struct!"

God damn! Tired of life at the tender age! Suddenly I felt very old and tired and alone. I looked quickly down at my desk, visualizing the plastic bottle of capsules there. I was nearly four times his age, I had that kind of right—but God, a fourteen-year-old boy?

On my scopes, I was finally getting some activity. A small spiking on the EEG, not much, but something, at least.

I increased the power input slightly. *Easy does it,* I told myself, *don't fry him.* I was curious to hear his version, provided I could land him, and it would be good work. Good work was something to be proud of, something else people rarely bothered with any more.

He had been a handsome kid when he was alive. Some medic had done a rotten job on a pair of matched leopard-fur shoulder caplets. They were the only transplants he'd been wearing when he'd died. A few scars were scattered over his body, remnants of past surgeries, but not all that many. Pretty conservative, for a teener.

I looked around the crematorium, noticing how nearly full it was. Looked like they'd have to run the ovens in a day or two, to clear the tables for the next batch. I could taste the bitter dregs of the holding-embalm left in the air by the air'ditioners, and I felt the cold worse because of the clammy dead, I fancied. I spotted only two guards roaming about, but I knew that there were others. There were certain . . . people in our society who had all sorts of uses for fresh bodies.

Another blip on my scopes—some ventricular fib on the ECG. The heart was tough, even after death. I began to think that I might get this boy moving after all. The timer said twenty minutes had passed, and that wasn't good, but there was still a chance out to half an

CHAPTER 9

hour. But five more minutes passed without any change. Then seven. Eight. Crap, the organs must be too far gone. *Sorry, kid,* I thought, as I reached for the power switch.

Just then, the body turned its head. The girl squealed and I turned up the strength on the booster-relay. I had gross muscle!

Three more minutes passed and then the fibrillation converted. Damned if I didn't get a spotty but definite sinus rhythm! A block, sure, but it was pumping! If autonomics were still workable, that meant some fine control was possible. Maybe even speech.

The EEG had steeled down to only a mild epileptogenic focus, so I fed the neural circuits more juice. Oxy-lack damage was difficult to overcome, but the polyvital could soothe a great deal of brain damage and rot—temporarily.

Now or never, I thought. I kicked in the bellows pump, and the lungs started to inflate. If they held. . . .

"Uuunnhhh." A windy moan, the voice of the dead.

"Roj? Oh, Roj! I'm here!"

His eyes opened. They were cloudy, of course, and blind. Optic nerves were always the first to go—very few Reconstructs were sighted, even those only a day or two gone. But the eighth cranial, the auditory, hung on for some reason. It was always the last to leave, so it was likely that he'd be able to hear.

"Te . . . Tefi?" Ah, some vocal cords. It was that eerie drone of speech I had heard so many times before. Mostly wind, rushing through a voice-box that had lost much of its elasticity. There was little tongue or lip involved.

"Oh, Roj!" She cried, reaching out to touch him.

"Don't!" I yelled, my voice an echo in the vast room. "You'll short him out!" She jerked her hand back, and I relaxed a little. *Likely short yourself out, too,* I thought. *Besides, you wouldn't like the feel of his flesh. It would be like a just-thawed steak.*

". . efi? . . . wh . . why...didn' . . youuu..uuhhh...you...uuhhh. . ."

The girl started to cry. "I'm sorry," she whispered with a sob. I watched as a tear fell onto the cryo-table. It spattered, and froze into a thousand smaller tears.

"After you, I mean, I was scared, after you were. . . ."

" 's okay. .swee'. .efi. . .uuhhh...'s..like they ssaid. . . ."

The dead boy struggled, fighting against the bellows pump which restricted his speech. He fought for air which had no other use to him now except to run his decaying vocal cords.

"..onderful.:here...like they ssaid...'eaceful. 'alm...sso.nice." Another pause, waiting for the air. "...friendss...here...all of the...but..youuu...."

She started to sob, her body shaking. The knobs of my instruments felt suddenly hard and lifeless in my hands. Even after all this time,

I could still feel the sadness. Even after all the people I'd brought back.

A self 'struct pact. Only she couldn't go through with it at the end. So she had brought him back. For what? To say she was sorry? Could that matter to him? Or to find out if it were really true, what they said about the Other Side? To hear it from one she knew and could trust, to know that Life After Death existed, after all.

But did she know? The boy's story was familiar. It was like, but unlike, many others I had heard. It was good to hear it, since I had almost decided. It helped to push my fears into the distance. It helped.

But looking at the girl's face, I wasn't happy. She was getting the same message—more, it was her dead lover saying it. *No,* I thought, *not you. Me, certainly, but not you, not at your age. Don't listen. Wait—thirty, or forty years, a hundred years, then decide. But not now!*

I jerked my eyes down, to see the digitals dropping. He was fading. It had taken every bit of my skill, along with a great deal of luck to pull him in, and now I was losing him. But I tried, for her sake—and my own. I punched in full power. The smell of burning hair grew stronger. The body shook, but it was no good. He was gone, this time, forever.

Once, we healed the sick. Now, we raised the dead. I was as bad as all the rest, I did it too. That ability, that power of godlike strength, that curse was going to be the death of mankind. I looked at the girl, and I knew.

"I'm sorry," I said, not meaning just the loss of the boy.

"Don't be," she said, smiling through the tears. "It's all right now."

But I knew that it wasn't all right. Not now, not ever. She had made up her mind, but it wasn't all right. It was wrong, and it was as much my fault as any man's.

I repacked my instruments. Even after thirty years as a medic, I still hated to lose a patient, regardless that he was already dead. All I wanted to do now was get out, into the city-stale but alive air.

Inside my ancient and much-repaired hovercraft, we sat quietly for a minute, letting the autoglide fly us back to my office. I knew what she was thinking, but it was wrong.

Why? shouted a voice inside my head. *Weren't you thinking the same thing?*

That's different, I argued with myself. *I am older. I—*

Hah! said the voice.

"So you are going to do it," I said. It was not a question.

She nodded, smiling and unafraid now.

"You can't! You're only a child!" I exploded.

CHAPTER 9

"Roj is waiting for me!"

"There are a thousand boys—"

"No! They are not Roj!"

"But to kill yourself—"

"So what? Here is only here! There is perfect! It's like everybody said, you heard him!"

Yes, I'd heard him. Him, and all the others. Still, I had to try.

"You don't know what life has to offer!"

"I do so! I'm not a baby! I've been places, done things! Why go through it all over again? Why does it even matter? Roj is *there*, waiting for me!"

"But—"

"You heard him!" She threw herself back deeply into the hovercraft's worn seat, her arms crossed to shut me out.

How could I argue with it? How could I fight a voice from the lips of her own dead lover? Who would not be taken in, convinced totally by the words of a father, mother, or a sister—or a wife?

I stared through the pitted plastic window at the city beneath us. Mostly deserted now, a far cry from the days before the Reconstruct process. Maybe if Mali had lived, had made it until the process had been perfected. . . . No. It was long past, and I'd never hear it from my own wife.

I turned back to the girl. "Listen," I said, feeling desperate. For some reason, it was important that she know, that she understand. I caught her shoulders, feeling her smooth skin and firm muscle under my hands.

"When the Reconstruct concept was first created, there were a lot of theories. One of the most important was thrown out, because nobody wanted to believe it. That theory says that what the dead say is not real!"

She shook her head and struggled, but I wouldn't let her go.

"It says that the human brain refuses to accept its own death, so it makes up a story, to convince itself that it will not die! That what the dead say when you bring them back is only that story, played back a final time, like a recording! That's why the stories are different, because they are subjective, not because there are really different realities on the Other Side!"

She stared at me, not wanting to hear it.

"Don't you understand? It could all be a lie! You could be killing yourself for nothing!" There. I'd said it. But who was I really trying to convince?

"You heard, you heard!" She screamed, starting to cry. "Roj said, he said, he said—"

I let her go, and slumped back into my seat. Yes. Roj had said.

The girl was gone, and I sat alone at my desk, staring at the drawer. Had I convinced her? Planted a seed of the smallest doubt? I didn't know. Probably not, but maybe. Somebody had to convince them, the young ones. What if the theory was wrong?

What, even, if the theory was valid? Suppose there was Life After Death—what then? Why would there be any point in staying alive? Or what point in being born in the first place? It was a question that had been debated by the best minds we had, and no answer had been found.

At least, not in this life. There was one way for anyone who wished to find out. I took the bottle of capsules from the drawer, and shook them about inside their plastic prison. I was older than most, surely I had the right to do as I wished. I had heard all the stories: It was Heaven, Valhalla, Nirvana, Paradise. Nobody ever said it was Hell—at worst, it was much better than here.

But if I did it, who would be left to try and keep the young ones going? And what if it were a lie? What if the whole thing was a massive con game, a trick of the human mind on itself; who would be around to try and keep the human race going?

I was supposed to be a healer, a life-giver, a medic. It was my job, wasn't it? But I was tired, and how much could one man be expected to do?

I poured the blue-and-green capsules out onto the desk, touching the slick-and-light one-way tickets to where? Heaven, or oblivion? I stirred them around with my finger, hearing the tiny sound they made on my plastic desk. I was almost sure, until I had met the girl today, and brought back her dead lover.

Was this the way the world was to end, not with a bang or a whimper, but with an expectant smile?

Could all those people be wrong?

There was only one way I could be sure, only one way.

Carefully, I put the capsules back into the bottle, and snapped the lid shut. *Not today,* I thought.

Not today.

Steve Perry got the idea for this story by daydreaming.

"One day, I flashed on a sign on the front of a doctor's office. There was the surgeon's name, then a list of his services, much like an old-time medicine man's wagon. It went something like: 'J.R. Johnston, M.D., Organ Transplants, Neurosurgery, General Surgery, including Healing the Sick, Raising the Dead.'

CHAPTER 9

"So: I had a title, and with it, a main character—a doctor who could somehow bring the dead back to life. I puttered with it.

"About that time, I did some study, including a seminar on death and dying, by Dr. Elizabeth Kuebler-Ross, on people who had been clinically dead and somehow brought back. And these people had some interesting stories. The stories had a lot in common, in that they were mostly positive; but they were also quite different as to actual details.

"I sat down to my banged-up portable and wrote the thing. It was, I think, my fourth story. When I finished, I wasn't happy with it; it didn't flow. I had no idea when I started writing it how it was going to end. Right up until the last paragraph, I had pretty much figured that the main character would suicide. Only, he didn't seem to want to; and I couldn't make him.

"It became a drawer story, after two drafts. I stuck it away, went on with my one-story-a-week schedule, and forgot about it. Two or three months later, I happened across it again. When I reread it, it seemed still to be a good idea. I saw a few places where the syntax was sloppy, so I cleaned it up in a final draft and sent it off to *IA'sf*—mainly because that was the only magazine bothering to send personal comments with rejections. That was on 27 March 1977.

"Less than a month later, I got a note back from the editor. He listed a few things he thought might improve the manuscript. None of the suggestions affected the story line; they were minor points that I'd goofed on, mostly, and one or two language changes more appropriate for a family magazine. I retyped the entire MS as fast as I could. It went out with the next day's mail.

"I'm still proud of that story. Oh, if I were writing it today, I'd probably do it differently. The dialog was terrible and not all that well done. I'd probably make it longer, and give myself more room to play with the theme. My medical background was pretty solid, and I wouldn't fool with the hardware aspect of the tale much. I'd still do it first-person, even though I've only done a couple in that voice since. Basically, I'm satisfied with 'Heal the Sick, Raise the Dead'; it said what I wanted to say, and not *that* badly. It didn't win any awards, but it got published; it made me a pro on my fourth try. I can't complain.

"The story also proved one of the cardinal rules of SF writing: once you've finished a story, you've got to submit it. If I'd been fainthearted, it could still be stashed in a drawer somewhere, turning yellow, wasted. Instead, it was the key that opened the door to the world I wanted to enter—writing SF. Since then, I've sold maybe fifteen other short pieces, finished up two books and part of a third, and am now a full-time writer. But that first one was the nicest reward I've gotten, when I finally saw it in print. I have the acceptance framed and on my wall—you only lose your virginity once."

TRAGEDY AND FUTILITY

There is conflict in this story. Neither the girl nor the narrator are wholly trapped by the situation; both must decide what they must do. The girl decides to die, while the doctor is sufficiently appalled that he is driven to live on. Note that the story follows the normal pattern of problem/complication/climax/resolution. As a futility story, it would have been nothing more than girl-decides-to-die-and-does,-and-doctor-does-too. Such a story, as the traders around the fire on Momus observed, would be pointless and futile, and no storyteller would be foolish enough to inflict it on his audience. You must not make that mistake, either.

This is not a tragedy in the formal, Aristotlean sense, even though it is very downbeat. No one rises to tragic stature, but all the characters are believable and sympathetic. The story works. All the elements of a complete story are present.

It is worth paying attention to what keeps this story from being merely a futility.

The conflict is on a human scale; the hero is not squashed flat by his problems. The doctor is not asked to save the human race, which would be impossible for this one man, but only to keep one girl from committing suicide, or to avoid it himself.

There is a real possibility of success or failure—the doctor's actions make a *difference*. He fails to save the girl, but he does save himself. In each case he had a chance, and the outcome is a result of what the characters did or learned or decided. The story is not merely one of a man overcome by the forces of circumstance.

The most important point of all is simply that a story isn't *required* for any external reason to be upbeat or downbeat. It must work on its own terms, and the ending must grow out of it, following naturally from what went before. A plausible ending is the one that your story should have. Do not arbitrarily tack on a happy one or a sad one merely because you want the story to end that way. As we remarked earlier, one of the reasons readers read fiction is to find order, to make some sense of the daily chaos. Your ending must make more sense than what is going on Out There.

CHAPTER 9

HUMOR: GETTING THE JOKE

There is only so much you can learn about humor from a book. A funny story is one that makes people laugh, and anyone who has to carefully analyze what makes people laugh will *never* be able to do it. By all indications, humor is not learned. It is innate and spontaneous. If you don't have a sense of humor, there's nothing we can do for you. But if you do have the basic talent, you can learn things about how to put that humor into a story.

There is something worse than not having people laugh at your humor. That's having them laugh when they're not supposed to. This chapter's purpose is to help make your intentional humor work.

The first thing to remember is that **humor alone does not constitute a story!** There must be a story beneath the jokes. A humorous story, like any other, must have a beginning, middle and end; it must have character change and a point to it all. Since we are talking about science-fiction humor, remember also that the story has to be inherently science fiction. The same rules apply as elsewhere. If the story could take place anywhere, or none of the essential elements have anything to do with the science-fictional content, the story is mainstream in a clever plastic disguise.

It is in fact a Bat Durston, about which much more later.

Not every line of a story can be screamingly funny. Whether you are writing situational humor, verbal humor (e.g. puns), satire, or parody, an overly heavy-handed approach will make the whole thing fall flat. Pace your humor. A large laugh at the front, perhaps, then a generally amusing tone as the complication builds, then another joke at the climax, and the biggest and best one at the very last. Often a humorous story delivers one funny item, then another; but fails because the last one is not nearly as good as the first few, and thus seems a letdown.

Don't overextend yourself. Very few humorists can keep it up over great length. Humorous novels, inside science fiction or out of it, are much scarcer than short pieces. A humorous story has to work absolutely. There is no such thing as a half-funny story unless it is a dull one. When Shakespeare wrote, "Brevity is the soul of wit," he wasn't talking about humor, but about intelligence in the sense that a stupid person is witless, but his truth still applies. (And of course the line *was* delivered in a funny scene, the humor coming from the incongruity of the long-winded, pedantic Polonius making a statement like that and totally failing to heed it.)

Always keep in mind that the most enduring humor (as in Mark Twain's work) grows out of the foibles of character, rather than sprouting from one-liners. Huck Finn is funny because of his way of looking at things; Tom Sawyer's reactions are funny partly because they are so in-character. A story doesn't even have to be a comedy to have humor—humor is a part of most people's lives and shouldn't be eliminated just because a story is "serious." The more serious the story, the greater the need for occasional humor to break the tension and give contrast to the darker moments.

Keep your humor in good taste. Standards vary between publications, but exploring new frontiers in bad taste is not in itself humorous. The shock of such a thing is the most ephemeral of all literary values, and such a story will seem sophomoric very quickly. But good humor, which has something to say about the way people behave, or which contains a genuinely funny and original idea, won't date. Some of the most standard gags in modern comedy derive from the Roman playwright Plautus and they still work today. But bathroom and bedroom references for their own sake will not amuse any but the most limited audience.

We stated earlier that the protagonist of a story is the person who changes, and that means—even in a funny story—the person who hurts. It is true that in most funny stories we are laughing at the trials and embarrassments of others; our culture teaches that this is permissible when fictional characters, clowns, or actors are involved. Such things happen to real people, but it's considered "impolite" and "wrong" to laugh at them. The kinds and degrees of such sufferings that are "allowed for a laugh," however, depend on personal taste.

CHAPTER 10

An old problem with SF humor is the "funny alien" who is essentially a green stand-in for the fool or cripple we are no longer culturally permitted to laugh at. This is not to say that cultural or physical differences cannot be used as a source of humor; but the best of such stories will see both sides of the joke, laughing as well at the silliness of humans seen through alien eyestalks.

Don't be obscure. An in-joke is something which is funny only to those who already know what it is about; those who don't will miss the point entirely. Some authors slip these into stories for the amusement of themselves and their friends, but they must be so unobtrusive that they do not distract the ordinary reader. At best, these in-references will be boring to the outsider; at worst, they are insulting (nobody likes to feel he is being talked past).

Because science fiction is a fairly close-knit field with many well-known figures, this kind of thing is tried frequently. But the same cautions still apply—and remember that the mere shock of recognition is not humor. Slipping in references to real persons or things is not of itself funny.

Avoid satires on topical issues. A humorous commentary on a particular politician's hairstyle may be outdated (by an election defeat, or a haircut, or baldness) before the story is printed. It is something else to write a satire based on *extrapolation* from current trends and issues—suppose a politican's TV image becomes so important that his hairdo matters more than his stand on issues? Frederik Pohl has written this type of story many times, sometimes using what is called *reductio ad absurdum*—carrying the trend so far that it becomes ridiculous. This is a difficult technique, because some part of the audience always fails to see that the writer is joking, and because by writing a deliberately absurd story you give up some of the readers' acceptance.

A satire cannot abandon the rules of fiction, no matter how absurd it is intended to be. Imagination, detailed examination of a premise, characterization as opposed to mere stick figures, and all the other elements of good science fiction are required. The technique is at least as old as Swift's *Gulliver's Travels*, but the story has to live on its own strength, rather than contemporary references. Thus Swift's satire on the political figures of his own day is lost to us, but the bit about fighting a war over which end of an egg to crack is sufficiently universal as an observation on human nature to remain valid forever.

A humorous phrase is often a serious phrase in a particular context. Read the following:

> He crumpled the doctor's report in his hands. "I'm going to *die*," he said.

Pretty grim. Now try the following:

Hustling a friend into a corner of the crowded ballroom, he pulled up his trousers to display his socks. One was blue. The other was yellow.

"I'm going to *die*," he said.

Get the idea? It's the exaggeration, and the juxtaposition of the terribly serious statement with the silly situation, that creates the humor.

We don't have an example among our first sales of a full-scale humorous science-fiction story, much less a good piece of social satire, because those types of stories are difficult to write and consequently rare even from expert authors. We do, however, have a specimen of that curious subspecies, the science-fiction pun short-short.

CHAPTER 10

THEY'LL DO IT EVERY TIME
by Cam Thornley

At 15, Mr. Thornley is our youngest author—a fact we discovered only after we had agreed to buy this latest entry in the horrible-pun contest. The writer also reports that he and his brother edit a school-oriented newspaper/magazine that is a lot funnier than you would think, and that he is a victim of unrequited love. This is his first sale.

The High Vavoom of Kazowie was in conference with the pilot of the scoutship which had just returned from Sol III.

"I am certain that you have much to tell us of the strange and fascinating ways of the barbaric humanoids, Captain Zot, but—"

"You wouldn't believe it, your Vavoomity! Why, they live indoors! They don't keep slaves! They even—"

"—but after skimming through your log, I have formulated a few questions which should provide the information necessary to determine whether or not the planet is ready for colonization. Now—"

"It's unbelievable, sir! They eat with pieces of metal! The men think they're better than the women! They don't—"

"—now I just want you to answer these questions as briefly and completely as possible. Do you understand?"

"They—"

"Good. First, what was the reaction of the natives upon first sighting you in the air?"

"Well, high sir, at the time I couldn't help noticing the resemblance to a glikhill that has had freem poured on it. The humanoids went into a frenzy and fired several projectiles at me, all of which fell short by several naugafrangs."

"I see. Now please describe your landing."

"Of course, high sir. When I approached the surface of the planet, I noticed that it was covered with wide black strips which appeared to be vehicular routes. As regulations strictly prohibit landing one's craft upon such routes, I looked for a better place to touch down. The only other areas that seemed to fit my craft's landing specifications were the hard-surfaced paths from the doors of the natives' houses (I will explain this later, high sir) to the vehicular routes.

"I set the ship down on one of these paths and went out to greet the humanoids. They all—"

"Wait a moment. This is extremely important. What was the reaction of the natives upon first seeing you in the flesh? Try to remember everything that happened."

"Yes, high sir. It seems that I bear a striking resemblance to one of their major religious figures. When I came out of the ship all the humanoids in the vicinity knelt and averted their eyes, and said something about the coming seconds. I think this was a reference to an event that was going to happen in the near future. At any rate, when the natives stopped talking they got up and started walking towards me with their arms stretched out in front of them. I didn't like the looks of this so I jumped into the ship and took off. The religious-figure-resemblance theory is strengthened by the fact that when I observed the landing site several weeks later through my reasonable-distance site-viewer I discovered that the natives had built a shrine there which always seemed to be full of pilgrims from many lands."

"Ah, yes. The familiar saviour-from-the-stars syndrome. It happens to every one of our astronauts on pre-colonization planets."

"What's that, high sir?"

"They worship the walk he grounds on."

"They'll Do It Every Time," according to Cam Thornley, was written in a fit of passion. "After reading Asimov's shaggy-dog story, 'About Nothing' in the Summer 1977 issue of the magazine, I said to myself, 'Hey, I can do better than that!' So I did.

"Actually, it was a little harder than that. My original manuscript, with a cheeky letter twice as long as the story, was returned several weeks later with a friendly letter from the editor explaining exactly what I had done wrong and why he didn't want to buy it. Huffily embarrassed, I almost didn't realize that he wanted me to rewrite the piece of fluff and send it back. I did just that [correcting every single flaw we pointed out in our letter], and soon 'They'll Do It Every Time' (my own clumsy giveaway title) was nestled in with greats and near-greats between the covers of a real science-fiction magazine. And what covers! My issue featured the classic scantily-clad young maiden and rippling-muscled young man, both wielding vintage 1940 rayguns and gracefully posed on a cover overflowing with assorted bizarre bits of machinery. This may well have contributed to the popularity of my story, but it is a tad embarrassing in terms of posterity. I mean, where's the BEM, for crying out loud?

"Well, after my first sale I knew I had it made. Everyone knows the toughest part of being a successful writer is breaking in, right? I figured I'd rattle off about four more stories before graduating from high school, and then really get swinging. So I spun another yarn and sent it to good old George Scithers, and good old George Scithers sent it right back, this time with a list of mistakes as long as my face and a polite letter that could not be mistaken for anything but a complete and final rejection. Hey, no problem. I just sat down and wrote another story. But this one didn't look right, and somehow I just never got around to submitting it.

"Meanwhile, however, a strange thing was happening—my story was being reprinted! First in an anthology, then in a hardcover edition of same called *Masters of Science Fiction*—'masters' no less!—then in a drugstore checkout counter paperback model, and now in a how-to-write-SF book. I may not have sold five stories while I was in high school, but I did almost as well—one story five times. And the future looks bright: novelizations, movie contracts, comic strips, bubble-gum cards . . . And you ask if I would write it differently now!! Ha ha! Of course I would.

"I would change the damned title."

This type of story was popularized, if not invented, by Grendel Briarton, whose adventures of Ferdinand Feghoot have graced the pages of several SF magazines. Consequently the technical term for this literary subgenre is the *feghoot*. (Note: Even though other people may write short stories ending in puns, the character Ferdinand Feghoot is the property of Mr. Briarton. We occasionally receive unauthorized Feghoots from beginning writers. They are unpublishable for this reason alone. Hands off!)

The basic trick is to set up a situation quickly, present a series of pieces of information, and then snap to a conclusion with a pun which is not only a pun but also the logical last line for the story.

"They'll Do It Every Time" is a complete story. There is rudimentary characterization through the dialog. We can tell by the way the characters speak that the pilot is young, inexperienced, and eager, while the High Vavoom is patient, used to this sort of thing, and doubtless patting Captain Zot gently on the head with a tentacle (or whatever) in an effort to calm him down.

One element which could have wrecked this story if allowed to get out of hand is the use of nonsense words; "a glikhill that has had freem poured over it" doesn't tell us very much, since these terms are not defined. Something is vaguely implied, and the terminology gives a sense of comical aliens in the same sense that the title "High Vavoom of Kazowie" does, but fortunately the author had enough sense to know when enough is enough and not go overboard on such a weak device.

A pun is created for the *ear*, not the eye. If you read a written pun aloud and the effect is lost, it is not a good one. If your character goes to Warsaw to get some "shoe polish," leave him there and junk the story. Since "Polish" and "polish" don't sound the same, such a pun won't work. But Thornley's will. It is particularly enhanced by its similarity to a common expression. (Another one, based on an old burlesque line, is probably the most horrid yet published by *IA'sf:* "What was that laser you sawed me with last night?" "That was no laser, that was my knife.")

A pun story has to follow the same rules any humorous one does, save that it is best that it be far *shorter* than other types. Don't strain to reach the pun. It must be a natural outflowing of the story itself. If it is obvious that the whole thing is a setup, much of the humor will be lost.

Don't be obscure. If the pun depends on some in-group or specialized knowledge, a large portion of your audience won't get it, and a pause of incomprehension is even more fatal for a pun story, where the pun is virtually the entire point, than it is for other kinds of humorous fiction.

Above all: puns must not depend on names invented to fit the wordplay.

Next, we come to another specialized type of science-fiction humor, the artistic satire. It is called this because it is about artforms, in this case, science-fiction space-opera stories and western movies.

CHAPTER 10

BAT DURSTON, SPACE MARSHAL
by G. Richard Bozarth

*Though Mr. Durston, under various aliases,
has roamed the space-lanes since—almost—
time immemorial, he first came to general
notice when, on the back cover of the very
first issue of* Galaxy Science Fiction,
*that magazine's editor, H.L. Gold, exposed
a suspicious similarity between horse
operas and the rocket-&-raygun story.
"You'll never see it in* Galaxy!" *Mr. Gold
vowed; and ol' Bat had to hang up his
blasters and anti-grav'd off into the
earthset—until, we thought, just this
once. . . . So here, with a hearty, "Hi-yo,
Lorenz-Fitzgerald!" is Mr. Bozarth's very
first sale. Now 28, he's been writing
since 12 and seriously so since 21.*

Bat Durston pushed the coffee dispenser button with a long,
brawny index finger. Behind a clear plastic door a biodegradable
disposable mug of authentic Nineteenth-Century American Western
Territories design plopped down beneath a spout. A second later the
dark, nearly black brew flowed steamingly into the mug.

At completion of the filling cycle, the clear plastic door automatically slid up. Bat Durston hooked the previously described index
finger into the mug's finger loop and tasted the brew. It was bitterly
strong-flavored to reproduce as accurately as possible what archae-
ologists had determined to be the flavor of the Nineteenth-Century
American Western Territories coffee.

If Bat Durston ever minded the emphasis on symbology that a
space marshal had to put up with, it never showed on his steady,
dedicated, ruggedly handsome face. The tall, broad-shouldered, nar-
row-hipped man had piercingly determined blue eyes and a steady,
sober, thin-lipped mouth. Clearly, he was a man who could clean up
his parsecs.

Bat Durston walked with quiet, strong grace to his Sector monitor
and sat down. He was surrounded by a winking, blinking, gleaming,
glowing, sophisticated array of electronic wonderments that contin-
ually reported the state of law and order in his Sector. He looked
like a starship pilot on a starship bridge.

If being nearly the sole foundation of law and order in his parsecs
bothered Bat Durston, he did not show it as he sipped the bitter
coffee and read the various video reports with unflinching eyes.
Folks could be secure with a man like Bat Durston on the job. He

would never say it out loud, but their confidence and trust sustained him in the performance of a hard, often dangerous job.

A flashing red light over one screen claimed his attention. The video readout reported the Bad Bart Blackie Gang had just robbed the Transgalactic Conglomerate of its credit transfer authorizations on PhiBetaCrappa IV. Angrily, Bat Durston's eyes narrowed a nanometer as he fed in the reported trajectory of the gang's starship. The calculated projection of possible destinations made the corners of Bat Durston's somber eyes crinkle with mirth.

Pushing a comm button with the same index finger he had already used twice before, he spoke in a low, serious monotone, "Andy, you there, son?"

"Right here, Bat, cleanin' up ol' *Igniter*," came the bubblingly enthusiastic reply of Bat Durston's young sidekick, Andy, known as Andy the Kid.

In calm monotones that betrayed his fury, Bat Durston explained what had happened, then said, "I reckon by computer figgerin' we can head 'em off at the Horse-Head Nebula. Reckon you'd best get *Igniter* ready for liftoff. I'll be over directly."

"Great full moons, I shore will, Bat!"

The room lights glinted grimly off Bat Durston's quiet eyes as he opened a door and pulled out a belt and holster. The gleaming synthetic permapolish leather holster held a proton blaster. Bat Durston pulled out the deadly weapon and thumbed the power-pack release. Into his palm plopped the rectangular cartridge. Its load indicator showed a full charge of six destructive shots of pure (yet environmentally safe) proton energy.

Before reloading the blaster, Bat Durston checked the action of the weapon. Due to safety regulations, it required two hands to fire the gun. The gun hand gripping the butt depressed a safety which opened the interlocks that prevented accidental discharges. The trigger was a centimeter-long switch on the top near the rear. It was activated by slapping it with the palm of the triggerhand. This was called "fanning" by gunslingers and space marshals.

Satisfied with the proton blaster, Bat Durston returned it to the holster and stood up with a lethal, yet moral, agility. He strapped the weapon onto his narrow hips, his thin lips in an even straighter line than usual. He did not like to carry a proton blaster, but he knew someone had to if these parsecs were ever to be safe for decent, respectable folks.

Suddenly into the Law Enforcement Command Control Center (locally termed "the Marshal's office") burst Miss Mary. She was a comely young woman with wide, innocent, easily emotional blue eyes and straw-blonde hair. Her father, owner of a robot repair facility, was a hard-working, upright citizen well thought of in the community. The room lights reflected warmly off Bat Durston's sober eyes as he saw Mary. She was the kind of decent, clean-living sort of girl a man would—well, would want to settle down with after his job was done.

"Howdy, Miss Mary," Bat Durston monotoned romantically.

"Oh, Bat!" Mary gasped, the tears springing to her eyes. "I saw Andy getting *Igniter* ready for liftoff. Oh, Bat! He—he told me!"

"Now, now, Miss Mary," Bat Durston monotoned nonchalantly.

"Oh, Bat! Don't go! Bad Bart Blackie and his gang are—are—they're so bad—they're—oh, Bat!"

With a burst of affection, Bat Durston took her by the shoulders and looked steadily into her wetly frightened eyes. "Now, now, Miss Mary," he said in his quiet, rugged, unvarying voice. "Yuh know I gotta. It's mah duty. But—well, thar's a mite more to it."

"More, Bat? Oh, Bat."

Bat Durston's nostrils flared a millimeter in embarrassment as he said evenly, "Well, yeah, ya see, I figger this here Bad Bart Blackie Gang is 'bout the last of the bad ones in these here parsecs. Well, I ain't gettin' much younger, so I'ma guessin' maybe when I got 'em locked up, I oughta—well, hang up my proton blaster and get me a fine, young—" But here words failed Bat Durston.

"Oh, Bat!" Mary cried, impulsively hugging the hard-muscled space marshal. She knew what he could not say and he knew she knew and she knew he knew she knew the unspoken words were the ones she had been longing for him to finally not be able to say.

In a rare burst of passion, Bat Durston pressed his thin lips briefly against Mary's willingly responsive forehead and said, "Now, now, Miss Mary." Avoiding an even more extreme display of emotion, Bat Durston chivalrously tipped his hat, then quickly stepped into a matter transmitter and transferred instantly to his trusty starship, Igniter.

The space marshal was greeted enthusiastically by Andy the Kid, called usually Andy by his friends and sometimes 'son', but only by Bat Durston. Being as Andy was a supergenius cloned in a recombinant DNA laboratory, he wasn't really anyone's son. However, Bat Durston had a fatherly affection for his living supergenius sidekick (standard government issue to all space marshals) and called him son. Bat Durston was not the sort of man to coldly think of Andy as simply another recomb clone; just another Ralph 124C41 + model.

Andy was a tall, slim drink of liquid nutrient with a clean, fresh face; quick, genius eyes; and sloppy blond hair. As soon as he saw Bat Durston, he said, "Ready for liftoff, Bat! I redesigned the quark accelerator this morning, so we can travel even faster than the speed of light than before. I also changed the sheets on our bunks."

"Good, son," Bat Durston said. "Well, thar's a job t'get done an' the Horse-Head Nebula is a fur piece down th' starlanes. Let's lift off."

"Alrighty, Bat!" Andy cried.

No starship was now faster than trusty *Igniter,* thanks to Andy's redesigned quark accelerator. They arrived at the Horse-Head Nebula well in advance of the Bad Bart Blackie Gang. Cleverly, they concealed themselves behind a black hole; a feat made possible by another of Andy's inventions, the Blackhole Nullification Concealatron.

Bat Durston easily waited stoically for the precomputed arrival of the Bad Bart Blackie Gang, but the tense pressure eventually got to the much younger Andy. Cracking under the strain, the recomb clone said, "Say, Bat."

"Yep, son?" replied Bat Durston quietly.

"I wuz thinkin', Bat."

"Yep, son?"

"Well, this here Bad Bart is 'bout the meanest of 'em all, ain't he?"

"Yep, son?"

"An' his gang is purty mean, too, ain't they?"

"Yep, son."

"Well, can ya take 'em okay, Bat?"

Realizing his young sidekick was nearly in a panic, Bat Durston took immediate corrective action. He stood up, squarely planting his feet shoulder-width apart. He hooked his brawny thumbs on his gunbelt and looked piercingly into some higher moral value somewhere beyond infinity. His square-cut chin thrust forward in a ruggedly reassuring way. Andy forgot his previous terror as he quivered with scarcely suppressed excitement, for he knew Bat Durston was about to deliver one of his rare insights into the true depths of life.

"The way I reckon, son," Bat Durston monotoned as the compartment lights glowed wisely off his clear blue eyes, "folks in these here parsecs sorta hanker fer a bit o' respite from th' frustrations of everyday life. I mean t'say, th' meaningless tragedies of everyday life sorta make decent folks want t'see happy endin's an' not more of th' same maddenin', frustratin' failures. So, figgerin' this inta things, I reckon I can take 'em okay. It's mah duty."

Totally awed, Andy sighed, "That there wuz profound, Bat! Why can't I ever thinka stuff like that?"

Managing to smile with fatherly affection without bending the sober, dedicated straight line of this thin lips, Bat Durston said, "Yo're young, son, an' figgerin' out human bein's is a mite harder than understandin' quark accelerators."

This wisdom allowed Andy to get hold of himself and wait out the

CHAPTER 10

ambush very nearly as calmly as Bat Durston. It was not much longer, though, before the Bad Bart Blackie Gang showed up. Instantly, from behind the black hole, the two defenders of law and order in *Igniter* sprang upon their quarry.

Well, criminals are notoriously foolish, so it was not surprising the Bad etc. tried to get away. They actually might have, had not Andy redesigned *Igniter's* quark accelerator. After a long chase, Bat Durston and Andy aboard trusty *Igniter* had cornered the Bad Bart Blackie Gang against a single-lined spectroscopic binary.

"Yo're under arrest, Bad Bart," Bat Durston monotoned over the radio.

"Yer gonna hafta draw down ta bring us in," came Bad Bart's sneering reply.

A lock of blond hair fell over Bat Durston's forehead with disgust at this necessary violence as he returned evenly, "I'ma comin' out."

"Let me go with ya, Bat!" Andy begged as Bat Durston got into his spacesuit.

"Not this time, son," Bat Durston replied. "If 'n—well, somebody has t'tell Miss Mary."

"Bat!" cried Andy.

"A man's got t'plan ahead, son. I guess anyone c'n figger wrong."

"Bat!" cried Andy.

"It's mah duty."

Outsider *Igniter,* floating in the weightless void and vacuum of space, Bat Durston, Space Marshal, faced the six evil men of the Bad Bart Blackie Gang alone, unafraid, asking only that if this should be his time, another would pick up his fallen star.

"I'ma givin' yuh one last chance, Bad Bart," Bat Durston said in his most persuasive yet unrelentingly brave monotone.

"I'ma givin' *you* one last chance, Bat Dummy," Bad Bart sneered. "There's just one of you and I count six of us."

"I figger we gotta draw down, then."

Seven hands flashed for seven proton blasters. Incredibly fast were the Bad etc., but faster still was Bat Durston. In a blur of fanning, six ruby-red proton energy bolts disintegrated the six blasters of the bad guys before they fanned off a single bolt. In Bat Durston's opinion, it was a poor space marshal who couldn't bring his men in alive.

Bat Durston thumbed the powerpack ejector as he pulled a full-charged pack from a belt loop. As the empty pack cleared the pack well, he slammed in the new pack. Realizing their hopeless plight, the Bad Bart Blackie Gang reached for the overhead portion of interstellar space.

"Oh, sizzlin' comets!" one criminal cursed disgustedly.

"This is ridiculous!" cried Bad Bart as he felt maddening, frustrating failure. "Nobody is gonna believe this! This ain't real life!

G. R. BOZARTH

Everything with you, Bat Durston, is nuthin' but space opera! How do ya do it?"

Bat Durston replied in his sober, dedicated monotone, "I don't reckon I know 'bout that. All I know is if'n this ain't real life, it oughta be."

The author reports that he got the idea for this story from a handout we once sent to him. "In it, among other informative things, you said that you didn't want 'space opera' with Bat Durston heading them off at the Horsehead Nebula and gunning them down with a proton blaster. Almost instantly, I pictured one of those lurid Golden Age pulp covers with the blazing title, **BAT DURSTON, SPACE MARSHAL** across it with an illustration of Bat confronting a BEM clutching a nearly nude beauty in distress.

"The idea of Bat Durston, Space Marshal wouldn't leave me—the satire possibilities were so obvious. It took about two days to mentally develop the idea. Actually, that was pretty easy. I had recently seen Gary Cooper in *High Noon*, and this suggested to me Miss Mary as well as the character I gave to Bat Durston. Andy the Kid came from any number of other '40s and '50s Westerns where the bold, dashing hero had a sidekick for comic relief. The character of Andy the Kid was a satire on the Tom Swift, Jr., books that were the delight of late childhood and early adolescence.

"When I physically wrote the story, I made no changes significant enough to remember. This is rare for me. Usually I have to make at least one major change in a short story. But 'Bat Durston' was all right there, complete the first time around; and I felt extremely satisfied with the finished product. I had no doubts at all about whether I could have done it better or if it needed to rest a while on the shelf before sending it out.

"Today, I wouldn't change it in any way. I feel that in it I fully satisfied my purpose to satirize the Bat Durston stereotype. I don't even want to make it longer by adding more incidents of the same nature. I feel that would be overworking the satire, as well as disrupting the pace of the tale."

The interesting thing about this story is that it is not what it pretends to be. It is not a transplanted Western. If this were shifted back to the Old West, most of the humor would collapse. The laughs are produced primarily by the incongruous juxtaposition of science-fiction and Western clichés. If the science-fiction elements were removed, this effect would be lost. The amusing part is how the author is able to explain the Western elements in science-fictional terms; hence science-fictional reasons for fanning a proton blaster, and for the marshal to have a bright young sidekick. The story becomes a satire on bad science fiction because in the usual transplanted Western, the product of a lazy writer, there is no attempt to rationalize the wholesale similarities between 1875 in Kansas and 2250 on a planet near the Horsehead Nebula. The clear implication is that if the typical space-Western situation were examined rigorously, it would come out like this.

At the same time, this story is a parody of the description-clogged, adjective-heavy archetype of bad fiction of any kind—and yet it *isn't*. Almost every noun in the first few paragraphs has two or more adjectives; most verbs have an adverb or two lurking nearby. But, something *is* happening—the coffee has a taste to it—and the setting and the cast are outrageous enough to be *interesting*. An important test of the effectiveness of any story is how it works on people who are unfamiliar with the particular genre or sub-genre being satirized; a story that requires too much prior knowledge belongs in a small-circulation magazine intended for long-time SF readers only. "Bat Durston . . ." does work for newcomers; sometimes too well, for we got a few letters berating the editors for bringing back the bad old days of space opera. For any humor to work, it must be appreciated by nearly all those who read it; and this story did meet that test of success.

SUMMING UP: LAWS NOT WISELY BROKEN

"There are nine and sixty ways of constructing tribal lays,
And—every—single—one—of—them—is—right!"
"In the Neolithic Age"—Rudyard Kipling

In this book, we have shown you a great array of observations, rules, and principles for *writing,* for writing *fiction,* and for writing *science* fiction. Many a beginning writer—and even half-seasoned writers who ought to know better—will object, "But rules are made to be broken," and quote Kipling, quite forgetting that one must know at least *one* of the nine and sixty ways and preferably several, and completely misunderstanding the nature of rules. Rules are *not* meant to be broken——

Rules are meant to be understood. Rules, especially in the writing game, are brief, sometimes even elegant summaries of basic, universal truths, worded more for easy remembering than comprehensive coverage. Consider, for an example, the Ancient Rule for Westerns: **Shoot the sheriff in the first paragraph.** The underlying idea is expressed with more precision, but at the cost of brevity, in Rear Admiral Pinney's Observation: **If you don't get a reader's attention in the first paragraph, the rest of your message is lost.** The common idea under both these expressions is the way that people read, the way that they pick what to read, and therefore the way that editors—even editors who are not working for Western adventure pulps—decide what to buy and what not to. Literally shooting the sheriff isn't necessary, nor is denting the villain's carapace (though that can't but help): the basic idea here is that a story must be interesting enough, from the very beginning, to make a casual reader into a fascinated one; and still more important, to convince an editor that his readers will find it so.

Sometimes—it's rare but it does happen—the author's past perform-ance and his reputation are what keeps reader and editors reading on past the first page, for it *is* true that a famous writer is trusted further than an unknown. And sometimes a well-crafted passage of description or exposition will catch readers' attention. The most re-liable way to start is still to dive into the middle of things, as did Homer; the *Iliad* begins, "I sing of the anger of Achilles, . . ." and he sings to us still, 3,000 years later.

As for holding attention, once caught, Mark Twain left us a set of Rules; they require:

1. **That a tale shall accomplish something and arrive some-where.**

2. **They require that the episodes of a tale shall be necessary parts of the tale, and shall help develop it.**

3. **They require that the personages in a tale shall be alive, except in the case of corpses, and that always the reader shall be able to tell the corpses from the others.**

4. **They require that the personages in a tale, both dead and alive, shall exhibit a sufficient excuse for being there.**

5. **They require that when the personages of a tale deal in con-versation, the talk shall sound like human talk, and be talk such as human beings would be likely to talk in the given circumstances, and have a discoverable meaning, also a discoverable purpose, and a show of relevancy, and remain in the neighborhood of the subject in hand, and be interesting to the reader, and help out the tale, and stop when the people cannot think of anything more to say.**

6. **They require that when the author describes the character of a personage in his tale, the conduct and conversation of that personage shall justify said description.**

7. **They require that when a personage talks like an illustrated, gilt-edged, tree-calf, hand-tooled, seven-dollar Friendship's Offer-ing in the beginning of a paragraph, he shall not talk like a Negro minstrel at the end of it.**

8. **They require that crass stupidities shall not be played upon the reader by either the author or the people in the tale.**

9. **They require that the personages of a tale shall confine them-selves to possibilities and let miracles alone; or, if they venture a miracle, the author must so plausibly set it forth as to make it look possible and reasonable.**

10. **They require that the author shall make the reader feel a deep interest in the personages of his tale and in their fate; and that he shall make the reader love the good people in the tale and hate the bad ones.**

11. **They require that the characters in a tale be so clearly de-**

fined that the reader can tell beforehand what each will do in a given emergency.

Dealing now with *how* you tell the story, Twain's Rules require that an author should:

12. *Say* **what he is proposing to say, not merely come near it.**
13. **Use the right word, not its second cousin.**
14. **Eschew surplusage.**
15. **Not omit necessary details.**
16. **Avoid slovenliness of form.**
17. **Use good grammar.**
18. **Employ a simple, straightforward style.**

And as for style, E.B. White says very much the same thing in his chapter, "An Approach to Style" in the book *The Elements of Style*. White goes into more detail: Twain's Rules are briefer, blunter, and easier to remember. Twain also goes into some fundamental principles of making your story—and above all, its cast of *people*—interesting, and believable, and true to what your readers know of life.

But all of these Rules and Examples and Observations are ways to obey an all-important Law: **You must seize, then hold, your readers' and editor's attention,** whether by reputation, or craft, or believability of characterization, or headlong flow of action, or otherwise. **Then, you must repay the readers' time and the editor's money by having something to share and sharing it,** whether information, or entertainment, or emotional involvement, or the like.

And this is a Law Not Wisely Broken.

Consider now exactly what reaches the printed pages of a magazine or a book: your choice of words and punctuation, the way you've wrapped the story idea in the English language . . . all that, yes. But not the actual pages that you've typed on; these are read by the editor, marked up by the copy-editor, and used by the typesetter to set the pages for printing—and go no farther. Your words and ideas are for the reader, but your manuscript is for the typesetter, and its format is set by what *she* demands.

Standardization is the first of those demands. A magazine may be typeset from a dozen manuscripts comprising some 300 pages or so; and the typesetter will have another, wholly different magazine to work on when she's finished that one. The only way she can cope is by imposing a standard format on all writers, by demanding consistency in page size, line-spacing, and the like.

Complete legibility is the second. The typesetter is not an English teacher nor a typing instructor; she is not at all concerned with how many mistakes you make in typing. What *does* concern her is to be able to read, without any ambiguity, every single word and punctuation mark on every page of every manuscript.

Closely allied to the need for legibility is clarity of instructions, as she translates what you have put down—limited as you are to the 88 or so symbols of your typewriter keyboard—into the five or six times that many symbols of her composing machine. Consequently, you must learn the typesetter's special language; and you must use it to tell her how to put your story into the form that the reader will finally see.

Innovation has no place in manuscript format: first, it hinders the typesetter, whom you want to follow instructions—quite literally—to the letter; second, innovation in format distracts your attention and that of the editor from the underlying *story;* and third, auctorial innovations in format are always misdirected. (Again and again we see manuscripts from authors who have suddenly "discovered" that typewriters are available with 1½ line settings as well as the conventional single-line-space and double-line-space; again and again we see return envelopes with postage "helpfully" attached by paper clip instead of glued to the envelope; again and again, we explain: double-line-space *means* double, not one-and-a-half, and affix postage means stick it onto the envelope!)

The appendix to this work contains complete instructions for manuscript format; the end-papers, a sample of a two-page story in manuscript form. Good format is invisible: the editor won't be distracted from the story, the copy-editor will have more time to spend on messier manuscripts, and the typesetter will—gratefully—find the story goes into type more easily. Good format is not at all the same thing as perfect typing, or even perfect proofreading; it is a matter of knowing *how,* and knowing *why,* and then *doing.* And, while good format cannot sell a basically bad story, too great a departure from acceptable format can make it very hard to sell a good story—and impossible to sell a marginal one.

The relevant Law, then: **You must put your story into a format which the editor knows the copy-editor can work with and the typesetter can set from.** And this, too, is a Law not wisely broken.

Many of you are terrified of rejection. We *know;* we've been there, too. We've commented elsewhere in these pages that it isn't you that is risking rejection; it's just some pieces of paper that have been typed on. And we know that this fact helps some—but not always enough. We know that many otherwise rational, moderately successful authors pursue a strategy of sending their stories to medium- or low-paying markets where they're sure of immediate sale, rather than sending each story first to the highest-paying market that might conceivably buy it, and only then working down the list to surer sales.

What we don't know is how to persuade authors to make more use of Scithers's Strategy: **It is more profitable to maximize income than to minimize rejections.** Nor do we know how to convince beginning writers that the *only* evaluation of their manuscripts that is at all significant is that of an editor who is paying money for manuscripts like theirs.

There is, of course, a Law, obviously not wisely broken. It is simply this: **You must put your work before an editor who might buy it.**

APPENDIX A:
MANUSCRIPT FORMAT

TYPING

All typesetters always insist that all manuscripts be legibly typed. Therefore, you must have some skill at typing, and you must have access to a typewriter.

If you lack both, we think that your first priority should be to get professional instruction in touch-typing. While it *is* possible to teach yourself this skill, most self-taught typists find that they have to struggle to un-learn a lot of self-taught bad habits later on. You will be better off, around the long orbit, to go to a good typing teacher at the beginning. Not only is typing a skill that is endlessly useful, but also your experience with the typing school's equipment will give you a very good idea of what to look for (and what to avoid) when you can buy a typewriter of your own.

Clearly, you must satisfy yourself with the *feel* of the keyboard; you must be comfortable with your machine's action. What matters to your editor is the legibility of the typed copy; and a 50-year-old, cast-iron-frame machine in good repair may well turn out better-looking copy than a brand-new, color-coördinated, electric portable. Typed characters should be in alignment, both horizontally and vertically; each keystroke should put a clear character on the page. Avoid battered typefaces, ribbon-mechanisms that miss part of any character or that don't reverse when they should, and rubber rollers (platens) that are hard and glazed from age. Editors and typesetters object to manuscripts typed in script or italic typefaces, in ALL CAPITAL LETTER typefaces, and in LARGE AND SMALL CAPITAL LETTER typefaces.

It is helpful but not essential to have the exclamation point (!) as a single character on your keyboard, rather than having to build it up from an apostrophe and a period. It is helpful to have the quotation mark and the apostrophe together on the key immediately to the right of the / key, because typing is just a little faster with this arrangement. Avoid typewriters whose capital **I** looks just like the lower-case **l**.

Since the red half of a red-&-black ribbon is useless for manuscript typing, buy all-black ribbons. Always have several on hand, and replace your working ribbon as soon as it prints gray instead of a clean, clear **black**. But watch for dirt building up on the type-bars (the things that actually hit the paper); before the letters **s, e,** and **o** begin to look like o's, clean the type-bars. Typewriter and stationery stores have the materials to do this, and their personnel can explain how to use them.

We don't think you should worry about getting a word-processor or other computer hardware until you are earning enough as a writer to pay for the equipment from those earnings. When you reach that point, the manuscripts you produce must still fit standard format. Editors do not like getting stories on long, fan-folded strips of paper, so you must produce standard, numbered pages. Typesetters have difficulty reading manuscripts produced by dot-matrix printers, because the lower-case letters **g, a,** and **s** from these printers look too much alike. Therefore, editors will not accept manuscripts produced by such printers.

Most word processors and other "smart" typewriters can justify the right margin. That is, they can vary the spacing between words, just as a typesetter does, to make the lines all come out even. Editors and typesetters do *not* want you to even up the right margin; we greatly prefer equal spacing between words, and justified margins do us no good whatever.

PAPER

Typesetters insist that you use *one* side only of each sheet of standard-sized, white paper. Twenty-pound bond paper is the weight most commonly used. Sixteen-pound is also acceptable, and saves on postage costs and storage space. Paper heavier than twenty-pound weight costs more, both for the paper and the postage, but doesn't make the story typed on it any more likely to be bought. Paper of high cotton-fiber content is more expensive; its one significant advantage is that such paper will last some decades longer in your files.

Standard size for paper is 8½ inches wide, 11 inches long. Paper that is 8 inches wide and 10 inches long will do if nothing else is available. Legal-length paper, 14 inches long, is not acceptable.

Stationery stores may try to sell you some kind of so-called easily erased papers, such as "Corrasable," "Racerase," "Ezerace," and the like. Refuse to buy *any* of them; insist on bond paper. The reason editors and typesetters hate the erasable papers is that they are slippery and hard to handle, typing on them smears easily, they take penciled or inked corrections badly, and they are translucent instead of opaque. Furthermore, you should never, never, *ever* make an erasure on a manuscript, because the erasure-and-retyping is never as unambiguously legible as an XXX'ed out word with the correction typed (or hand-printed) above or after the error.

If you are very good with Liquid Paper or other brand of correction fluid—essentially fast-drying white paint—you may use that. It's especially useful if you've made a correction and want to un-make it, or if you want to correct a punctuation mark; but we don't recommend it for more than two or three words at a time.

There is a kind of correction paper and tape that works by typing a chalky white material onto the error. Unfortunately, when the chalky material wears off again, as it inevitably will in handling, it's impossible to tell what's error and what's correction. Please do not use the stuff!

There is an entirely different kind of correction paper and tape that works by *lifting off* the error. Editors and typesetters have no objection to this kind of correction. However, remember that editors and typesetters are not grading your manuscript on appearance; XXX'ed out errors are perfectly acceptable to us and lots faster for you.

MARGINS

Leave about one-half inch between the top of the paper and the heading or page number, because your manuscript will probably be photocopied and most such machines won't reproduce anything too close to the edge. Leave a full inch margin between the top edge and the body copy.

Leave a full inch margin at the left edge of the paper

Leave at least a one-inch margin at the right edge of the paper. We recommend that you set the position of the bell of your typewriter 1-¾ inches from the right edge of the paper (that is, 18 spaces on a pica typewriter, or 21 spaces on an elite typewriter), then follow the rule: never start a new word after you hear the bell. Start a new line when you finish whatever word you're typing when that bell rings. Don't worry about the rare word that will extend to within a half-inch of the right margin; but if an end-of-line word should be even longer than *that,* cross out the whole word, start the next line, and put the word there. And never—ever—break a word with a hyphen at the end of a line in manuscript typing, because if you *do,* the typesetter will have to stop and decide: does this hyphen-broken word keep or drop that hyphen when it appears in the middle of a line of type?

Leave a full inch margin at the bottom of the page. Don't be afraid to put a visible mark, with a pencil or a pen, at the left edge of each sheet, an inch from the bottom, so that you will stop at the same place on every sheet.

The reasons for margins are to give the copy-editor room to put corrections or special instructions for the typesetter, and to make it easy to hold a sheet of manuscript without hiding part of the text with the fingers.

FIRST PAGE

Put your name and address in the upper left corner of the first page. This is the name to which the editor will make out the contract and check; this is the address to which the editor will return the manuscript; this is the single most important information you put on a manuscript (yet some writers leave it out!).

Put the word-count of your manuscript in the upper right corner of the first page. You won't know this number when you begin the manuscript; put it in when you've finished the manuscript and counted it.

Put the title of your story about 3½ inches down from the top of the first page, centered between the right and left margins. Put your by-line—the way you want your name (or pseudonym) to appear on the published story—directly under the title, similarly centered between left and right margins.

Begin the text of your story about 5½ inches down from the top of the first page; continue until you reach the bottom margin. (It is not necessary to put "more" or "continued" or the like at the bottom of any page of copy that reaches the bottom margin, and you should not do so.)

CONTINUATION PAGE

Put the heading of the next page—and of all following pages—in the upper right corner of the page about one-half inch down from the top edge. The reasons for top *right* are to reduce the chance that an unwary typesetter might start setting that heading into type and because manuscripts are usually paperclipped in the top *left* corner by the editor and others, which hides whatever might be in the left corner.

The heading should contain your name (last name alone if it's an uncommon one; initials and last name if you are Smith or Jones), then one word from the title of your story, and then the page number.

There are important reasons for each of these items. Your name serves to identify a stray page from your manuscript, should it come adrift in the editor's or the typesetters' offices. A significant word from the title of the story serves to identify a similar stray page in *your* office. And the page number is essential for putting the stray page back in its proper place in the manuscript.

Thus, you might use a heading such as **Thornley/Time/2,** or you might use **P Smith/African/5.**

LAST PAGE

It's necessary to have a very clear indication that this *is* the last page and nothing is missing. Some writers use a **- 30 -** centered between right and left margins. Some use a line of # # # # # symbols, because this is the typesetter's symbol for space. We think the most unambiguous way to show the end of a story is to type the word **END,** centered between right and left margins, below the last line of text, then draw a circle around the word and mark with a "delete" symbol, as shown in the endpapers.

SEPARATE TITLE PAGE

Some writers prefer to use a separate title page, especially with longer works, such as novellas and complete novels. A separate title page is just like a first page, except that it contains no text, just headings, title, by-line, and word-count. In a manuscript with a separate title page, page number *one* is the first page *with text*, and the title page does not get a page number.

The advantage of using a separate title page is that, should the top page of a manuscript be damaged or worn and need retyping, it's easier to replace. The disadvantage is that there's one more sheet of paper to buy and to pay postage on.

CHAPTER HEADINGS

Many long novellas and novels are divided into chapters. Some writers will end a chapter, skip a couple of extra lines, insert the name or number of the next chapter, skip a couple of extra lines, and begin the text of that chapter. Others will leave blank the balance of the page on which a chapter ends, inserting the note: **END CHAPTER 3** with a circle around the note and a delete symbol so *that* note won't be set in type; and then put **CHAPTER 4** about 3½ inches down from the top of the next page, with the text of that chapter beginning about 5½ inches down from the top of that page. Either is acceptable, so long as you stick to one system or the other throughout any given work. In any case, the copy-editor will mark up the chapter headings to conform with the design of the magazine or book, telling the typesetter about spacing, type-styles, and so on.

TEXT or BODY COPY

Set the line spacing of your typewriter so that it will "double-space," which means that you will advance the paper two full lines every time you return the carriage. Some typewriters can be set for 1½ lines; do *not* use this setting. The reason you must use the full two-line setting is to provide a full blank line between every pair of typed lines. This gives you plenty of room for corrections; this gives the copy-editor plenty of room for more corrections; this makes the manuscript easier for the typesetter to read.

Use this full double-line-spacing for *all*—we **do** mean *all*—manuscript text. If you want an excerpt, such as an extended quotation, to be set off, then tell the copy-editor what you want by a pencilled marginal note and by leaving an extra couple of blank lines at the beginning and end of the excerpt. If necessary, put in pencilled notes such as "continue set-off " and "end of set-off " on following pages of a multi-page item. But *your* typing must be all fully double-line-spaced. The copy-editor will decide what spacing and type size will be used by the typesetter, and mark the manuscript accordingly.

Set the first tab of your typewriter for an indentation of exactly five spaces. (Standardization here is an aid to word-counting, as well as reducing the chance of the typesetter misreading your text.) Indent the first paragraph—and all following paragraphs—five spaces. Note that in ordinary dialog, each new speaker gets a new paragraph, with customary five-space indentation. (Very rarely, you may want to have the typesetter indent a line by more than the customary amount. To tell her to do this, make a marginal note, **Indent 2-M,** for double the normal indentation.)

Note carefully how quotation marks are placed in the end-papers; note that the quotation marks closely surround the quoted material and its associated punctuation. If one speaker speaks without inter-ruption for more than one paragraph, just as in the authors' comments at the end of each of the stories in this book, then each paragraph of that speech begins with indentation and quotation marks, but only the *last* paragraph of his speech will close with quotation marks.

If you wish to indicate to the reader that there is a break between paragraphs of greater than routine importance, as for a scene change or a lapse of time, tell the typesetter to leave a blank line there (re-member that typeset, printed copy is set single-spaced, so one blank line is very noticeable) by skipping *three* blank lines between para-graphs in your manuscript, inserting the # symbol in the middle of that extra blank space. Do *not* skip more than the customary one blank line between paragraphs elsewhere in your manuscript; reserve the extra space for definite breaks in the flow of action.

WORD COUNT

There are several ways to count words. The most generous of the accepted ways to do this, "printers' rule," is obviously the one that you should use. If the editor to whom you have submitted a story prefers another way of counting words, it's up to that editor to say so. This word count actually measures space, rather than "counting"; it works like this:

1. Put a ruler along an average-length, mid-paragraph line in your manuscript, that is, a line that looks to be longer than about half the mid-paragraph lines on a typical page, and shorter than the other half. By counting and measuring, find out how many typed characters plus spaces plus punctuation marks there are in that line (e.g., 10 characters and spaces per inch and a 6-inch line equals 60 characters and spaces to the line).

2. Divide this number by 6.

3. Multiply the result by the number of lines per manuscript page.

4. Now, multiply that result by the number of pages, correcting for partly-filled pages at the beginning, the end, and so on. This number, then, is the number of five-letter-plus-one-space "words," assuming that all short lines are counted as if they were full lines.

Since the typesetter will be leaving short lines and blank space in about the same proportion that you have in your manuscript, this "count" gives an accurate estimate of how much space your typeset story will occupy. Put this word count in the upper right corner of the first page (or title page if there is one) of your manuscript.

RIGHTS OFFERED

This is a subject where you must know what you are doing before putting words down on paper. If you are dealing with the specialized SF magazines, or if you are offering a complete novel for sale to a reputable hardcover or paperback publisher, no note is necessary. With these magazines, the rights they want to buy (strictly speaking, they are renting the use of the story under certain conditions, but the phrase "buying rights" is customary usage) are specified by contract or by an endorsement on the check offered in payment. Generally, magazines buy First North American Serial Rights. Some buy certain foreign rights as well; some take an option on certain non-exclusive anthology rights. In every case, the signed contract or the endorsement on a check that you sign overrides any notation you may have made on a manuscript.

Book publishers buy an entirely different set of rights, and these cannot be summarized in a single phrase. Book publishers buy material by means of detailed, printed contracts that must be signed by all parties to the transaction. Consequently, there is no point in trying to put down what rights to book-length material you are offering; wait for the publisher to send back a contract and then start negotiating. (Elsewhere we've recommended that when you get an acceptance from a book publisher is the very best time to find an agent to negotiate the contract, with the understanding that you and the agent might want to continue the relationship.)

Is there any point in specifying rights offered at all? Very rarely. If you submit a story to markets which try to buy substantially more than First North American Serial Rights plus *specified* foreign and anthology rights—some men's magazines, for example, will try to buy "All Rights" or to specify that yours is a "Work For Hire"—it's well to put them on notice that you are going to argue about such an offer.

And if you should sell a story to a market that is so casual in its dealings that it simply sends out a check in payment without a clear, written understanding of exactly what rights have been offered and accepted, then the notation **First North American Serial Rights** may save a lot of argument later.

First here means that the manuscript has not been published in any form anywhere in the world, and that you agree that you will not permit any other publication until after it has been published by the buyer. **North American** is generally taken to mean publication in the United States, in English, with primary distribution to the United States and Canada (or simultaneous publication in the United States and Canada), along with some distribution of copies of the publication throughout the world. **Serial** means in a magazine or newspaper, whether in one installment or several, instead of book publication.

Leaving out any part of this phrase changes the meaning more than you might expect. **First North American Rights** means the right to print the work in a magazine *and* a book *and* to produce the work as a movie *and* to use it on tee-shirts . . . do you get the idea? Similarly, the phrase **First Rights** means the buyer can have the work published on tea bags in Sri Lanka. (If what you want to say is that the story has never been published before, use the phrase **Not Previously Published.**)

The phrase **All Rights** means exactly that: *all.* The phrase **Work For Hire** is even worse; it means that you agree that you were an employee of the buyer, that the work was done at the buyer's direction, and that the buyer owns everything connected with the work *forever.* We strongly recommend that you avoid such an arrangement unless you are actually producing a work to order, such as advertising copy or the like.

To summarize, then: Don't specify what rights you are offering unless you think you must. If you do, put down the entire phrase **First North American Serial Rights** in the upper right corner of the first page (or title page) of your manuscript, right under the word count. Anything more complicated than this belongs in a cover letter, where you can explain, in plain language, exactly what you mean.

HYPHENS, DASHES, & ELLIPSES

The hyphen (-) and the dash (—) are completely different marks of punctuation, both in meaning and on a typeset, printed page. To tell the typesetter you want a hyphen, simply type one in place. If you are putting a hyphen in by hand, use the = sign, with a circle around it to make it more noticeable (unless you can put the = in the middle of a word). Use the = sign, circled, next to any end-of-line hyphens if the hyphen is to be retained when the word is put in the middle of a line by the typesetter. (You shouldn't break words at the ends of lines at all, when typing manuscript copy; but if you forget and break "mother-in-" on one line and "law" on the next, this is how to tell the typesetter to keep the hyphen after "in" when setting. If you broke "sis-" and "ter" onto two lines, then mark the hyphen after "sis" with the delete symbol. Until you have trained yourself never to break words at the ends of lines, check over each completed manuscript to so mark any end-of-line hyphens.)

The dash, which is used to set off phrases—like this—and to show an abrupt interruption, especially in dialog ("That's imposs—"), doesn't appear on your typewriter keyboard. (Yes, we know that you can imitate one by using the underline key; please don't.) To tell the typesetter that you want the standard, "one em" dash: leave a space, type *two* hyphens, then leave a space, like -- so. (Some writers use *three* hyphens and no spaces; this is also acceptable. Whichever you use, be consistent.) The reason for using more than a single hyphen is to make it easy for the typesetter to tell that it's a dash that you want. If you insert a dash in a manuscript by hand, put in **1/M** or a **1** over a horizontal line over an **M**.

For special situations, such as expressing dates like 1812–1945, the typesetter has a "one en" dash, which you can call for by typing two or three hyphens, then printing a **1** above and an **N** below the hyphens. There are also 2/M and 3/M dashes available, called for as shown.

In formal writing, scholarly papers and the like, the ellipsis is used to show an omission: "If you don't get a reader's attention in the first paragraph, the rest of your message is lost," becomes: "If you don't get a reader's attention, . . . your message is lost." Note that the ellipsis itself, three periods, has spaces between the periods, as well as before and after the set. Punctuation—in addition to the ellipsis itself—goes in as needed to make sense. "What do you hear? What do you see?" becomes: "What do you hear? . . . see?" But "What do you hear?" can become: "What do you . . . ?" One exception to the spacing rule: quotation marks close up to the periods at the beginning or the end of an ellipsis which they enclose. Thus: "You must *finish* what you write," becomes: ". . . *finish* . . ."

Both dashes and ellipses are used in dialog and to a lesser extent in narration to show irregularities in speech or thought that cannot be easily shown by conventional punctuation. Generally, a dash at the end of a word or word-fragment shows an abrupt interruption; a dash in the middle of a line of dialog shows an abrupt change of subject. An ellipsis, on the other hand, shows the speaker's voice fading away rather than being interrupted, shows faltering speech instead of abrupt shifts; in both speech and narrative, an ellipsis can show an uncompleted thought. Thus: "Call for help—bandages—stop the bleeding!" and, "It hurts . . . getting weaker . . . can't keep . . ." by rescuer and victim, respectively.

TYPESETTERS' SPECIAL FONTS

The basic type-font which the typesetter is using in this paragraph is called "roman," sometimes "upright." It is the most readable font available, is used for the bulk of the text being typeset, and is what the typesetter will set if not told to do something else. To call for something to be set in roman when there is a chance for confusion, as an isolated word to be set in roman in the middle of a line of some other type, or to make a change in what's called for, use the marginal note **Rom** and circle the words to be set in roman.

This paragraph is set in italics. Since it is not as easy to read as roman type, you should not use it for more than a short paragraph or so at a time. Italics are also used for foreign words, especially when you want the reader to realize that they are foreign; for emphasis; and for the titles (typed in capitals and lower case) of books, magazines, movies, and ships. Tell the typesetter to use italics by underlining; please do not shift to an italic typeface in your typewriter, because a typewriter italic face is not as easy to spot as underlining is. The marginal note, **Ital,** *can be used as needed, especially for long paragraphs like this one.*

The usual way to show emphasis and so on in the middle of a line of italics is to reverse back to roman type, thus:

Is this all *there is?* he thought to himself.

And, as just shown, italics are sometimes used instead of quotation marks to set off what your characters are thinking, rather than saying aloud. Titles of stories shorter than whole books, of chapters, and of TV programs are set in roman type, within quotation marks. Names of buildings, bars, and the like take initial capitals, in roman type, without quotation marks. Thus: the Empire State Building and Gavagan's Bar, the *Millennium Falcon* and the *U.S.S. Enterprise,* "The Tryouts" and "They'll Do It Every Time," *Isaac Asimov's Science Fiction Magazine* and *Newsweek, Dune* and *Double Star,* "Night Gallery" and "Star Trek," but *Star Trek—the Motion Picture* and *The Empire Strikes Back.*

Bold face type, like this sentence, is less often used than italics. Call for bold face with a wiggly line under the words to be so set, plus the marginal notation **Bold** or **B.F.** This font is used for emphasis when italics are somehow inappropriate, as in a paragraph already cluttered with italicized foreign words, book titles, and the like. It is also useful to set off words or single letters: "He entered the **M** wing, strolled past the **Keep Out!** and the **TRESPASSERS WILL BE EATEN!** signs, and finally reached his destination: . . ."

Some typesetters also have ***BOLD ITALICS,*** as in **TRESPASSERS WILL BE EATEN!** but some do not. In any case, you will seldom need them.

SMALL CAPITALS, called for by underlining with two parallel lines and the marginal notation **SC** or **Small Caps,** are used for 6:00 A.M.,

4 P.M., 436 B.C. (but note that it's A.D. 1776). Small capitals can also be used to set off words less emphatically than bold face: ". . . reached his destination: a door modestly marked DEPARTMENT OF ANTHRO-POPHAGY." Note that some small capitals are indistinguishable from lower case: c, o, s, v, w, x, and z.

Typesetters also have a variety of symbols available, such as the Greek letters and what is called the "pi font"; here are some:

£ ¡ ℓ ° ◇ ¿ ⋙ [⑂ ○ □] ℞ ˏ ˘ ‡ ˜ ` ´ ¶ ® ♀ ♂ © § ☆

However, it is not all that easy to set these symbols; please hold your use of them to a minimum. It's all right to describe something as ☆-shaped, or to mention the £-symbol; but a page of "♂ said" and "♀ said" is more than most editors will put up with.

COVER LETTERS

It's usually best for the writer to say as little as possible about his story in a cover letter. On the other hand, cover letters often save editors no end of time and trouble by—quite inadvertently—telling the editor that the manuscript is quite hopeless without putting the editor to the trouble of reading that manuscript through. Telling the editor how desperately you need money, or mentioning which other editors have rejected the manuscript—and why—won't help your chances of sale at all. We generally say that if you want to write a cover letter for a short story, do; and if you don't want to, then don't.

There are two situations where a cover letter *is* essential: first, when the rights offered or previous publishing history are at all complicated ("This 90,000 word novel, *Warring Stars,* is expanded from a limerick by the author which appeared in the June, 1976 issue of *Arthur Clarke's Science Fiction Magazine.*"), and second, when this story is being re-submitted to an editor who has seen it before ("This story was sub-mitted to you in June, 1980. You rejected it because having the Sun go nova at the end made for a futile ending. Accordingly, I have completely rewritten everything past page 23, resolving the basic prob-lems of the heroine and her three house-husbands. Minor changes were also made on pages 6 and 12.").

If you feel you simply must say something so that the editor will begin to recognize you as more than just another name in the man-uscript-heap, then go ahead—but for Goodness' sake, be cheerful and friendly about it. If you keep files on everything—and you really should—then a formal letter ("Dear Madam: The enclosed story, 'Wars and Stars,' is submitted for your consideration.") will provide, by means of a dated carbon copy, a written record of when you sent the story out, and to whom.

MANUSCRIPT FORMAT

COPIES

Never send out your last copy of any manuscript. If you have access to photocopying services, make a good copy of your finished, copy-edited manuscript. Mark that copy, **Not a simultaneous submission** (which simply means that you are not sending another copy of this manuscript to anyone else at this time—magazine editors refuse to read material that is being seen by some other editor at the same time), then keep the original in your files and send out the photocopy.

The photocopy must be wholly legible—legible enough, in fact, for another photocopy to be made from the one you've just made. Plain paper copies, like those made by Xerox or IBM brand copiers, are best. Other kinds of photocopies are acceptable, provided that they are clear and legible, and provided that they can be marked on with pencils, ball-point pens, and ordinary pens.

If you don't have access to a photocopying service, make a good carbon copy of the manuscript as you type it. Copy all your corrections onto the carbon copy, and then keep that carbon safely in your files.

COPY-EDITING & CORRECTIONS

For the writer, copy-editing is going over one's manuscript after the final typing is completed, checking for mistakes—from making sure the heroine's name is spelled the same all the way through the story; through checking for omitted words, typing errors, and the like; and on to marking up those errors, making other marginal notes like **Small Caps** or **Greek letter alpha**—and generally making the manuscript ready for the publisher's copy-editor.

For the copy-editor, copy-editing is catching all the mistakes the writer missed. Obviously, the better you do your job, the less chance that an error will slip by both of you. More important, perhaps: the better you clean up your mistakes and the more professionally marked-up your manuscript is, the less the copy-editor is likely to meddle with the way you want your story to appear.

Basically, then: put a just-finished manuscript aside for a day or so, long enough so that you can come at it afresh. Then read it carefully, word for word, with a spelling dictionary at hand, checking everything: spelling, punctuation, capitalization; your characters' names, their appearances, their speech mannerisms; *everything*.

Ghastly errors may require retyping a page or two; for others, slip a page back into the typewriter and type in the correct word or words in the space between the already-typed lines, always putting the corrections *above* the errors. If there is more correction than will fit between the lines, either retype that page, or—sometimes—type a few lines (*always* double-line-spaced!) on a sheet of paper, trim it to fit, and carefully paste or glue it over the mistake. Do *not* use cellophane tape to affix your correction sheets, because it's impossible to make corrections on that slick surface. Minor corrections may be inserted—carefully and legibly!—by hand-printing above the mistakes, remembering to distinguish between capital and lower-case letters.

If you must add a page in the middle of a short manuscript, renumber the following pages to fit; similarly with removing a page. For a very long manuscript, you may use **A** and **B** pages thus: add **-A** to the page number of the page immediately before the added page. Then give the added page the same page number, but with **-B** instead of **-A.** If necessary, go on to **-C.** Right under the page number of the final page of a run of added pages, put **next page is page number** —— and fill in the appropriate page number. Thus, page numbers might run: 26, 27, 28-A, 28-B, 29, 30, . . . And on page 28-B, you would note: **next page is page 29.** If things get any more complicated than this, renumber the whole manuscript.

If, on the other hand, you come up with one less page in the middle of a long manuscript, put in a full-sized, otherwise blank page with just the author-name/story-name/page number in the upper right corner.

A correction, with or without an adjustment for page numbers, may leave a page with just a few typed lines at the top and the rest blank, somewhere in the middle of the manuscript. Do *not* retype the rest of the manuscript! Simply type (or hand-print) the words **run on, no paragraph** if the text should indeed continue without beginning a new paragraph; or **close to new paragraph** if that's what's intended, or **close to one line space** if there is a scene break at that point. In every case, circle these instructions and attach a delete symbol, so that the typesetter won't be tempted to set them into type.

What you may *not* do—ever—is to ask the typesetter to stop in the middle of a manuscript page, go find an insert on another page, and then go back to the first page again. You must *always* put the manuscript into the order that it is to be set, no matter how much cutting and splicing of pages or even retyping that requires you to do.

Some of the typesetting symbols $\frac{|}{M}$ the
special language of writers, copy-editors, and type-
setters $\frac{|}{M}$ are useful in making yourself clearly
understood, like the delete symbol on the word
typesetter, above. Note how we've asked the   /BF
typesetter to use bold face, both above and   / BF
here. To call for italics, simply underline;
please do not shift to an italic typing element.
¶ Since we should have begun ~~this sentence with~~
here,
a new paragraph∧ but forgot to indent, we've
~~marked~~ put in the ¶ symbol.
Whenever you take out a letter with the
delete symbol, as above, you must show whether
the typesetter should close up, like this; and
when she must leave a space, as here. (Exception:
you don't have to show either close up or leave
space when the correction is this obvious.)

When you insert a period by hand, put a

circle around it, so that it's clear it <u>is</u>

a period, not a bit of dirt on the paper⊙

When you ma~~c~~k a transposition err~~n~~g, you can   //𝓉𝓏

use the transposition symbol, as above. But it
                    clearer
is even ~~cleaarre~~∧ if you ~~ccrss~~ cross out the

scrambled word and put in the correct version.

Some of the typesetting symbols—the special language of writers, copy-editors, and typesetters—are useful in making yourself clearly understood, like the delete symbol on the word **typesetter,** above. Note how we've asked the typesetter to use **bold face,** both above and here. To call for *italics,* simply underline; please do *not* shift to an italic typing element.

Since we should have begun a new paragraph here, but forgot to indent, we've put in the ¶ symbol.

When ever you take out a letter with the delete symbol, as above, you must show whether the typesetter should close up, like this; and when she must leave a space, as here. (Exception: you don't have to show either close up or leave space when the correction is this obvious.)

When you insert a period by hand, put a circle around it, so that it's clear it *is* a period, not a bit of dirt on the paper. When you make a transposition error, you can use the transposition symbol, as above. But it is even clearer if you cross out the scrambled word and put in the correct version.

To insert a hyphen, use the = sign, as
we've done with "son in-law" here. If the word "son-
in-law" had been broken at a hyphen that should
be retained when it's put in the middle of a
line, mark that hanging hyphen as we did above.

#

Note the section-break symbol, above. for
putting a letter into capitals, triple-underline,
then put Caps in the margin. On the other
hand, to lower-case a letter inadvertantly
typed in capitals, Run a diagonal slash through
it and marginally note L.C. For small caps,
double-underline; the marginal note is Small
Caps or just S.C.
In principal, one can correct individual
letters in a word. In practice, it's better
to change out the entire word. In principle
you can cancel a correction and go back to the
original version by running dots under the
mistaken correction and putting stet in the
margin; in practice things get very messy
very quickly, and you'd best reach for the

```
correction fluid or else make a marginal note.

    Two final words: make your copy-editing

corrections carefully and very legibly; and        /BF
                          #a
don't be afraid to spell out exactly what you

mean in a marginal note ⅂ that's what margins
                        ⁀
are for.

                    #
```

To insert a hyphen, use the = sign, as we've done with "son-in-law" here. If the word "son-in-law" had been broken at a hyphen that should be retained when it's put in the middle of a line, mark that hanging hyphen as we did above.

Note the section-break symbol, above. For putting a letter into capitals, triple-underline, then put **Caps** in the margin. On the other hand, to lower-case a letter inadvertently typed in capitals, run a diagonal slash through it and marginally note **L.C.** For SMALL CAPS, double-underline; the marginal note is **Small Caps** or just **S.C.**

In principle, one can correct individual letters in a word. In practice, it's better to change out the entire word. In principle, you can cancel a correction and go back to the original version by running dots under the mistaken correction and putting **stet** in the margin; in practice things get very messy very quickly, and you'd best reach for the correction fluid or else make a marginal note.

Two final words: make your copy-editing corrections *carefully* and **very** *legibly;* and don't be afraid to spell out exactly what you mean in a marginal note—that's what margins are for.

PROOFREADING

Briefly, proofreading is the same process as copy-editing, except that you're working with typeset copy with no blank lines for corrections. Thus you have to mark the *location* of your correction in the copy, and explain what's wrong with a marginal note.

Most dictionaries give a list of proofreading symbols. The ones that you'll have the most use for are these:

Show an apostrophe's location by a small **v,** coming from above just like the apostrophe itself; in the margin, draw an apostrophe, again in a **V** in order to distinguish it from a comma.

Commas, then, are located by a caret (**∧**), rather like a capital **A** without the cross-bar, coming from below, just as the comma itself does. The marginal notation is, again, a hand-drawn comma within a caret.

Quotation marks, obviously, are much like apostrophes; "coming from above," and are drawn in a **V** in the margin. In the body of the text, location is marked by a small **v.** When necessary for clarity, especially when it's possible to mix up single quotes and apostrophes, show which way these marks curve as you draw them. A common error to watch for is reversal of quote marks so that they hook away from the enclosed material, instead of hooking toward that material, as they are supposed to do.

Circle words that should be in roman type instead of italic; marginal note: **Rom.** Underline words that should be italic instead of roman; marginal note: **Ital.** or **Italics.** Similarly for bold face and so on.

Circle misspelled words; spell out correctly in the margin. Mark location of missing with a short vertical line; spell out in the margin. For punctuation marks other than apostrophes, commas, semi-colons and quotation marks, mark location with a vertical line and show in margin; then circle the correct punctuation mark you've drawn in the margin to make it clear this *is* a punctuation mark and not a random squiggle. Careful penmanship will make clear the difference between the colon(:) and the semi-colon (;), but most writers and proofreaders prefer to put the semi-colon under a caret to avoid confusion. Since a circled question mark can also mean, "What's going on here?" it's well to put the word **set** beside the circled **?** when you do want it inserted at the location marked.

[Here, now, is the section on proofreading, reset with corrections.]

PROOFREADING

Briefly, proofreading is the same process as copy-editing, except that you're working with typeset copy with no blank lines for corrections. Thus you have to mark the *location* of your correction in the copy, and explain what's wrong with a marginal note.

Most dictionaries give a list of proofreading symbols. The ones that you'll have the most use for are these:

Show an apostrophe's location by a small **v,** coming from above just like the apostrophe itself; in the margin, draw an apostrophe, again in a **V** in order to distinguish it from a comma.

Commas, then, are located by a caret (**ʌ**), rather like a capital **A** without the cross-bar, coming from below, just as the comma itself does. The marginal notation is, again, a hand-drawn comma within a caret.

Quotation marks, obviously, are much like apostrophes; "coming from above," and are drawn in a **V** in the margin. In the body of the text, location is marked by a small **v.** When necessary for clarity, especially when it's possible to mix up single quotes and apostrophes, show which way these marks curve as you draw them. A common error to watch for is reversal of quote marks so that they hook away from the enclosed material, instead of hooking toward that material, as they are supposed to do.

Circle words that should be in roman type instead of italic; marginal note: **Rom.** *Underline* words that should be in italic instead of roman; marginal note: **Ital. or Italics.** Similarly for bold face and so on.

Circle misspelled words; spell out correctly in the margin. Mark location of missing words with a short vertical line; spell out in the margin. For punctuation marks other than apostrophes, commas, semi-colons and quotation marks, mark location with a vertical line and show in margin; then circle the correct punctuation mark you've drawn in the margin to make it clear this *is* a punctuation mark and not a random squiggle. Careful penmanship will make clear the difference between the colon (:) and the semi-colon(;), but most writers and proofreaders prefer to put the semi-colon under a caret to avoid confusion. Since a circled question mark can also mean, "What's going on here?" it's well to put the word **set** beside the circled **?** when you do want it inserted at the location marked.

MANUSCRIPT FORMAT

RETURN ENVELOPE

This is almost the final step. Get a *new* 9 inch by 12 inch envelope. (Use a 10 by 14 if you must.) Address it legibly to yourself, with the address parallel to the 12-inch length of the envelope. Weigh the envelope plus your manuscript. Mark the envelope either **First Class** or **Special Fourth Class: Letter Enclosed.** If you mark it **First Class,** put on postage in the proper amount; if you use the other endorsement—which means that you are paying at the lower rate for books and other literary materials *plus* postage for the editor's reply to you—then put on postage equal to the book rate for that weight *plus* whatever the postage is for a first-class letter at that time. In either case, stick the stamps to the envelope, in the upper right corner of the envelope. Do not *ever* paper clip the stamps to the envelope.

If the envelope won't fit into your typewriter so you can type the address parallel to the 12-inch length, type the address on a gummed label and stick that to the envelope. If your manuscript has six pages or less, you may use what stationery stores call a business or number ten envelope—about 9½ inches long, about 4 inches wide. If your manuscript is too big for a 10 by 14 envelope, you'll have to send it in a box of some kind; for the return, include a self-addressed label that is big enough to comfortably hold the return postage as well, and affix the postage to that label. Do not in any case send a padded "bubble" or "jiffy" bag as a return envelope. (If your manuscript won't fit in a 10 by 14, it's probably too long to appear in one issue of a magazine; *Asimov's* does not buy serials, *Analog Science Fiction* and *The Magazine of Fantasy and Science Fiction* do.)

If it's cheaper for you to have the editor throw away the photocopy of the story that you send him while you make another photocopy for the next submission, rather than enclose return postage for the whole manuscript, tell the editor, "Dispose of this copy if not bought." But you must still enclose a letter-sized, self-addressed envelope with first class postage affixed for the editor's reply; and you must never tell an editor to dispose of what appears to be the original copy of a manuscript, because if you do, he will decide you don't think much of the material—and he won't either.

If you cannot get U.S. stamps for the return postage, either include International Postal Reply Coupons—three will be enough postage for an ordinary air-mail letter across the ocean—or an International Postal Money Order or Bank Money Order, payable in U.S. dollars, for the estimated amount of return postage. Or, if the return envelope and manuscript weigh just a few ounces, some magazines (*Asimov's* is one) will accept a few colorful, local postage stamps for our stamp-collecting friends.

OUTGOING ENVELOPE

Fold the 9 by 12 envelope once, with the fold *across* the middle, parallel to the 9-inch width. Address a second, new 9 by 12 (10 by 14 if necessary) envelope to the editor you're submitting the manuscript to. Be sure to put your return address in the upper left corner of the envelope. Put the manuscript on the return envelope, the cover letter (if any) on top, and put on one paper clip that is big enough to comfortably hold them all. Put manuscript and so on into the outgoing envelope. Seal. Weigh. Affix postage as before. (If you don't include a cover letter, you don't have to use the "letter-enclosed" part of the marking, or the extra postage for same.) Be sure postage is adequate. If you feel you must reinforce the flap, it's better to do so with gummed tape than with cellophane (or "Scotch") tape; and remember to leave the corners free so the editor can get a letter opener in easily.

Do *not* staple manuscripts. Do *not* enclose them in folders. Do *not* include cardboard stiffeners in the envelope. Do *not* use padded envelopes; if the manuscript is too big for a 10 by 14, use a small box for it.

If the manuscript is six pages or less, you may use a number ten envelope to send it to the editor; in that case, fold the return envelope twice, parallel to the short dimension, into thirds, so that it will fit easily into the outgoing envelope.

Since the *only* protection that you have against loss of your manuscript, whether in the mails or in the editor's hands, is keeping a good copy—or the master copy—safe in your files, it is a waste of your money and the editor's time to send manuscripts by insured, certified, or registered mail.

Once the manuscript is mailed, get to work on your next one. If you don't hear from an editor in about 30 days, send a brief, polite letter, giving the title of the manuscript, your name and address, and the date you sent the manuscript; and ask if the editor received it. It's helpful to include a self-addressed, stamped postcard for the reply.

APPENDIX B:
THE RULES

The first group of Rules are those that do not appear elsewhere in the text; the second, those that do.

Le Guin's Rule for Writing SF:
    If you wanta write it you gotta read it.
Obis's Law:
    Somebody else probably has the same idea—so (a) get started, (b) plan to do it better.
Grizzly Pete's Advice:
    The most successful liar is the one who lies the least. (Col. William C. Hunter)
William Sloane's Essential Query:
    Who is the reader *being* as he reads?
Occam's Razor:
    Entities ought not to be multiplied except from necessity. (William of Occam, XVIth century) (See also H.G. Wells's Rule, below)
Whitehead's Warning:
    Seek simplicity—and distrust it. (Alfred North Whitehead)
Nolan's Observation:
    The difference between smart people and dumb people isn't that smart people don't make mistakes. They just don't keep making the same mistake over and over again.
Old Boy's Law:
    You don't learn anything the second time you're kicked by a mule.
Greener's Law:
    Never argue with a man who buys ink by the barrel.
Tromberg's Law:
    Just because you can do it doesn't mean you can make a living at it.

King of Hearts' Rule: [page] 1
    Begin at the beginning, and go on till you come to the end; then stop.
Asimov's General Principles: see pp 1-4
The Truth of the Matter : 5
    A writer is one who *writes*. You become one by writing.

Heinlein's Five Rules for Writing: see pp 8-10
Campbell's Remark: 10
> The reason 99% of all stories written are not bought by editors is very simple. Editors *never* buy manuscripts that are left on the closet shelf at home.

Scithers's Saving Statement: 10, 193
> Editors do not reject people; they reject pieces of paper that have typing on them.

William Sloane's Goal of Writing: see p 12
James Gunn's Outline: see pp 13-15
John M. Ford's Suggestion: 13, 18
> Observe, don't imitate.

H.G. Wells's Teaching: 14
> [You] must trick [the reader] into an unwary concession to some plausible assumption and get on with [your] story while the illusion holds.

The Ancient Rule for Westerns: 14, 190
> Shoot the sheriff in the first paragraph.

Linus Pauling's Ideation: 17
> The best way to have a good idea is to have lots of ideas.

John W. Campbell's Observation: 19, 117
> The future doesn't happen one at a time.

H.G. Wells's Rule: 19-20
> The thing that makes such imaginations interesting is their translation into commonplace terms and a rigid exclusion of other marvels from the story.

Sturgeon's Definition: 57
> A science-fiction story is a story with a human problem, and a human solution, that would not have happened at all without its scientific content.

Campbell's Categorization: 57
> For above all else, a story—science fiction or otherwise—is a story of human beings.

Sherlock Holmes's Reproof: 57
> You *see*, Watson, but you do not *observe*.

Sir Alec Guinness's Reassurance: 57-58
> In every kind of fantasy . . . there must be an anchor in reality, to contrast with all the bizarre elements.

Schweitzer's Law: 59
> Ugliness for its own sake is not realism.

Gunn's Paraphrase on Characterization: see p 61
Delany's Character's Observation: see p 61
Sharon Webb's Theory: 98
> Reading is a vicarious experience in which, for a short time, order can be perceived in existence; the reader can thereby hope for order in his or her own life rather than futility and chaos.

Aristotle's Dictum: 100
> A likely impossibility is always preferable to an unconvincing possibility.

Mark Twain's Obligation: 100
> Truth *is* stranger than Fiction, but it is because Fiction is obliged to stick to possibilities; Truth isn't.

THE RULES   217

APPENDIX B

AN ANNOTATED BIBLIOGRAPHY

On Writing:

Writing is an idiosyncratic business, and what works for one person may well not work for another; the value of any book on writing is limited to pointing out mistakes, showing how to avoid them, and getting you to think about various aspects of your craft that you haven't considered before. No book can teach you how to write (that must be learned at the typewriter), much less *what* to write (that comes from your life, your perceptions, and your imagination), but those listed below can help.

Strunk, William, and White, E.B. *The Elements of Style.* Third edition. Macmillan Publishing Co., 866 Third Ave., New York NY 10022. Hardcover and paperbound editions available. A classic; absolutely essential. You may begin by learning from this book, then by disagreeing with it, and still later by realizing that the authors were right all along. White himself observes: "Writing good standard English is no cinch, and before you have managed it you will have encountered enough rough country to satisfy even the most adventurous spirit." Many of you will see nothing wrong with the sentence: "A period of unfavorable weather set in." This book shows you that it's better to say: "It rained every day for a week," and *why.* Buy the hardcover edition, for you must re-read this book over and over again. Of it, William Sloane wrote, "Get hold of the Strunk and White essay on style and you better believe it."

Barzun, Jacques. *Simple & Direct: a Rhetoric for Writers.* Harper & Row, Publishers, 10 East 53rd St., New York NY 10022. Hardcover and paper. A clear exposition of the basics of good English prose, this book covers the material that most books on writing *assume* you already understand. There are chapters on word choice, diction, tone, meaning, composition, and revision. Exercises and examples are included.

Zinsser, William. *On Writing Well: An Informal Guide to Writing Nonfiction.* Harper & Row, Publishers, 10 East 53rd St., New York NY 10022. Hardcover. More practical advice. Particularly strong on humor: "If you're trying to write humor, almost everything that you do is serious." (Zinsser more than justifies this statement.) On the need for revision: "But the secret of good writing is to strip every sentence to its cleanest components."

Swain, Dwight V. *Techniques of the Selling Writer.* Second edition, revised. University of Oklahoma Press, 1005 Asp Ave., Norman OK 73019. Hardcover. A careful, detailed exposition of the principles of good story construction. His discussions of "motivation-reaction units" and how to arrange a scene are particularly helpful. Swain suggests that you use his rules not as dogma, but as a way of spotting and correcting flaws in what you have written—good advice for any book on writing.

Sloane, William. *The Craft of Writing.* (Edited by Julia H. Sloane.) W. W. Norton & Co., 500 Fifth Ave., New York NY 10036. Hardcover. Assembled posthumously from a series of notes and lectures. Sloane was not only a brilliant science-fiction writer (his *Edge of Running Water* and *To Walk the Night* are both classics), but also an editor with a clear sense of what his writers needed to be told. As he wrote, "Art cannot be taught. No more can the greatness that it conveys. What *can* be taught is technique, craft, method, understanding of the medium. Any writer or would-be writer would be advised to reflect that a mastery of craft is just exactly that and has nothing to do with greatness or power except to enhance it." Sloane is particularly good in the discussion on "the means of perception" (that is, viewpoint), which is the fiction writer's most useful means of getting his readers' participation.

On Writing Science Fiction

Science-fiction writers have been writing on how to write science fiction for a long time; H.P. Lovecraft's essay (now pretty obsolete) dates from 1927, the year following the appearance of the first SF magazine. Here are a few books on the topic we think you'll find useful.

Bova, Ben. *Notes to a Science Fiction Writer.* Houghton Mifflin Co., 2 Park St., Boston MA 02107. Paperbound. As the cover blurb puts it: "straight-from-the-shoulder talk to the short story writer from the editor"—Bova was editing *Analog Science Fiction / Science Fact* magazine when he wrote the book; he is now editor of *Omni.* Very practical. Discusses Character, Background, Conflict, and Plot, with examples from his own work.

Longyear, Barry B. *Science Fiction Writer's Workshop—I: An Introduction to Fiction Mechanics.* Owlswick Press, Box 8243, Philadelphia PA 19101. Paperbound. The author assumes you know nothing about writing, and builds up from there. For the complete beginner, the most practical guide around, complete with exercises, examples (all from Longyear's own work, including How Not To from his rejected stories), and ways to recognize and correct common flaws.

de Camp, L. Sprague. *Science Fiction Handbook: The Writing of Imaginative Fiction.* Hermitage House: New York. The original, 1953 edition is now out of print. This is the original, classic, writer's guide and history of the field. Much of the first edition is still of great interest, and even the material that has become obsolete—such as the 1953 market reports, profiles of then-leading authors, and the like—has considerable curiosity value.

de Camp, L. Sprague and de Camp, Catherine Crook. *Science Fiction Handbook, Revised.* McGraw-Hill, Inc., 1221 Sixth Ave., New York NY 10020. The historical sections of this edition are condensed, but those on writing are improved, and a new (and invaluable) chapter of the business side of writing is added. Very hard-nosed advice on everything from keeping accounts through dealing with agents and on to how to word the bankruptcy and out-of-print clauses in a contract. (An expanded edition is in preparation; it will incorporate much of the deleted history from the first edition, updated and enlarged. Owlswick Press will be the publisher.)

Knight, Damon. *Creating Short Fiction*. Writer's Digest Books, 9933 Alliance Rd., Cincinnati OH 45242. Hardcover. An understanding, detailed text, concerned not only with how stories are written, but also with how the beginning writer develops. Based on Knight's years of teaching experience at the spectacularly successful Clarion workshops.

Eshbach, Lloyd Arthur. *Of Worlds Beyond*. Advent:Publishers, Box A-3228, Chicago IL 60690. Hardcover and paper. A symposium on writing SF, with articles by Robert A. Heinlein, John Taine, Jack Williamson, A.E. van Vogt, Edward E. Smith, L. Sprague de Camp, and John W. Campbell, Jr. The first work of its kind, originally published in 1947. The Heinlein essay is still essential. Some of the others have become obsolete, but most have something of interest.

Bretnor, Reginald (editor). *The Craft of Science Fiction: A Symposium on Writing Science Fiction and Science Fantasy*. Harper & Row, Publishers, 10 East 53rd St., New York NY 10022. Hardcover and paper. Definitely an advanced text. Essays include Norman Spinrad's "Rubber Sciences," Jerry Pournelle's "The Construction of Believable Societies," Frederik Pohl's "The Science Fiction Professional," John Brunner's "The Science Fiction Novel," and many others. The authors assume that you know the basics of writing (and may even be a selling writer) and address special matters. You'll find the relative usefulness of the articles shifting as your career advances. Keep this one around and dip into it several times a year.

Dictionaries

The most commonly-seen size, the "college" or "collegiate" dictionary, is a bad compromise: it's too big when all you need to look up is the spelling of a commonplace word, yet it's too small to contain all the words you need to look up the meanings of. Instead, we recommend you fill these two needs with entirely separate books:

Ellis, Kaethe. *The Word Book*. Dictionary Division, Houghton Mifflin Co., 2 Park St., Boston MA 02107. Hardcover. An excellent spelling dictionary, priced at less than five dollars, and widely available. Contains no definitions, except where required to distinguish between words which are easily confused, like capital & capitol, or stationary & stationery. Other spelling dictionaries are available; be sure the one you buy has a sturdy binding and a typeface that you can comfortably read.

Little, William; Fowler, H.W.; and Coulson, Jessie (editors). *The Shorter Oxford English Dictionary on Historical Principles*. Third edition. Oxford University Press, 200 Madison Ave., New York NY 10016. Hardcover. About the size of a "Webster's unabridged," this is far superior; it is a shorter version of the monumental, 13-volume *Oxford English Dictionary*. (Should you ever run across the complete *OED*, either as a 13-book set or the 2-volume set with a magnifying glass, and at a bargain price, buy it if you possibly can. At full, list price, however, the complete *OED* is something that can wait until you've made enough money from writing to easily afford it.)

Morris, William (editor). *The American Heritage Dictionary of the English Language*. Houghton Mifflin Co., 2 Park St., Boston MA 02107. Hardcover. A good, general-purpose dictionary, with biographical and geographical entries.

Webster's New Dictionary of Synonyms. G. & C. Merriam Co., 47 Federal St., Springfield MA 01101. Hardcover. Particularly good for defining the *difference* between words of similar meanings, and thus far more valuable thān a thesaurus. (If you simply *must* have a thesaurus as well, don't overlook *The New York Times Crossword Puzzle Dictionary,* available in hardcovers and paper from Warner Books, 75 Rockefeller Plz., New York NY 10019.)

Quotations

All of these delight by the sheer spectacle of so many people expressing themselves elegantly and with style. They are also endlessly useful as sources for story titles, story ideas, and unexpectedly useful wisdom. Do not overload your fiction with exhibitionistic erudition; if Xenophon never said anything about the subject at hand, don't quote him. (The present volume goes about as far in that direction as one can safely go, and perhaps a little over.)

Bartlett's *Familiar Quotations, Revised & Enlarged.* Fifteenth and 125th-Anniversary edition. Little, Brown & Co., 34 Beacon St., Boston MA 02106. Hardcover. Of Bartlett's, Winston Spencer Churchill wrote: "The quotations when engraved upon the memory give you good thoughts. They also make you anxious to read the authors and look for more."
The Oxford Dictionary of Quotations. Third edition. Oxford University Press, 200 Madison Ave., New York NY 10016. Hardcover. The *Oxford* is arranged alphabetically by author; Bartlett's, chronologically by the author's date of birth. The *Oxford* is stronger on poetry; Bartlett's, prose.
Dickson, Paul. *The Official Rules: the Definitive, Annotated Collection of Laws, Principles, and Instructions for Dealing with the Real World.*
Dickson, Paul. *The Official Explanations: the All New, Annotated, Illustrated, and Even More Definitive Collection of Laws, Principles, and Instructions.* Both published by Delacorte Press, 1 Dag Hammarskjold Plz., New York NY 10017. Hardcovers. What Murphy (*that* Murphy) originally said was that if there was any way for a person to make a mistake, eventually someone would; this is entirely distinct from the common version of his law.
Peers, John. *1001 Logical Laws, Accurate Axioms, Profound Principles, Trusty Truisms, Homey Homilies, Colorful Corollaries, Quotable Quotes, and Rambunctious Ruminations for All Walks of Life.* Doubleday & Co., 245 Park Ave., New York NY 10167. Hardcover. Peers has more laws; Dickson has more to say on each of a smaller selection.

Manuals on Manuscript Format

These works cover almost every question that may come up in punctuation, capitalization, and other inconspicuous but essential details of the process of putting ideas down on paper.

Young, Bruce, and Seybold, Catherine (editors). *A Manual of Style.* Twelfth edition, completely revised. The University of Chicago Press, 5801 Ellis Ave., Chicago IL 60637. Detailed and authoritative.
Skillin, Marjorie (editor). *Words into Type.* Third edition, revised. Prentice-Hall, Englewood Cliffs NJ 07632. A ghastly choice of typeface mars

what is otherwise an excellent manual.

Theory

Lewis, C.S. *An Experiment in Criticism.* Cambridge University Press, 32 East 57th St., New York NY 10022. Hardcover. Not a critical work in the usual sense, nor a book on writing, but a book on *reading.* A thoughtful and incisive exploration of how people read, and what various audiences get out of various types of literature (and non-literature). Any writer should be aware of this work.

About Science Fiction

Gunn, James (editor). *The Road to Science Fiction: From Gilgamesh to Wells.* ———: *From Wells to Heinlein.* ———: *From Heinlein to Here.* New American Library, Mentor Books, 1633 Broadway, New York NY 10019. Paper. Science fiction from Lucian of Samosata (circa A.D. 170) to the mid-1970s, with excellent, historical introductions and an exhaustive bibliography of the field.

Knight, Damon. *In Search of Wonder: Essays on Modern Science Fiction.* Second edition, revised. Advent:Publishers, Box A-3228, Chicago IL 60690. Hardcover and paper. A collection of book reviews, which constituted the first serious attempt to critically examine science fiction from within. Knight is generally regarded as the first outstanding critic of this field; and his judgements have for the most part been confirmed by time, with the exception of his virtual blind spot for fantasy. Knight here shows enthusiasm, a refusal to tolerate less than the best, and a clear understanding of what works, what doesn't, and why.

Blish, James (writing as William Atheling, Jr.). *The Issue at Hand* and *More Issues at Hand.* Advent:Publishers, Box A-3228, Chicago IL 60690. Hardcover and paper. A series of critical essays on various aspects of SF, such as religion, the New Wave, the use of first-person narration by Heinlein, and so on.

Nicholls, Peter (editor). *The Science Fiction Encyclopedia.* Doubleday & Co., 245 Park Ave., New York NY 10167. Hardcover and paper. A true encyclopedia, not entirely free of errors, but more reliable and wider-ranging than any other available. Entries on authors, themes, magazines, films, artists, editors, critics, etc. Particularly useful are the articles on themes, such as Time Travel, Aliens, and Perceptions, which give the reader a quick entry into each area.

Williamson, Jack (editor). *Teaching Science Fiction: Education for Tomorrow.* Owlswick Press, Box 8243, Philadelphia PA 19101. A collection of essays about science fiction, the relationship between science fiction and other fields such as politics and religion, and more. An excellent, broad-spectrum introduction to the entire field. Particularly useful to the writer is the bibliography by Alexei & Cory Panshin of twentieth-century SF, which lists about 100 important titles.

Brown, Charles N. (publisher & editor). *Locus: The Newspaper of the Science Fiction Field.* Locus Publications, Box 3938, San Francisco CA 94110. Essential, broad coverage of the whole field.

Porter, Andrew (publisher & editor). *Science Fiction Chronicle: The Monthly Newsmagazine.* Algol Press, Box 4175, New York NY 10163.

Greater emphasis on publishers and publishing, but less total content per issue.

Science Fiction

The one author whose works are indispensable is H.G. Wells. You cannot write good science fiction today without a thorough grounding in his work. He invented many of the basic techniques of the form and introduced most of the major themes. As a stylist and literary technician, he far outranked anyone to follow him for decades. These five are his most important novels: *The Time Machine* (time travel, 1895), *The War of the Worlds* (extraterrestrial invasion, 1898), *The Island of Dr. Moreau* (biological wonders, 1896), *The First Men in the Moon* (interplanetary travel, 1901), and *The Invisible Man* (1907). These are available in many editions; but the most convenient collection is *Seven Famous Science Fiction Novels of H.G. Wells* from Dover Publications, 180 Varick St., New York NY 10014.

It is hard to make a good, short list of other works, since science-fiction experts have never really been able to agree on a canon of novels. Jack Williamson once surveyed 80 reading lists for science-fiction courses and found 12 titles recurring most often:

Asimov, Isaac. *I, Robot.* (1950)
Bradbury, Ray. *The Martian Chronicles.* (1950)
Heinlein, Robert A. *The Moon Is a Harsh Mistress.* (1966)
———. *Stranger in a Strange Land.* (1961)
Herbert, Frank. *Dune.* (1965)
Huxley, Aldous. *Brave New World.* (1932)
Le Guin, Ursula. *The Left Hand of Darkness.* (1969)
Miller, Walter M. *A Canticle for Leibowitz.* (1960)
Pohl, Frederik, and Kornbluth, C.M. *The Space Merchants.* (1953)
Silverberg, Robert (editor). *Science Fiction Hall of Fame, Volume I.* (1970)
Wells, H.G. *The Time Machine.* (1895)
———. *The War of the Worlds.* (1898)

One of these, the Silverberg anthology, is discussed below; the rest are available in various hardcover and paperbound editions.

The first important anthology of SF short stories was that edited by Healy, Raymond J., and McComas, J. Francis. Originally published as *Adventures in Time and Space* in 1946, it is currently available as *Famous Science Fiction Stories, Adventures in Time and Space,* in hardcovers from Random House, Modern Library, 201 East 50th St., New York NY 10022. The stories are from the late 1930s through the middle 1940s, all but three from *Astounding Science Fiction* under the editorship of John W. Campbell. Most are classics.

A follow-on volume to the Healy-McComas anthology is that edited by Silverberg, Robert, and Greenberg, Martin. *The Arbor House Treasury of Modern Science Fiction.* Arbor House Publishing Co., 235 East 45th St., New York NY 10017. The stories range from 1947 through 1975; it is the best single volume of contemporary SF available.

Silverberg, Robert (editor). *The Science Fiction Hall of Fame, Volume I.* Doubleday & Co., 245 Park Ave., New York NY 10167. Hardcover. Also Avon Books, 959 8th Ave., New York NY 10019. Paper. This anthology was selected by a poll of the members of the Science Fiction Writers of America as the best short stories of all those written before 1965. A good selection, though SF writers (like other people) tend to remember the stories that most impressed them when they were young and uncritical.

Bova, Ben (editor). *Science Fiction Hall of Fame, Volume II-A* and *II-B*. This anthology covers novellas (short novels); other details as for the first volume, described above. Particularly useful since novellas are rarely anthologized because of space limitations, and much of the very best science fiction is written at this length.

Fiction

The science-fiction writer must know *fiction*, not just science, not just science fiction. Make sure your literary education doesn't end in the classroom; any formal literature course, at best, is a *beginning* of your continuing education. Below, a short list of works you should have read; many are of such stature that they are the standard that measures one's education. More to the point, when an author alludes to something in one of these works, he may expect to be understood by any well-read reader.

Homer: The *Iliad* and the *Odyssey*. Shakespeare, William: major plays, such as *Hamlet, Othello, Macbeth, Romeo and Juliet, Julius Caesar,* and *The Tempest*. Dickens, Charles: *David Copperfield*. Poe, Edgar Allan: short stories. Hawthorne, Nathaniel: *The Scarlet Letter*. Melville, Herman: *Moby Dick*. Twain, Mark: *The Adventures of Huckleberry Finn* and *A Connecticut Yankee in King Arthur's Court*. Conrad, Joseph: "The Heart of Darkness" and *Lord Jim*. James, Henry: *The Turn of the Screw*. Shaw, George Bernard: *Caesar and Cleopatra* and *Saint Joan*. Joyce, James: *Portrait of the Artist as a Young Man*. Kafka, Franz: short stories. Fitzgerald, F. Scott: *The Great Gatsby*. Hemingway, Ernest: *A Farewell to Arms*. Nabokov, Vladimir: *Lolita*. Borges, Jorge Luis: *Labyrinths*.

Science

You must get your science right, but you don't need doctorates in a dozen fields to do it. Read some of the scientific magazines, such as *Scientific American, Smithsonian, Natural History,* and *The National Geographic;* but remember that your colleagues are doing the same. The magazine *Science* is too technical for most people, but there are excellent review articles; and if you know a particular field of science, you can follow articles on that specialty there. Beware of pure popularizations; a scientist working on research may not write as gracefully as a full-time science-writer, but the content of his material is closer to the advancing edge of scientific discovery. However, for a general survey of many areas of knowledge:

Asimov, Isaac. *Asimov's Guide to Science*. Basic Books, 10 East 53rd St., New York NY 10022. Hardcover. First published under the title. *The Intelligent Man's Guide to Science*.

INDEX

This index covers the Foreword, the 11 numbered chapters, and Appendix A. The various Rules, Laws, and Observations in the text are listed, with page numbers, in Appendix B.

INDEX